Séan Ó Tuathaigh

OUTLANDERS

Stories of the Displaced

MERCIER PRESS

MERCIER PRESS

Cork

www.mercierpress.ie

© Séan Ó Tuathaigh, 2019

ISBN: 978 1 78117 680 1

A CIP record for this title is available from the British Library.

Printed and bound in the EU.

Author's Note

Half the royalties of this book will be donated to Samos Volunteers.

All these stories are true. In some instances, however, names and details have been changed to protect identities, and on occasion fictional characters have been introduced to represent endemic problems within certain systems. Any factual errors are my own.

This book is dedicated to the hardened-hearts
and the blind-eyes.

I was a stranger and you welcomed me.
- Matthew 25:35

Ignorance leads to fear, fear leads to hate and hate leads to violence. This is the equation.
- Ibn Rushd

He went on a long journey, was weary, worn out with labour. Returning, he engraved on a stone the whole story.
- The Epic of Gilgamesh

CONTENTS

INCENSE

Somalia

'you have to understand,
no one puts their children on a boat
unless the water is safer than the land'
- from 'Home', Warsan Shire

A TEENAGE GIRL CROUCHES OVER her clay stove outside the tent. She stirs the coals. They are red-hot, shimmering, like the rising sun that has dispersed grey twilight from the camp. In the distance, silhouetted, are the antennas and minarets of Mogadishu. All along the dusty street of tents, other women, in their many-coloured, multi-patterned hijabs, are nurturing lazy trunks of smoke.

Saadia stares into a rising ember; she is troubled by the dream she has just woken from. There had been a herd of goats, munching quietly in the sunset, when a great black beast had leapt among them, its mane trailing smoke, its claws glinting. She shudders and fans the fire again. The neighbourhood hums with chatter and gossip, but Saadia keeps to herself, yearning for solitude. It is found in focus: breakfast needs to be cooked. She places the pan over the flames and pours from a jug of mixture onto it, spiralling inwards to make a circle, which bubbles and steams, coalescing into a pancake – canjeero. Soon there is a stack of them.

Inside, under a billowing ceiling, her family sits around on rugs and cushions, passing teapots about, filling cups to wash down their meal of canjeero, bananas and sugar, drizzled with sesame oil. Saadia is the eldest child; she has two brothers and five sisters. Her mother rubs sleep from the baby girl's eyes, while her father hurries the other children.

'Eat up! You will be late!'

When breakfast is eaten, the tent empties. The younger children trudge off to Quranic school, the older ones zip outside to their friends, and Saadia's father shuffles across to the neighbours, to speak and smoke. There are no jobs. Saadia and her mother tidy away the bowls and cups and sweep the floor.

'We will have fish for lunch,' her mother says, lighting some incense.

'Yes, Hooyo.'[1]

'Get some tuna, the usual amount.' She digs in her purse. 'Here you go.'

Saadia takes the shillings, nodding.

'What has come over you, Saadia? You are very quiet this morning.'

Saadia pauses. She wants to blurt out her nightmare, to tell of the vicious creature, of its knife-like teeth and the mangled kids scattered about the meadow. She wants to explain the sounds she heard: bleating, shrieking and then silence – a deep, immutable silence. But she does not, she just smiles.

'It's nothing, Hooyo, just a dream. I'll tell you about it later.'

Her mother tuts good-humouredly and rubs her shoulder.

---

1   Mother.

Saadia clings to the handrail as the bus jolts into another pothole. It is packed and sweaty; morning rush hour is in full flow. Outside, the tents and trees give way to huts and then to multi-storey buildings. The bus navigates around craters and chunks of masonry, and frequently jerks to a halt in the traffic: donkey drays, handcarts, the occasional car rattling past.

The scars of war are all around. Bullet holes spatter every edifice like a pox, and the crumbling, undulating parapets above grin and gape like the lower jawbones of so many skulls. There are gaps where entire buildings have collapsed: weeds and scrub tangling upon heaps of debris.

Saadia came into the world in 1991, just as the Somali government was prodded out of it. She is unversed in the workings of a stable society. Sprawling graffiti proclaims the ascendancy of warlords and factions who vie with each other unceasingly. There are periods of tense truce that collapse suddenly into skirmishes. Then the dust settles and life resumes – with shifted alliances, new boundaries and, inevitably, the haunting laments of mothers.

Checkpoints occur along the borders of these tectonic polities, each exacting a toll from those who would pass through. Saadia's bus pays two along the way. Sometimes, a gang of boys – with no education or employment to offer hope – will set up their own roadblock and demand their slice, aping the militiamen. They cannot be scolded or mocked: very often they will be strutting about with impossibly long assault rifles slung from their skinny shoulders. For some this will be a boyish experiment, a boisterous phase with lessons learned. For too many, however, it is an apprenticeship into a life by the sword.

The bus shudders to a halt. Saadia keeps her hand pressed against her purse as she steps out onto the street, though it is well buried in the folds of her dress. She emerges into a jostling shoal: women surge around her carrying bags and baskets; a scooter darts through with a shark balancing and bouncing behind the driver; young lads, sons or nephews of fishermen, plod with swordfish as big as themselves across their shoulders, and above all this looms a building – squint-inducing in its whiteness – the length of the block, with high, semi-circular windows. It is a miracle the arcade has survived at all, but somehow it has weathered almost two decades of deadly hail: mortars, rockets, grenades. Today, thankfully, only seagulls fly overhead.

The whiteness of the fish market is almost ghostly among the other tattered buildings. It is a visitation from an earlier time, an era Saadia has only heard talked about among elders. On a wrinkled postcard she once saw it: a splendid city on the sea, of white cubes and domes – 'The Pearl of the Indian Ocean' they had called it, when Somalia had been a paragon of peaceful decolonisation. Saadia finds this difficult to imagine; it is somewhat improbable, falling into the realm of mythology.

She gazes down the street while queueing to enter the fish market. She would like to forget about her chores for a minute – or an hour – and stroll down to where the sturdy fisherboys are streaming, to weave through the ruins and out onto the waterfront, where the stench of aquatic entrails is breezed away and the jetty swerves far into the ocean. Those murmuring waters do not retain bullet holes, they do not permit graffiti. She longs to sit by the water's edge, with her back to the crumbling roofscape, to let her feet splash and watch the blue turn to lavender, pink, orange, red; she longs for her shadow to stretch towards the horizon and for the stars to peek out one at a time. She considers it, but then the queue lurches forward into the shadows of the arcade. There is food to secure and it is unwise for a young woman to wander solo in this city.

She knows exactly where to go, who to haggle with and when to come to terms. In minutes, she has squeezed back outside and onto the bus, a cool parcel of diced flesh in her hands. The buildings shrink, thin out, huts replace them and trees sprout up, while the seats empty. She steps off at her stop, among tents now, and strolls around a corner into her street.

There is a crowd at the end of it. How strange, she thinks. As she approaches, she sees that more and more people are joining the crowd, their faces curious and frightened. There is a babble bubbling up from them like a boiling pot. There are also people drifting away, looking ashen, shocked. A little girl, her neighbour, turns, sees Saadia and looks to the ground. More faces turn and stare, the crowd parts, and there, by the opening of her tent, two boys lay crookedly. The dust beneath them is purple, sticky, congealed. They are utterly harrowed: shot through with bullets.

Her friend Fadumo approaches. She appears sickly, not smiling or joking like she usually would be.

'The militia, they came for your sisters. They took your parents too. Your brothers tried to resist …'

Saadia sinks to her knees, sways, and there are arms embracing her, women praying, weeping, wailing. The day passes in a blur: in someone's tent, being fanned, told to drink, to eat, refusing it all.

This is not the first time her family has encountered militia; they have not always lived in a tent. Five years previously, when Saadia was eleven, they had lived – by Somali standards – a fairly normal, if difficult, life in some rooms of a townhouse in the middle of Mogadishu. One day, there came a rap on the door. Militiamen, bullets strapped around their torsos, wearing keffiyeh and berets and jabbing gun barrels, had barged in demanding the property. As simply as that. Saadia's brother, the eldest child, stood up to them and was summarily shot before the whole family. They grabbed her parents and her other two brothers, and shoved them aboard a pickup truck. Saadia and the other children were left with their brother as he bled out on the kitchen floor.

He was buried and life went on, somehow. The children lived alone, in terror, occasionally sleeping in neighbouring houses when the fear overwhelmed them. Saadia grew up very fast. She was not simply the eldest now; she was the mother, the manager of the household.

Five months later, there was another knock on the door. It was her parents and brothers. They had been released on the condition they hand over the deeds to the property. They gathered their belongings and fled, ending up in a tent on the outskirts of the city.

That had been the end of the violence, until today.

In the evening, 'Uncle Hussein' – a distant cousin of her father – arrives and takes Saadia away from the camp. He is older than her father, tall, with stooped shoulders and a grey beard. His household consists of three portable cabins, side by side, with his wife and three adult sons. It is not far from the camp, only a few minutes' walk; she has been there many times and knows these people reasonably well. They will be her family now.

Two years have passed. Saadia is eighteen years of age. There are a number of people gathered in the front room of the cabin this evening, sitting on cushions, candlelit and wreathed in incense: her aunt, Ubah, and Uncle Hussein, their three sons, a handful of friends and an imam.[2] A delicious aroma wafts in from the back room, where a feast awaits on platters: spiced meat, rice, canjeero.

---

2   An Islamic clergyman.

Saadia is in her finest dress and is holding a bouquet in her lap while the dowry is discussed and agreed upon.

She gazes down into the flowers and recalls what Uncle Hussein had said, some weeks previously: 'You are not a young girl any more, Saadia. It is time you thought of marriage. He is a good man, a solid man, and he has a job – that is a rare thing in this country, you know that. He'll never get rich, chopping fish, but he'll never be poor either. People will always need fish.'

'Yes, Adeer.'

Saadia knew it was reasonable. Perhaps it would be something new that might dispel the unshakeable sadness that had clung to her since the day her family disappeared. She still cried every day, and rarely left the house. This self-imposed cage was forged not merely from depression but from a profound terror that the men who had destroyed her family would one day return.

'Anyways,' he continued, 'a woman needs a protector. Otherwise, terrible things can happen.'

She nodded and the arrangements were made.

The ceremony goes smoothly. Prayers are murmured, the food is eaten and dancing follows before a ring is slipped onto her finger by her new husband: Hussein's eldest son, thirty-three-year-old Ahmad. At the end of the night, he scoops her up, amid cheers and blessings, and carries her to their new home: the portable cabin next door.

Saadia is pregnant before long. In the summer of 2009, a daughter is born. Life has a purpose again; she is kept busy. The flood of tears slows to a trickle.

They do return, though, as she had feared. *They*: the beast among goats.

Saadia sits on her doorstep, her baby in her arms, enjoying the last glimmers of the evening, when a truck roars around the corner. Men pour out of the back of the vehicle: green uniforms and ammunition pouches, with black keffiyehs wrapped around their faces. Only their eyes are exposed, burning with ferocity. The side of the truck is painted black, with a large blob of white in the middle, covered in script. It is Al Shabaab.[3]

The leader steps forward and says: 'We order that the men of this household assemble before us. There are three men of fighting age living here, we know this.'

Ahmad edges out of the middle cabin, where he has been playing cards with his two brothers. They peek out of the doorway.

'What is it you want?' asks Ahmad.

'Are you infidels?' asks the officer.

'No, we are not. We are Muslims.'

'Good. Then you will be pleased to hear that you have the honour of joining our ranks. You will fight the jihad, as all good Muslims should.'

Ahmad sighs, looks sadly at the ground.

'Come. Say your goodbyes,' the officer orders.

'I cannot,' Ahmad stutters. 'I have a wife and a child. I have a job. Who will protect them?'

'We provide for all dutiful wives. You needn't worry.'

Ahmad meets the officer's gaze now, defiant. 'I will not go. I will not shoot people, chop off hands and feet and heads. I refuse.'

A militant steps forward and rams the butt of his Kalashnikov into Ahmad's stomach. He topples forward and is hoisted into the truck.

Ahmad's father now emerges from his doorway, his skin turned almost as grey as his beard by what he sees unfolding. He is trembling and looks ancient, as though a sudden wind might sift him away like ash. Auntie Ubah stands behind him, hand to her mouth.

---

3   Al Shabaab is a Jihadist fundamentalist group affiliated with Al Qaeda. They operate in Somalia and throughout East Africa.

'Stop it,' he croaks. 'What are you doing? Do you think that God wills this?'

'God operates through us,' says the officer. 'We are his tools on earth.'

The fear seems to evaporate from the old man: he clenches his fists and strides forward.

'Where have you found such arrogance?' he growls. 'How can you claim –'

A shot rings out and the old man crumples into a heap. Auntie Ubah screams and the two younger brothers duck back inside their cabin, but several militants charge in after them. There are shouts, rumbling furniture and a glass smashes. The brothers are dragged out, limp, and flung into the truck on top of Ahmad.

'God is great,' says the officer, lowering his smoking pistol.

'God is great,' cry the men, thrusting their rifles at the heavens. They hop aboard the truck and it roars off.

Ubah runs out and tries to pick up her husband, but his head lolls back. You can see it, a blankness in his eyes – he is dead. Saadia's aunt lets out a great, beseeching howl.

Saadia knows now that she needs to leave Somalia. Her life here is over. This is the first real decision she has ever made.

Within a few weeks she is ready. A minibus arrives one morning and picks her and a dozen like-minded neighbours up, mostly young people. Only she has a baby. She waves goodbye to Ubah, who has two streams running down her face. There was no convincing her to leave: she refused to be budged from the home she had made, though to Saadia it is now scarcely warmer than a tomb. She recalls one of the arguments. It had escalated until finally she screamed out:

'They're gone, don't you see?'

'They'll come back.'

'They won't, and neither will Hooyo or Aabbe or my sisters or brothers, or any of them. They're all dead!'

'No!'

Both broke down, whimpering, clasping each other.

The bus trundles southwestwards and very soon civilisation is far behind. As daylight fades the refugees find themselves in a baked wasteland, its scrawny trees streaking sinuous shadows across the red earth. They veer off-road and rattle along for an hour until they reach an old creek bed. Here they disembark, sling their luggage upon their backs and follow the guide into darkness.

At some point, under that vast dome of stars, they cross the border into Kenya. They are alert, like owl-fearing rodents; they have all heard tales about the Kenyan military, about corruption and brutality, detention and ransoms. But the alertness gradually fades into exhaustion: the struggle of putting one aching foot ahead of the other. Several times, in the middle distance, Saadia notices – she is sure of it – pairs of eyes, green-glowing, which follow their progress. She says nothing.

After many hours trekking, with dawn's filament on the horizon, they lay down in a herder's shack. They passed a bottle of water around, gulped it down, wide-eyed. By sunrise they are asleep. Saadia, though, is woken by the gurgles of her baby and gently hums a lullaby, rocking her back and forth, swatting flies away in the unbillowing heat. A bus arrives as the sun departs and they ride through the night. At dawn, they lay low again. There are two more nights of this.

Nairobi is a shock after the nocturnal pilgrimage through the wilderness. The bus crawls along avenues that are tree-lined and traffic-thronged, with great glinting towers of steel rising into the blue to either side. Buildings are different here compared to Mogadishu: freshly painted, clean, unblemished by bullet-pox. Saadia sees some houses of God, though they are crowned with crosses, not crescents. She peers up into a leafy treetop: vultures stare back at her.

They soon arrive in a denser district: streets of cheap hotels, shopping malls and unfinished multi-storey tenements, crowded with stalls, vehicles and pedestrians. The road is a marsh in places, soupy puddles and sucking muck. Everywhere rubbish rolls, glides, accumulates. There are mosques in this district, hijabs are worn and, as they pass a hookah den, she catches a waft of that same old incense from back home. She has arrived in Eastleigh, otherwise known as 'Little Mogadishu'.

But all this upheaval – the new sights and sounds, the harsh uncertainty – cannot alone account for the churning sickness that has been engulfing Saadia for the last few days. She feels weak all the time, but it is especially torturous in the mornings, as if some malignant organism within her is writhing its tentacles. There is something growing within her, she realises, but it is not an otherworldly creature. She is pregnant again.

Unable to work, she lives on the kindness of near strangers, spending a week here, ten days there, as she is passed among the Somali diaspora, from household to household, apartment to apartment. She sleeps on couches and rugs, in kitchens and attics. Sometimes, a bedroom is cleared for her. It is a complicated pregnancy: there is frequent, debilitating nausea, much bleeding and constant fatigue, all caused or exacerbated by recent traumas. Finally, she gives birth to another baby girl, who, miraculously, is healthy.

Within a few days, however, a deep depression sets in. Saadia is a female refugee, utterly exhausted, with two children, no support, a paltry and ever-diminishing budget and zero prospects on the horizon. Ahead she sees only misery and chaos; behind is the heartbreak of her homeland.

Almost a year has passed in Kenya. Saadia and the babies are living in an apartment with several single women, who toil in the fruit stalls along the footpath downstairs, or as maids in other neighbourhoods. Saadia has tried to balance motherhood with earning a few bob by helping her roommates here and there, but it is not easy. In truth, it is miserable: much of the illness that accompanied her pregnancy lingers on and her living arrangements are still temporary.

Saadia is going to cook dinner this evening when they return from work. She does this for her hosts every day; it is her way of contributing. She leaves the babies with a neighbour and descends the dark, cluttered staircase into the bright busy street. Her brow is beaded with sweat instantly – she longs for an ocean breeze, even for a moment, to surge through the heat. But the ocean belongs to a previous life.

On the way back from the market, laden with bags, she sees a group of young women gathered around the doorway of a hotel. On the steps stands a man in a suit and a tie, which lies along the curve of his big belly. He is not local, or even African. He has a thick, neat moustache, sunglasses and his dark, slick hairline is receding. A Somali in a much cheaper suit is translating for him.

Saadia listens as he speaks: '... young ladies, attentive and hard-working. Most of all, to work with us, we require a girl to be respectful. She must follow the teachings of The Prophet, peace be upon Him. If you can prove yourself to be all of these things, you will do well. Life can be good. It is better there; there are more opportunities, more services. I have many contacts; I am well-known, well-respected, in my homeland. I will look after you and make sure that all is arranged smoothly: the visa, the flights, the work. You repay me by earning your salary. It might not sound cheap, but it is a bargain – you girls will thank me one day.'

Saadia nudges the young woman beside her.

'Who is this guy?' she whispers.

'He is a businessman, an Arab. He is doing interviews this afternoon.'

'For?'

'Maids.'

'Is he … honest?'

The girl shrugs.

Saadia sits at a desk in a tight office with ancient filing cabinets and a wobbly ceiling fan. The Arab sits opposite, leaning forward on his elbows, steepling his fingers. His shirt is a crisp desert, with an oasis under each armpit, the smell of which pokes through a curtain of cologne. He has been staring at her for over thirty seconds, at the tears gathering in her eyes.

'Look,' he says, 'I am not sure you are what we are looking for. I mean, two babies …'

Saadia hardly waits for the translator to finish.

'Please, Sir, I promise, I'll –'

The Arab holds his hand out, stopping her short. He leans back in his chair, sighs. 'This is what I am going to do,' he says. 'I can see you are in a bad situation. You are a good girl. Your story pains me. I will arrange your visa, the flights for you and your daughters. When you land in Egypt, you are free to do as you please. You will not pay me back. You will not ask my name, or my address, and you will never speak with me or of me again. Is that understood?'

As the translation comes through, Saadia's face changes from desperation, to confusion, to astonishment. She tries to hold them, but the tears burst forth and her hand covers her mouth.

'Thank you, thank you, thank you.'

The Arab fidgets with the sunglasses in his breast pocket, smiles awkwardly. Then he coughs, frowns and informs the translator that the interview is over.

Cairo is not a huge improvement, not for Saadia. She lives far from pyramids and tourists and luxury resorts. The air is dryer here, the surroundings sandier. In fact, everything looks to be built from sand: the buildings, monuments and streets, whether of concrete or blocks or plaster, are uniformly beige. Occasional palms offer a welcome dash of green on this arid canvas.

She lives in a poor neighbourhood in the Nasr district, sharing a stifling apartment several stories up with a single woman – a fruit vendor – who has little room but even less money to pay rent. Saadia finds it difficult to make ends meet, and her illness still lingers. There are droves of Africans, including Somalis, crowded into these residential towers, where the washing lines along the balconies flap like bunting and the hum of old box fans is constant.

Like many of her compatriots, she works as a maid for the affluent denizens of Nasr. Or seeks to work. She drifts from household to household, sometimes surviving a week, other times a day, but in the end she is always let go. The reasons are always the same:

'We are not looking for mothers.'

'I feel that childrearing distracts you.'

'Your baby cries too much. We cannot take it any more.'

But she cannot leave her children behind; crèches and babysitters are expensive.

She travels across Cairo one morning, from bus to bus, and spends the day waiting in line at an office: the United Nations High Commissioner for Refugees (UNHCR). After a thorough interview and examination of documents, she is told her case has been accepted for processing.

'What do I do now?' she asks.

In their crisp shirts and cosy chairs, the interviewers smile back at her rosily.

'All you have to do is wait,' they say.

Wait, she thinks. Wait and somehow hold down a job, pay the rent, feed the children. That's all.

She sits on a bus. It is dark, the near-empty interior swept occasionally by passing street lamps. Her current boss, a haughty housewife, has sent her out on an errand: to exchange fifty US dollars for some Egyptian genēh, God knows what for. Saadia wishes she were already done because of the man lurking a few seats behind her. She can see the bulk of him out of the corner of her eye, leaning forward on the seat in front of him. They are the only two passengers. She knows he is staring; she can sense it.

She will be fired if she returns empty-handed, she knows this with absolute certainty. One little task and then home, she promises herself. Here we go, this is my stop.

She steps out and peers down the street: light comes from a few curtained windows, dim music throbs somewhere.

Is the shop still open? she wonders. Ah, there it is; the lights are still on, thank God.

An arm reaches from behind and clamps her against the chest. As she struggles she feels warm panting on her neck – a cloth is rammed against her nostrils and chemicals surge up into her brain.

She awakes in shadows. The smell of rubbish surrounds her, a drain gurgles overhead. An alleyway. She raises herself slowly, gasping. Pain everywhere: on the outside, on the inside. Her clothes are dishevelled, her headscarf trailing loosely.

Another year has passed. Saadia is between jobs, cleaning a diaper in the heat of the apartment. Her three-month-old, lying on her back, is peddling her chubby little legs in the air.

Saadia's phone begins ringing. It continues: shrill, insistent. She bins the nappy and grabs the phone.

'Hello?'

'Saadia? Is it you?'

She feels behind her for the arm of a chair and guides herself down into it.

'Ahmad?'

When she arrives at the square she pushes through the crowds towards where the roof of a bus arises. There he is, standing by a lamp post with a throng of other passengers who are removing their luggage or embracing friends. They are mostly youngsters; he is the oldest by far. When he spots her he breaks into a grin. They hug for a long while and then stroll into a café. Over tea, he tells his story.

'As recruits we were … *unenthusiastic*. They threw us into one of their jails, in the middle of the desert. I will not linger on the details. But one thing I will never forget is the smell. It is an awful thing to smell men confined, packed together, without hope: hungry, thirsty, inactive. But worst of all was the stench of fear – every day waiting to be dragged outside, for a sword to swing. I often imagined the cold of the steel.'

Ahmad puts down his cup, rubs the narrow nape of his neck. He has aged, flecks of grey in his once jet-black hair. His beard reminds Saadia of his father.

'We rotted there, the three of us, for months. One morning there was gunfire. It was distant, but it grew closer, more frequent and then there were explosions. This continued all day. The federal government was fighting back, we discovered.[4] In the evening there was an assault on the prison. Machine guns barked and rattled all about, the garrison screamed back and forth to each other, the wounded were shrieking, all rising and rising until we were almost deaf. Then grenades went off somewhere in the building. A guard sprinted past our cell, into the corridor. A gunshot cracked. Then government soldiers poured in, unlocking our cages. The battle was still raging outside and the prison was right in the thick of it. Me and my brothers waited for the right moment and made a sprint for safety. Hussein was hit, but Hassan and I survived.'

Saadia touches his hand. Her chin quivers.

'We made our way to Mogadishu,' he continues. 'I had had enough. Enough of the chaos, the killing, the complete lack of hope. I had had enough of Somalia. I wanted out, but Hassan said it was too expensive, too dangerous. So he stayed behind and I left the country on my own. Europe was my goal, I had heard great things about Italy. I got as far as Libya. I was hoping to get on one of those boats – they have these guys who you can pay to bring you across the Mediterranean. It's very expensive, though; they can smell the desperation. I tried to figure out how to get enough scraped together. My God' – he picks up a spoon, places

---

4   Al Shabaab have controlled vast swathes of Somali territory in the civil wars that have ravaged the country since 2006.

it back down again – 'it was terrible. I was living the life of a sort of fugitive, an outlaw. There is no work for people like that. Many of us were there, many Somalis. It was from them that I heard that you were still alive. "She's in Cairo," they said. It didn't take long to ask around and find your number.' He shrugs his shoulders. 'So here I am.'

She smiles.

'So,' Ahmad says, 'how have you been?'

The smile stays on her lips but leaves her eyes.

She is kneeling over the toilet, grasping its rim, her hair a tangle. The sickness is back, just as it was the other three times. She wipes her mouth, flushes, splashes her face in the sink a few times. A weary woman looks back at her out of the mirror: pouches under the eyes, eyelids shiny with fatigue. How will this stranger survive? Saadia wonders, as she presses back a mushrooming horror. Three children are difficult enough.

She is still renting the room in the little apartment from the fruit vendor, who lives there too. Now it is herself, three daughters and a husband in that single bedroom. The youngest, the baby, is lying on a rug, screaming, when she opens the bathroom door and steps out into the cluttered kitchen/living room. The red curtains are closed, but the sunlight makes them glow and flutters in through the box fan. Ahmad, in a ragged grey vest, is on the opposite side of the room: arms folded, smoking a cigarette, while staring at the child blankly.

'Can't you see she's crying?' asks Saadia.

'I'm busy,' says Ahmad, jolting into action. 'I have that, eh, meeting.'

'Meeting?'

'Yes, with Said,' he says, pulling a shirt on over his vest.

'With Said? Ahmad, I thought we talked about this?'

These meetings with Said, who 'knows people who know people', involve planning a voyage across the sea.

Ahmad glowers. 'Look, there are no jobs. I've been here three months already. I've looked high and low.' He shrugs. 'They hate us here, they don't want Somalis.'

'Be patient, Ahmad, please!'

'No. There is nothing here for us. Italy, we must go to Italy.'

'Ahmad, I heard they are looking for someone at the petrol stat–'

'There are jobs *over there*. The guys say it is good, Jama owns a car.'

'How do you know? They are exaggerating –'

'I can't take this any more. The boredom, the apartment, that fucking …'

He gestures at the baby.

'Go on,' she says, 'say it.'

Ahmad hurls his cigarette against the wall. 'We have nothing here. Nothing! In Europe we might have a chance. It's just a quick boat ride, a few days at most and then –'

'I'm scared,' she sniffs. 'It's too dangerous. I don't want to drown.' She frowns suddenly. 'Do you want your babies to drown?'

'*My* babies?'

Ahmad clenches his fists; he puffs vigorously, squeezing his eyes shut. Then he storms out. The door slams with a bang and Saadia bursts out crying. The youngest starts wailing again and then, in the bedroom, the other two.

He returns that night, drunk, and falls straight into a snoring slumber. He sulks about the apartment for the next few days, refusing conversation. She comes back from work a week later and he is gone. Her immediate theory is later confirmed: he set out for Italy by himself.

Some weeks later, she answers the door to a knock and Ahmad is standing there. He is quiet; ashamed and yet unrepentant. The Egyptian police had intercepted the boat, detained its passengers and then deported them. He simply returned through the porous borderlands: Somalia, Ethiopia, Sudan, Egypt.

He tries for Italy again a few months later, and again his plans are foiled by the authorities. This time he does not even make it as far as the vessel: the police raid some of the crewmembers' homes after being tipped off by informants, catching themselves a haul of traffickers.

Saadia gives birth again, a boy this time. She has neither the time nor the money for maternity leave; she is a maid again within days. As before, she must bring her babies, which means no job lasts long. Ahmad is pleased with his male heir for a while, but soon descends into brooding, filling the apartment with cigarette smoke or wandering off for hours at a time, sometimes overnight. He takes to chewing khat, a habit that brings him into certain circles and routines, none of them conducive to finding work.[5]

One day, soon after the newborn stops breastfeeding, Saadia returns from work and Ahmad has disappeared, along with his meagre possessions and the boy. No note, no phone call. Her heart breaks and she collapses inside, but she must continue to pay for food and shelter. She cries only at night, hidden in the bathroom. The girls must not see.

Soon, the morning sickness is back. She toils right up until the contractions, gives birth to her fifth child, another daughter, and once again returns immediately to her job.

A year drags by in an endless cycle of drudgery, barely scraping together enough for food and rent. She has never heard back from

---

5   Khat is a flowering plant, native to the Horn of Africa, and a popular
      stimulant in the region.

the UNHCR. Long ago resettlement became a childish dream, an improbable fairytale, one, therefore, not worth clinging to.

Meanwhile, the children are growing all the time: eating more, wearing more, filling the little apartment. The eldest is seven years old now. At night they shuffle and knock against each other on the mattress. By day they leap around the room or hang from the furniture. As much as possible, Saadia shoos them out to play with other children in the corridors.

In January 2017, while at work, scrubbing kitchen tiles, Saadia receives a phone call. It is the UNHCR.

'So, congratulations, Saadia! Your case has been accepted. You are going to be resettled.'

It is so preposterous that she is not shocked. She continues the conversation mechanically.

'Where are you sending me?'

'The USA,' she is told.

It is only afterwards, on the way home, that her mind begins to swim: memories of her old world and visions of the new wash over her like whitecaps on shingle.

Back in the apartment, she manages to get the three girls sitting down and hushed. The baby is asleep in the corner.

'What is it, Hooyo?' asks her eldest, twirling her braids.

'We are going on a holiday,' she tells them. 'It's an adventure, like in the movies. We will have to pack our bags and get ready.'

She sends the news throughout the community, hoping people will get word to Ahmad.

At the end of January, she receives her travel itinerary – her flights have been booked. They really are going. She prepares for the journey, selling whatever she can and receiving loans from friends. Her housemate, the fruit vendor, begins searching for a new tenant. Saadia is helping her do this one of the afternoons when she gets a call from the UNHCR. When she hangs up the phone, her smile has evaporated.

'What's wrong?' asks the housemate.

'They cancelled. They won't allow us in.'

Both glance around at the apartment, which looks both neat and empty for the first time in years.

'Why?'

'I don't know,' Saadia admits.

Far away, across the sands and beyond the ocean, in a big white building, a white man in an expensive suit had signed an executive order and obliterated Saadia's hopes for her children.[6]

But then, in a smaller building, in another American city, another white man – a judge – blocks the executive order. Saadia's flight is rebooked.

A month later, in March 2017, Saadia and her four girls arrive in the Midwestern United States. They are settled by their agency in an apartment, their own apartment. Small by American standards, it is palatial compared to what they have just left behind. It is in a street of low, brown housing units with grassy strips and plenty of trees.

Her first act, after unpacking, is to jam the whispering crack under the door with old towels, to block its cold rumourings of the outer world. She cranks the heater to its maximum setting. The girls pull on extra socks and sweaters.

The mosque is not far, she often sees other women in hijabs strolling past her house. She meets them in the Middle-Eastern shop nearby and begins to make acquaintances. Her eldest girls

---

6   Executive Order 13769 was put into effect by the US president on 27 January 2017, halting refugee admissions for 120 days, drastically reducing the yearly intake and banning travel from selected countries, including Somalia, for ninety days. Over 700 travellers were detained, and 60,000 visas were revoked.

are enrolled in school and Bilqiis, an old friend from Somalia, turns out to be living just down the road. Bilqiis tells Saadia not to worry, that the weather will get warmer soon.

Saadia eventually makes contact with Ahmad, who agrees that their boy should go and live with her in America. But this will be a tricky process. He had not been born when she first applied to the UNHCR, and his father had taken him away by the time their resettlement had been agreed and she was listing the children. Her application was granted and the flights booked in such rapid succession that she had been frightened to intervene and report him, in case it invalidated her case. The executive order had only stoked her fears. She worries constantly about her little boy, so far away. With any luck, her petition will be accepted and he will soon join his sisters. It is uncertain yet whether Ahmad will travel.

But overall, despite these issues, things are better. She is safer. Often, she walks down the street to Bilqiis. Their girls play games together while they prepare food and chat. They fry the familiar mixture and smell the familiar smells: sesame, banana and sugar on canjeero. As Saadia chews, she remembers rows of rippling tents, buildings poxed by bullets, fisherboys lugging tuna, militia jammed into jeeps and the aroma of that old incense that her mother loved so much. Regardless of the distance she travels, or the time that passes, Saadia will always be haunted by that sad tattered city on the sea.

ANTIQUE LAND

Palestine

PERCHED ON THE EDGE OF the bed, Tuqa takes one last look around her room. The rug and the patterned tiles, the gently billowing lace curtains. Dawn is creeping over the old quarter of Ramallah, uncovering flat roofs and palm tops. A rooster croons. Faintly, a helicopter rumbles. The room is a blur through her awakening eyes, her easel leers out of a shadow like a slender man, canvases jostle each other along one wall, paints and brushes and sketches clutter her desk, books jam her shelves. Last night, after a long tribunal, she selected four, which she jammed into her suitcase among all the clothing.

There is so much, she muses, so much in this wide room, under its high ceiling, and so little I can carry.

It is January 2017.

'It will be all right, Mama,' she said the night before. 'I will be back soon. It is only for two weeks.'

It was her last supper, over at her mother's place, a short walk deeper into the old town.

'You can't be certain of that. You know what they're like!'

'Mama, I'm sure it will be fine. I promise. I will return.'

It was a lie. She was not sure.

'It could ruin your whole life.'

'My life is ruined,' she exhaled, 'if I can't live it. What sort of life is it if I can't do simple things? It's just a college trip. I'm not a criminal; I'm not a danger to anyone. Other students travel all the time. Why can't I just be normal?'

'You're not normal, Tuqa. You're Palestinian.'

Ramallah has been her home for half of her life: twelve years. It has formed her, informed her, polished the lens through which the world appears.

A breeze carries the call to prayer into her bedroom, a whisper of tradition. Tuqa does not kneel forward, but rather lies back, gazing up at the ceiling. How soft this quilt is, how safe. Her dark curls tumble around her, her cardigan is loose on her collarbones, her ankles are bare below her baggy trousers. She squints at the tiny cracks in the plaster above: roads, ravines, borders, perimeters, walls.

An engine rumbles outside, a handbrake cranks, straining: it is a sloped street, typical of the old town.

Time to go.

Tuqa lives in an apartment complex in the midst of ancient townhouses. Herself and her sister share it: three bedrooms, a bathroom, a kitchen/living room. Neighbours in the hallway, a stairwell down to the foyer. And it goes deeper, underground. It is wise to be aware of the basement. And how to get there in a hurry.

Her sister waves down from the balcony.

'Message when you arrive!'

'I will, Luebna.'

'You better!'

The boot clunks shut.

'Ready?' says Omar.

Tuqa nods at him, glad that he will be with her for what lies ahead. The Scouts brought Omar into their family. The den he founded was the best in Ramallah; young children flocked to it. For the poorest of them it was a kind of salvation, a redemption amid the poverty, the endless privations and humiliations. Tuqa and her sisters all went. They loved it. The eldest, Maysera, was a senior Scout, then a supervisor. Omar fell in love with her. And Maysera fell in love with him, enamoured by his dry humour and his tireless work in the community. They have a house now on the far side of Ramallah, close enough to drop their two boys in with Auntie Tuqa for babysitting duties.

Omar picks up two of Tuqa's classmates, then four coffees to go, and soon they are speeding down the open road as the sun splashes the surrounding crags and cliffs pink.

'So,' asks Omar, into the rear-view mirror. 'How long have you been friends with Tuqa?'

'Since the beginning,' says one. 'Enrolment.'

'Yeah,' says the other. 'Over three years.'

'I'm sorry for your troubles,' says Omar.

'Oh shut up,' says Tuqa.

They chuckle.

'We're not taking the ziggy-zaggy road?'

'No,' says Omar, 'we'll take the direct route. The checkpoint shouldn't be too busy this early.'

Tuqa feels a momentary relief; plenty of cars have tumbled from the ziggy-zaggy road, the slopes below littered with rusting scrap. There are no yellow number plates among those crooked bumpers, only white ones.[1] But the choice of road they take to Jericho, whether vertiginous corkscrews or smooth asphalt, is the least of her troubles.

---

1   Number plates are segregated: yellow for Israelis, white for Palestinians.

They swoop down from the mountains into the flat fields of the valley. The air warms, the scene greens. Fertile valleys, stolen settlements, sweep by. Melons, bananas, lemons, eggplants, cucumbers. Shekels, dollars, euros.

They queue five minutes at an internal checkpoint, one of many, before they are waved through. Soldiers peer from under the rims of helmets, olive uniforms tucked into black jackboots, bullpup rifles slung across lumpy chests. They do not peer so much as scan. Machine men with machine minds and machine hearts.

'You are not machines,' Tuqa whispers. 'You are not cattle.'

She feels grateful to them for letting her pass, then remonstrates with herself. A sick feeling overwhelms her. She is travelling abroad; it is suddenly very real. They have no time for ancient Jericho with its springs and palm trees, where the conquest of the Promised Land began all those ages ago. They dash through the outskirts and the first crossing of the day looms up: the Palestinian Crossing.[2]

Omar finds a space in the car park. They haul their baggage up to a low building. Inside, under strip lights, they queue, show passports, have their bags scanned. It is smooth, steady, they pass through and climb aboard a bus.

Though she has lived under the gaze of Israeli muzzles her whole life, under gunships and towers and armoured personnel carriers, she has been inside Israel itself only once. This will be her first time out of the occupied territories, other than her childhood journey, which had been from Gaza to the West Bank. What an odd day this is.

The bus spills them out and they trudge into another building. A low, plane-less airport: glaring strip lights, belt barriers, booths. And tension.

---

2   The point at which one leaves Palestinian Authority territory and enters the narrow strip of Israel which surrounds it. To leave Palestine, one must pass into Israel.

She is glad to see their fellow travellers in line. There are five of them going in total. They greet each other, nervous but giddy for the adventure. Omar smirks at their optimism.

The first student reaches the booth, shows her documents, passes. Then the second. And third. Tuqa swallows. The air is stuffy, thick; there is a deadness in it. She looks at the booth, the stern woman inside it, olive tunic and tight ponytail, looks away, too quickly, looks down, suitably distant, taps her toe, stops, rearranges her cardigan. She feels sick again. She feels like an animal at the market. Or the abattoir. Perhaps they'll examine her teeth or lift up her hooves.

'To?'

'Eh, Jordan.'

The soldier squints.

'Passport.'

Tuqa hands it over. The stern eyes flash over it, like a scanner, twice, and she scowls.

'Show me your ID.'

'Yeah, of course, eh …' Tuqa fumbles, quivering, digging in her pockets, cursing her trousers for clinging, then yanks it out.

'There. Sorry.'

The soldier grabs it, scrutinises.

'You are from Gaza?'

Tuqa nods. Her address was never changed, all those years ago. She is, technically speaking, illegal in the West Bank. In her own country.

'Sit over there.'

She points at a row of seats in the corner, grimacing. Omar chuckles bemusedly.

'The Gaza chair,' he whispers to Tuqa.

The others out beyond the booth look back, inquiry in their eyes. Tuqa shakes her head.

Omar sits with her.

'It's okay,' he says.

'I can't believe this. The guy in the PA office said it would be fine. That I moved before 2007.'[3]

'They're always shifting the goalposts. One minute they announce one rule, the next …'

'What if they send me back?'

'They won't. They're on a power trip. They did this to your sister.'

'Same as this?'

'Exactly the same. She cried so much.' He chuckled. Maysera had a West Bank address on her ID, but Gaza mentioned as a birthplace was enough to cause consternation. 'You know how she is. You better not cry like that!'

Tuqa smiles briefly.

'Thanks Omar.'

She is glad to have him here. She feels like crying. Two men trudge over from the queue, sink into chairs opposite. They are muttering rapidly. She can hear it: the thickness of it, the 'Ah' sounds like gunshots, the Egyptianisms.

'You see,' chuckles Omar. 'These are the Gazan chairs.'

She recalls the drinking fountains of America, in those parched parks of the deep south, where your origins determined whether you would slake or thirst.

'You, you're the Gazan student?'

An olive uniform looms into sight. Sweat, tobacco, boot polish. The assault rifle dangles inches from her face: rugged, compact, futuristic, even alien-looking. A scratch glints in the matte black. A silvery notch. An account of action. A headshot? A headline?

---

3   PA: Palestinian Authority. The self-governing body in limited sections of the West Bank. Its autonomy or lack thereof is a matter of much controversy.

'Well, are you or aren't you?'

A square hard jaw under the beret. Eyes like bolts.

'Yes.'

'You Gazans don't go through. You should turn around; you're wasting your time here. Wasting our time.'

Tuqa bows her head. Her chin wants to wobble but she refuses to allow it. Tears well, but she breathes out.

'You people never learn.'

He turns on his heel, stamps away.

'Don't listen to that prick,' hisses Omar. 'He wants you to feel like that. To feel like a criminal, like an animal.'

'An invertebrate.'

Metamorphosis complete, she thinks. I am a cockroach in the abode of a superior species.

Gaza. Her earliest memories. Al Rimal, the Sand, a villa overlooking the sparkling Mediterranean. The jasmine-lined path from the front gate. The white limestone; thick immemorial blocks, cool in summer, warm in winter. It was a leafy avenue, salubrious. Wealthier refugees, many from Jaffa, had flocked there in 1948: al Nakba, the Catastrophe.[4]

In the garden she would make mud cakes while the others hurled mud balls. Her older sisters and cousins said she was too little to join them inside their ramparts made of clay and hay. They were redoubts, shelters from incoming mud bombs, crenellations from which to unleash your own. Israel they called one fort. Palestine the other. These tags the sole incursions of the conflict into their innocent bubble.

She remembers the cool interior, the patterned tiles and lofty ceilings, the artefacts and heirlooms adorning every wall.

---

4   The 'Nakba' or 'Catastrophe' refers to the exodus of Palestinians which occurred when the state of Israel was formed. This was a period of mass dispossession and displacement, along with massacres and the demolition of villages.

Tapestries, potted palms. A towering portrait of her grandfather: an infamous lawyer. His austerity offset by the fashion sketches of her mother and aunts: tall, leggy, colourful sylphs. Much pink, many florals. She recalls bobbing on her father's knee, him poring over magazines, reading to her, pointing at pictures, her mouth forming clumsy consonants in between dribbles.

Days on the beach, her mother teaching her to swim, uncertain strokes, gurgling, splashing, laughter under the sun. The sand in her toes, her hair, the unseen maze of her ear. The hunger as the picnic was set out. Her father never came, preferred to stay at home in his armchair, early signs of the rift with her mother. But at the seaside that was far off; all that mattered was the turquoise sparkle, gulls guttering overhead, schools of minnows surging past her hips, monsters of the deep. A fish was a leviathan, a crab a kraken, an eddy a whirlpool. Foam licking at the foot of a sandcastle was an unfolding Atlantis, a beautiful old city by the sea, crumbling into ruin. Fishermen were homecoming Argonauts, who would whistle and call to each other from their striped boats – green and yellow and blue – darkening as the sun set behind them.

Gaza.

Hamastan, Netanyahu now calls it. The 'great' leader. The strongman. Tuqa feels repulsed when she thinks of his smug grin. In his own malformed way, the Israeli leader is right; people have been brutalised. When you yank away the rug of democracy, the ability to be heard, to debate, to protest even, then you cannot be surprised when extremes present themselves. Hamas fires rockets, often provoked by Israeli bombings, often as negotiations seem to be appearing just around the corner. Bulls pricked by the master matadors. Hamas provides welfare, care that wins it favour as Gaza slips further into its slow-motion apocalypse.

By 2020, the UN says, it will be unfit for human life. Others would say that it already is. That it is a human rubbish heap, a sinking ship, an open-air prison, a cradle-to-grave cage, a concentration camp, a ghetto, a toxic slum. The water is slowly poisoning two million inhabitants, half of whom are children. Three-quarters are refugees. Four-fifths rely on international food aid. Typhus and cholera lurk, poised to engulf the suffocating warren.

Hamas has offered a long-term ceasefire, in return for a lift of the blockade. Netanyahu ignores this. The economy of the Palestinians, dislocated, incontiguous, quarantined, is in tatters, a fraction of Israel's GDP. The Israeli government complains of extremism, of violence, of ignorance, while it blows to smithereens electricity generators and cultural centres and schools, while it phosphorises enlightenment, tightens the barbed noose. Pax Israeliana.

A gaunt child, sick of watching his siblings turn paler and paler, stands up and hurls a rock at Goliath. The pebble pings off Goliath's steel chest, harmless, insignificant. A Lilliputian on Goliath's shoulder pulls his trigger. The other snipers cheer and clap him on the back. He can expect the jingle of medals, not the jangle of handcuffs. Purity of Arms.[5] And then, in their scopes, through the smoke, a medic appears.

Tuqa stares blankly at the queue as it passes through in slow jerks. Three hours have elapsed. Or rather, crawled. She wonders have her fellow travellers reached Amman yet and what they might be up to. She envies them. Still no word from the booth. Her mouth is dry. A strip light flickers.

The olive shadow looms again, the tobacco twang. The soldier thrusts the passport at Tuqa.

---

5 'Purity of Arms' is a central tenet in the Israel Defence Force's code of ethics. It states: 'The soldier shall not employ his weaponry and power in order to harm non-combatants or prisoners of war, and shall do all he can to avoid harming their lives, body, honour and property.'

'Go.'

She frowns, clears her throat.

'Go?'

'Go, go on.'

He waves her, impatiently, up and out the exit.

'You see,' whispers Omar. 'Told you.'

Tuqa smiles back, but quickly straightens her face.

An apology for the delay is not considered by either. It would be less outlandish if the soldiers offered her a shadow puppet show or a can-can performance. On the first page of her passport it says: *the Palestinian Authority requests all whom it may concern to allow the bearer, a citizen of Palestine, to pass freely and without hindrance and to afford the bearer all necessary assistance and protection.* Words. Ink. Nothing more.

There is an elderly man being interrogated as they pass through.

'Go on ahead,' says Omar.

'Why? What are you –'

'I'll catch up in a minute.'

Omar is already speaking with the man, reassuring him. Tuqa hesitates but passes through a turnstile, into fresh air. The vast lot is empty, apart from a single bus, shining under high noon. Last departure of the day. Time is crawling on and they still have to make the Jordanian Crossing before closing time. Tuqa slides her suitcase into the storage bay, glances back across the shimmering asphalt to the low building. No Omar. The bus driver frowns into the mirror, taps his wrist.

'We will have to go soon,' he says. 'The Jordanian border will be closing.'

'Please, one minute.'

The handful of other passengers mutter, shift about.

In her seat she checks her phone. Twenty minutes have passed.

A bee-eater, lime-green and gold, lands on the fencing outside, tilts its head, chirps, flaps away across the valley. Such liberty. There is a vapour trail in the sky. She can see herself dashing through the airport only to stop and stare out the window of the boarding gate: a rising airliner, an empty seat. She closes her eyes. Tries to breath, tries not to think of the soldier. But she imagines his voice whispering to her:

Even if we do let you through, do you think you will ever get back in? You never will. At best, you will be sent to Gaza, your real address.

Gaza, where her childhood home has been demolished, where happiness no longer exists, where the striped fisher boats rot on the shore, where only an embittered father remains, far from her college, her neighbourhood, her mother, sisters, nephews, friends. Her uncle and aunt, the cousins who lobbed mud bombs, left Gaza long ago for Qatar. The darkness is unhelpful, she opens her eyes.

'Omar.'

'There you are.'

'What happened?' she asks as he wriggles into his seat. The engine rouses with a growl.

'Ah, I tried to help that old fellow. He was from East Jerusalem, you know how that is.'[6]

'They turned him away?'

Omar nods.

No man's land zips past. Camels eye them through long lazy lashes, munching on scrub. Are they proud, those dromedaries? Do their humps swell with love of the motherland? What do *they* call it? Yisra'èl? Filastīn? Are they settlers? Or mere wildlife?

A streak of verdure appears ahead, treetops rising improbably

---

6   The Israelis conquered East Jerusalem in 1967, during the Six-Day War. Most of the Palestinians living there became Israeli residents, rather than citizens, which makes travel awkward.

out of the desert, in the shadow of a row of concrete piers and trusses. Allenby Bridge. It is named after the British general who chased the Ottomans out, with help from Lawrence of Arabia on his desert flank. This victory laid the ground for the Sykes-Picot Agreement – Britain and France carving up the Middle East among themselves, as well as validating the Balfour Declaration, which had promised to help establish a national home for the Jewish people.

Tuqa glances downstream, through the bridge railings and trusses blurring past. The River Jordan is underwhelming, a bed of wet rocks and rivulets. More a brook. Jesus, they say, was baptised right down there, among those reeds and rills, under the electrified fences and the gleam of circling drones.

A gatehouse looms up, painted white. Big blue lettering says: Welcome to Jordan, in Arabic, Hebrew and English. A large crown sits atop, gold and crimson. The car park is empty. It is five to three. Inside the booths the staff are standing up, stretching, chattering tiredly, happily.

Tuqa rose with the sun but now, somehow, may be too late.

Out front, a guard pulls on a smoke, frowns at the passengers, like a waiter might frown at last-minute customers who make him reset the table. His uniform is camouflage, not olive.

'We are closing. Why do you come so late?'

He clucks, spits.

Tuqa has heard that Gazans go to booth seven. There is a booth seven, so she breaks with the herd and goes up to that window. The guard is tidying his desk and looks up at the sudden shadow, irritation immediately vanishing as he sees Tuqa, her hippie style: unveiled curls, beady bracelets, make-up.

'Hello,' he says in English, beaming. 'Welcome to Jordan!'

My God. He thinks I'm a tourist.

'Hi.'

'How was your holiday?'

'I'm from Gaza,' she replies, in Arabic.

His eyebrows plunge.

'What?' He nearly topples off his chair. Terrorist, not tourist.

'Stay there,' he says. 'Don't move.'

He barks out the door. He stuffs chewing gum into his mouth, pouts. A superior officer enters.

'Yes?'

'Gaza,' says the guard, pointing at Tuqa.

'Mmhmm.'

'Three o'clock,' growls the guard, holding up his watch, tapping it violently.

'This is your wife?' asks the officer, looking over Tuqa's shoulder at Omar.

'No, no, I'm –'

'Who is she to you?'

'My wife's sister.'

The Jordanians glance at each other.

'Ah,' says the officer. 'I see. Well, show me your passports.'

They hand them in.

'And your green card? Or, sorry, your blue card?'

'I don't have it,' says Tuqa.

'First time?' asks the guard.

'Yes.'

'Okay. We'll issue you one.'

'Thank you.'

'Wait. You've been living in the West Bank?'

'Yes.'

'So we should issue you a green card then?'

'Em … I don't know …'

I don't care if you give me a rainbow-coloured card, just get me out of here.

'No, no, no,' says the officer. 'She is from Gaza. Officially, at least. It must be blue.'

Gaza, West Bank. Both are Palestine. How can you be officially from only one part of your country? Finally, the papers are issued, the stamp bangs, and Tuqa and Omar pass under the blue and white arch. Another car park greets them, along with shimmering asphalt, wire fences. Beyond is the same scrubland. Could this truly be another country? A new world?

'Is it ...' asks Tuqa. 'Are we?'

'Yes,' laughs Omar. 'No more checkpoints.'

Tuqa's eyes widen. She laughs. This is freedom? How utterly odd, how ethereal. A weight lifts off her shoulders. She has never in her life been out from under the jackboot. Her heart is flapping wings, rising out of occupation, an ember above the inferno.

'The sky is so blue,' she says.

'It is.'

Omar has pre-booked a rental car; they are soon whizzing into the east, towards low mountains. The radio blares tunes out the open windows.

'Here we are,' he says. 'Big Ramallah.'

Tuqa grins. Ramallah is nicknamed Little Amman. And not without reason, she now sees. Amman too is nestled in hills, lined with palms, has an old quarter of masonry, and a new quarter of glinting skyscrapers and glaring signs, of towering banks and cathedrals of consumerism. And tenements hidden around the corner, where refuse burns in the alleyways and tiaras of glass glisten along the wall tops. On the outskirts villas lounge, fattened on neoliberalism.

Amman is far larger than Ramallah. It has been – relatively – free to flourish. Omar spins around the city, gives her a quick tour.

He, like many West Bankers, knows the city well, its sprawling souqs and crumbling columns, its amphitheatre, citadel and palace, its casual treasures, Byzantine and Umayyad. There is time to dine in a downtown restaurant, but then they must hurry to the airport. Here she is reunited with the other students; they greet her at check-in, hug her, interrogate her.

'What happened?'

'Are you okay?'

'It was fine,' she says and changes the subject, slamming down a tsunami of dread.

Do you think you will ever get back in? You never will. You will be sent back to Gaza.

'Goodbye, Omar. Thank you. So much.'

'Be careful over there! Don't drink whiskey!'

They laugh. And then he is gone, still waving as she drifts into security clearance.

She is asleep as they fly over the Eiffel Tower, misses the bright lights of the City of Love. The jolt of the landing gear startles her awake. A layover in France; too brief to venture outside the airport. It is witching hour in the terminal: few shops open, pools of light in the shadow, contraptions polishing the floor, thrumming. The others thumb their phones or flick through magazines or try to snooze. Tuqa rings her sister, who has been living in Paris for over two years.

'Leulwa?'

'Hi! You're in?'

'Yeah, just landed. You must be tired, sorry to wake you.'

'I couldn't sleep; I've been checking your flight.'

'How long since we've been in the same city?'

'Oh my God. Two, three – three years and two months.'

'I miss you.'

'I wish you could stay in Paris. Even for a day,' Leulwa says.

'Come to Ireland with me!'

Leulwa laughs. There is a heaviness in it.

'So close, ey?'

But so far.

Drizzle slicks the cobbled courtyard. Tuqa is surrounded on all sides by colonnades, rounded arches, low grey roofs under a low grey sky. A verdigris clock tower streams. The minibus brought them straight here from the airport. The Irish Museum of Modern Art.

The director, streaming silver hair, striped sweater, welcomes them.

'Now,' she says, 'if you would like to follow me.'

She shepherds them in from the rain.

'I'll show you to your rooms. This was a military hospital once. See there? Those were the stables. Now they're your studio for the next two weeks.'

One of the students snaps a photo.

'I'm sure you're all exhausted.'

They nod.

'Well, lunch won't be until one. You can rest in your rooms until then.'

They are chirpier after the sleep, and showers and food. There is a buzz around the table, ice breaking, birthing, melting away. February gusts on the windowpanes but they are warm. Sitting among the Palestinian students are the Irish staff and Emily Jacir, award-winning Palestinian artist, who has graced galleries across the western world. It is she who has arranged the whole trip, a two-week workshop to run in tandem with her major exhibition, here in IMMA. She knows many of the students already, having lectured them several times back in the West Bank.

'How was the journey?' she asks them.

'Fine.'

'Oh, Tuqa,' blurts one, 'tell them what happened to you!'

Faces turn to Tuqa, sunflower-like.

'It was nothing, really,' she says.

She smiles into her glass and drinks.

Shut up. Leave me alone. Don't remind me.

There is an awkward pause. But soon the banter swallows it up again and it is forgotten. Yet Tuqa can smell the sweat and tobacco, see the bulletproof vest, the black muzzle.

You will be sent back to Gaza. You will never see your mother again.

The lax lunch was their last respite of the trip. Strict routine has taken over. Breakfast: seven sharp. Lectures: eight. They study Irish history, culture, politics. Analyse the similarities with home. The Plantations are discussed, and Captain Charles Boycott.[7] Debates in the evenings.

On the cold quays of the Liffey, they watch the wretched waxen faces, their ragged skeletons ghosting along the pavement. Trapped in bronze. They departed long ago, these phantoms – never to return, always to remain.

'The Irish are a tramping race,' they are told. 'Distant shores embraced us or entombed us or were simply inundated by us.'

In Belfast they see the peace walls, so familiar and yet, in this place, so seemingly mild. And in stasis. Not ever-creeping.

---

7   When Boycott attempted to evict tenants in 1880, during the Irish Land War, he was subjected to ostracism by the local community; thus the term 'to boycott' was coined.

In Derry more bulwarks: the old walls, cannon-crowned, impenetrable. And then the new walls, the gaudy gable murals: YOU ARE NOW ENTERING FREE DERRY. Nelson Mandela, Che Guevara, Martin Luther King. Hunger strikers. FREE PALESTINE! The Star of David. A king on a white horse. FOR GOD AND ULSTER. NO SURRENDER. The students are bombarded with dates: 1690, 1798, 1916, 1972, 1998.

Children in tracksuits traipse past, curved sticks over their shoulders. They laugh. When can the children of Palestine laugh? Where is their Good Friday? How will they clamber up out of the dust and the rubble?

The bus dips into the southwest. A moonscape surrounds them, striped, scraped and welted all the way to the horizon. The Atlantic out there somewhere, clouds brooding above it.

'Not enough water to drown a man,' they are told, 'wood enough to hang one, nor earth enough to bury him.'

The words of a roundhead commander. Cromwell's man.

Dry-stone walls snake, intersect, hem in precious scraps of grass. Dark limestone, jagged, tottering, unlike the white limestone of home, solid and squared.

They spend three days at the Burren College of Art. There are hikes, workshops, more discussions. It is brisk February weather, a cold glint in the sun. At the Cliffs of Moher, Tuqa leans into the winds, peers down at the briny turmoil below. Then out to the curving earth. Up at the soaring gulls.

Back in the workshop, she paints a landscape, entranced by how dusk daubs the grikes and the karst.

The whirlwind coughs them out in Dublin. Fortnight almost up.

The en suite door cracks open, sucking steam out.

'Are you coming?' asks her roommate. 'To lunch?'

'Yeah, I'll follow you down.'

The door clunks. Tuqa dries herself, dresses and stuffs everything into her suitcase. She makes rapid choices. The paints, tubes cracked and crusty, will stay. Rain jacket? Yes, crucial. Red sweater? My favourite, but too bulky. Burren landscape? Oh God, I can't. Photograph it then, quickly. *The Ship* by Jabra I. Jabra? Above all else. Forsake not thy favourite tome.

Fat rain batters the window, renders molten the outside world, makes a Dalí of the grey wing of the museum and the verdigris clock tower. She marvels at it: the rounded arches, unpointed, the Europeanness of it, built on a crusader priory to house old redcoats. The last of them were harbingers of a Mandate, sent packing by a Free State. 'Outremer' they called her home, long, long ago. 'Beyond the sea.'

She has the flu; dull throbbing temples, clogged sinuses. Her eyes are ringed darkly in the mirror. She has not slept soundly since leaving Palestine. She kept busy during the days, letting her senses overwhelm her. The nights have stalked her, though. Dark contemplations, unavoidable conclusions. The phone call home decided it, confirmed she was not going crazy.

'Don't come back,' her friend said.

'They were serious, weren't they?'

'You wouldn't be the first. They have you on file now, guaranteed. They will crush you for that address.'

'I was twelve.'

'You think they care? They imprison twelve-year-olds all the time. They shoot them. They know you live in the West Bank, but if you admit it, they'll crush you. If you don't, they'll send you to rot in Gaza. You can't win.'

'But how can I not go back? Ramallah. It's my home. My bedroom. What about college? What about mama? This can't be real.'

'Calm down. You have to keep calm. Take a breath. You're alive. You're safe. You're in a safe country.'

Last night, when her roommate was snoring faintly, the darkness started to swim and her lungs panicked, the air coming thick and tight, sluggish. She heard the voice of Edward Said echo: 'It is a fate of Palestinians. Not to end up where they started, but somewhere unexpected and far away.'[8]

Staring at the ceiling, into the milky dark, she made her final decision.

Tuqa looks at the husk of herself in the mirror, runs her trembling hands over her face. She mouths a word:

'Asylum.'

Then grabs the suitcase and pulls up her hood.

She pauses in a wide puddle, under the eave of the front door, its surface shivering. Before her is a courtyard. It is a mere thirty feet to the other side, but she will be visible throughout the crossing to her colleagues in the dining hall, where they are eating their last lunch of the trip. Complete exposure for ten seconds. She and her suitcase in the pouring rain. Alarming.

Yeah, I'll follow you down, she had told her roommate.

She has decided on a disappearance, a secret escape; she feels somehow that her colleagues would intercept her, detain her, haul her back aboard the plane. She is sick and exhausted, paranoid. But life is quite simple in this moment: reach the other side of the yard unseen, or suffer in a toxic slum forever.

She breathes. Then the water is splashing, the suitcase wheels spraying, a wake rippling behind her. Life as she knows it slips into the profound abyss of that puddle. She looks neither left nor right. And there it is, the museum facade. She has made it across

---

8 Edward Said was a Palestinian-American professor of literature, made famous by his book *Orientalism*, a cultural critique of western attitudes towards the Middle-Eastern 'Other'.

the courtyard. Unseen. She turns a corner, around a hedge. An avenue, flanked by linden trees, sinks into a distant perspective. She drags her suitcase forward, scrunching gravel, into the vanishing point.

Tuqa reaches the street and enters the strange wet greyness of Dublin city, drifting along the gleaming footpaths like a paper boat in a gutter. Soggy and lost, with whirlpools ahoy. She worries her suitcase is not waterproof. All she has is in it.

An umbrella hovers towards her.

'Sorry,' she asks. 'Where is Jervis Shopping Centre?'

It is the only shelter she can recall, after a brief shopping afternoon there with the group.

'You'll have to cross the river,' says the umbrella, spinning about, shooting droplets. 'That way, yeah, for a fair bit. Then take a left.'

'Thank you.'

'No worries.'

There are palms along the riverside boardwalk. But they are puny compared to home, they droop under the onslaught, weeping. Walls of wet wind sweep up the river. In Jervis Shopping Centre she clasps a coffee, inhales its steam. She pecks at a croissant; she should be hungry, but isn't. Her socks are saturated. She gets the WiFi code, makes some staticky calls.

A friend of a friend has a friend with a couch. A poky little apartment. Mildew in the hall, space heater blasting in the kitchen/living room. She crashes there, thankful for the tea and Lemsip and soup, though less so for the questions. Her headache is worse, but she trawls through the Internet as her boots steam on the radiator. Asylum in Ireland.

She finds the website that helped her make her final decision, rereads it, corroborates with blogs, articles. The International Protection Office. Right in the city centre, not too far. She looks up the buses.

Next morning, she arrives there. Closed. Until after the bank holiday. The knot in her chest, the heart garrotte, tightens another notch.

Her suitcase rolls under the flaps, into the belly of the X-ray. There is a metal-detecting gate and beyond that stretches a wide expanse of gleaming linoleum, a low ceiling, rows of chairs bolted to the floor; something between dentist and airport, a bureaucratic limbo. Alcoholic wafts from the gel dispensers glide on the stale atmosphere. It is reminiscent of the Israeli border crossing, but instead of air conditioners struggling with the heat, it is heaters struggling with the shivery morning seeping in through the windows.

'Step forward.'

Tuqa hesitates. She is unsure. The whole atmosphere brings her back home, back to the checkpoints, the searches, the interrogations. Constant humility and fear. Olive uniforms. Helmets with baggy covers. Tear-gas launchers.

'Yes,' drones the security guard, 'through there.'

He shakes his head, beckons her with exaggerated motions, as if she is a rather slow child. She wonders how he would like a day in Hebron, with a trip through the Cave of Patriarchs.[9]

'Okay, take a seat,' he orders, once she's through the gate.

Tuqa loosens her scarf, then wraps it again. She is cold and sweaty. On the seat, in the farthest corner, she curls into herself, clutching her elbows, shivering. The man sitting in front of her turns around.

---

9   A holy site for both Jews and Muslims, it is heavily fortified and requires worshippers, especially Palestinians, to endure lengthy queues and numerous security checks. Hebron itself is highly militarised and the scene of frequent intercommunal violence, even by West Bank standards.

'Don't worry,' he says. 'You will be okay.'

He is Zimbabwean, she learns. She wants to believe his reassurance, but it does little against her sickliness and nervousness. The conversation quickly trickles away into silence. The security guard chatters with a clerk, a phone rings insistently in some hidden office. Trust no one, Tuqa. It is you and you alone. Her mind blurs. She tries to count the kilometres to Ramallah, to coffee with her sisters on the sun-kissed balcony overlooking the old town.

She is called to the booth. Forms slide out.

'Fill these.'

She returns to her seat. Takes her time, reads and rereads before penning anything. Simple things stun her. Her date of birth becomes a painstaking inquiry, a trick question, a schizophrenic dialogue. There must be no errors, she reminds herself. An incorrect stroke of ink will condemn her to a toxic slum. Finally, she returns the forms. Relieved to be rid of them. Terrified of a mistake.

'Take a seat. We will be with you soon.'

She has been hailed in Ireland wherever she went, among artists and academics, in the shops and the cafes and the streets. In cities and villages. Smiles, greetings, self-deprecating asides. That chapter is over now, she realises. Again she sits, again she curls into herself, like a startled spider.

The minutes scrape slowly by, glacial.

What on earth am I doing?

She grabs her book, *The Ship*, plunges into brute escapism.

Where are we escaping to? I may escape into these paintings, which I only show to a very few people, or I may withdraw into silence that lasts for many days, flirting with my own thoughts. These thoughts usually revolve around my homeland, and my silence – a kind of internal silence, like a cosmic night whose spaces cannot be spanned …

Pages zip past, hours.

> Through all the years of my experience, black and painful, there still lurks that innocent, simple, loving, heedless youth, Fayiz'[s] twin, aged fifteen, sitting on the threshold of the old building eating a small pretzel with thyme and sketching people's eyes, overflowing with the fountainheads of life itself.[10]

Tuqa savours the last words. Rolls them around. Ponders sadly. It is dark outside now, car lamps flash the raindrops on the glass.

'Ms Sarraj?'

They lead her and a handful of others down a corridor and outside to a side street and into a minivan. The heaters are roaring and the door slides shut with a bang. Streets slip past, cones of lit drizzle.

There are five Pakistanis, three African women. Nobody speaks. For Tuqa, it is the same silence as after the gavel strikes, the bleak musings from courthouse to jailhouse. Or of aristocrats in a tumbril. Each locked in their own inner dungeons.

Tuqa sees girls outside, in short dresses, dashing from a taxi into a pub. They are her age. The van zips across a bridge and Tuqa glimpses a black Styx between the quay lamps, dappled yellow. The future yawns: unknowable, dark. The past washes away 'like tears in rain'.

---

10 From *The Ship: A Novel*, by Jabra Ibrahim Jabra, translated and with an introduction by Adnan Haydar and Roger Allen. Copyright © 1985, Jabra I. Jabra. Used with permission of Lynne Rienner Publishers, Inc.

They file up the step and into reception. It has the feel of an overgrown youth hostel, or a bleak and basic hotel. More forms to fill. Repetition of submission. Lines for ill-behaved school children. Some plastic chairs along the wall, a draft of night air, a noticeboard: English Lessons, Sewing Class, Summer Crèches, Clinics. This place is known as a 'Direct Provision Centre'.

A staff member, a young man, Irish, hands Tuqa her supplies:

Bedsheet.

Pillow.

Keycard.

'This way.'

She follows down a corridor. Him with the suitcase. The carpet, once floral, is now a faded palette of greys. The walls are dull, with inexplicable skid marks here and there, and generic still lifes at measured intervals.

'And where is it you're from?'

'Palestine.'

'Really? There's a load of solidarity here. In Ireland. With Palestine.'

She smiles politely.

'So,' he continues, 'have they filled you in? Have they explained the rules?'

She shakes her head.

'You can come and go whenever you like, as long as you're back in your room by curfew – nine o'clock. There's a special bus we run every morning and afternoon, if you need to go to the city. And then there's the allowance, of course. Twenty-one sixty per week.'

Before she can reply they come to a stop in front of a door.

'Here you go,' he says. 'Your room.'

He knocks and opens, leaves her with her suitcase.

'Good luck.'

'Thanks.'

There are three beds, three wardrobes and a desk. It is spartan, impersonal. A smell of dust and deodorant. Another door, in the corner, swings open and a woman emerges, wrapping a towel around her hair. She gasps.

'Who are you?'

She is blonde, a Balkan lilt.

'I'm Tuqa, I just got here –'

'I can see that.'

She grabs clothes off her bed.

'This is my room. Nobody told me about this.'

'I … I'm sorry.'

The woman takes her clothes into the en suite and slams the door.

'I am a rock,' Tuqa hums. 'I am an island.'

There is a bra on the desk, splayed like a fallen hatchling, some chocolate wrappers, a half-empty bottle of diet cola. Tuqa wishes there was a lamp, charcoal, paint tubes and brushes, a windfall of sketches. Like home.

She hauls the blanket up to her chin, lies in the dark, listens to her new home. A rustle from the opposite bed. A wet patter on the window. Some pipes thumping, deep within the building. Through the thin walls, she hears muffled conversation, giggles, bedsprings, squeaking at first, creaking then, and bouncing. The dark is paling when she finally shudders into sleep.

In the basement, stark-lit, the washing machines rumble and shudder, like crates of wild beasts in a hold, lint dancing in their warm updrafts. The Balkan woman is there alone, hauling her load up and into a dryer.

'Hi,' Tuqa says.

A bulging plastic bag dangles by her side.

'You get the liquid at reception.'

The receptionist is young and fed up. Sharp nose under a chestnut fringe, eyes close set, make-up mottled. She hands Tuqa detergent and a timetable:

Breakfast: 8.00–9.30

Lunch: 12.30–14.00

Dinner: 18.30–20.00

'Have you applied for your PPS yet?'

Tuqa shakes her head, then spends the next few minutes nodding, as she is told something about yet another application, and public services and correct documents and some office with an address and something about a bus.

'Okay?'

She nods once more and walks away none the wiser.

The dining hall is wedged, a long queue trailing back from the servers. She mimics the others, picks up a tray, stands in line. There are tables full of people, leaning in, bantering, arguing, and other tables with loners staring into their cups. My God, she thinks, which is worse? Where will I sit?

'Egg?' the server asks.

'Sorry. Yes please.'

The server fishes two out of the tray from among the dozen other eggs rolling about in the greyish water. He wears a grubby apron and a baggy kitchen cap. He winks at her and grins broadly, scanning her up and down. But suddenly he turns to the old man in the queue beside Tuqa, scowling.

'Please,' says the old man. 'Can I have some more?'

'More?' The server's eyes flash; he holds up one finger in the man's face. 'One egg is all you get here, old timer!'

Tuqa shudders.

At the next counter she dips into a white expanse with a ladle, wrinkles the skin, splashes a token amount of the milky substance into her bowl. A dribbly mystery. She queues again for toast, grabs a little foil-wrapped butter and a strawberry jam. Another line for the tea, big hot water dispensers, counter splashed in milk, sprinkled in sugar. Time to sit.

She carries the tray among them, skinny shoulders, broad backs, bright kerchiefs, bald folds, tangled locks, children swinging out of seats with jam-sticky fingers, slapping their siblings. She clenches the tray tighter than is necessary, steps carefully, as if on a tightrope, eyeing the sloshing tea in her cup. There is an empty little table on the far side of the hall. She lands the tray, shimmies in beside it, throws glances up from it now and again, furtively.

White plate, white eggs; white bowl, white substance. It is food made without love: you can chew the futility, the hopelessness. She pines for colours, for golden-brown bread and falafel, green olives and cucumber, red tomato, yellow lemon. Her mouth waters for creamy hummus, balled yoghurt, sour-spicy sumac. Thyme and oregano. Her heart aches for her sisters, her little brother, Yazan, her nephews, her brother-in-law. She misses her new father-in-law, Salim, the librarian, and all of his quiet suggestions and recommendations. She misses her mama. How little she appreciated their Friday tradition, the stroll around the corner to the baker; fresh kaek, bagel-like, crunchy and soft, sesame-sprinkled. The warm aroma mixing with the fragrance of the jasmine trees. The chatter and gossip and laughter at her mama's table. Mint tea afterwards in glass cups.

She nibbles at an egg and some toast and trudges back to her room.

✢ ✢ ✢

Lunch is the same. Alone in a hall full of people. Queue. The server's broad grin. Damp pale salad, bland rice. Chicken wings look the best part, but she must not allow this place to change her, to conquer her. She is a vegetarian. An artist. A Palestinian. Still, despite all.

There are other loners dotted about the hall, depression wafting off them, their silence thunderous amid the clatter of cutlery and chatter. They let this place change them, Tuqa thinks. Let it shuck the personality out of them. And into the void pours despair.

Her next choice tortures her: shorten the bleak afternoon in her room or shorten this awkward sitting.

She glances about at the other inmates. Who kept me awake last night?

Dinner: the server's broad grin. Damp salad, bland rice. Don't take the chicken. She is charging towards the wall, eyes glued to her seat. Don't make eye contact. She has made it safely and then:

'Peace be upon you!'

There is a face framed by a hijab, a short woman, smiling. She has rosy cheeks, dimpled. She seems to be in her thirties.

'You are an Arab?'

'I am.'

'My name is Maryam.'

Her eyes are friendly but nervous, darting here and there. She gesticulates constantly, fidgets.

'I'm Tuqa.'

'Can I sit? Thanks.'

She slides her tray beside Tuqa's.

'We will be friends, yes?'

Tuqa labours a smile.

Trust no one. Be an island.

Another dark night. Sheets rustling, pipes thumping, bedsprings creaking. She longs for poetry, to read some Mahmoud Darwish, seek his solace, but there are no poems in this place. She quarries down into depths of memory. She peeks through the curtain, up at the darkness, at the continents of cloud snailing by, edges frayed by hidden stars.

The quarry strikes a seam. A quote from Darwish comes to mind: 'A moon will rise from my darkness.'

But the clouds do not part.

Tuqa trudges down to the basement early in the morning, laundry liquid in hand this time. She is stuffing socks into the machine's mouth.

'Peace be upon you, Tuqa!'

'Ah, Maryam. Morning.'

Tuqa is trying to close the machine door, but it refuses to click.

'Oh,' says Maryam, 'that's a tricky one, you need to' – she bangs the door with her hip – 'there!'

'Thanks.'

'How did you sleep?'

'Oh, you know …'

'You look tired.'

'Yeah …'

'So, I don't know what you've got planned for the morning, but, I was thinking, if you like, maybe we could get the bus together?'

'The bus?'

'To the city? To go to Parnell Street.'

'Okay …'

'For your PPS. I thought I could help. I've been there before.'

'Really? Thanks Maryam. That would actually be … very helpful.'

Maryam beams back at her.

An island. Still an island. But perhaps an island with a ferry service. Or even a drawbridge.

Tuqa is on her bed, pulling on her shoes, sighing. It is evening, almost limp lettuce time. Tuqa has lost weight these past two weeks, lost colour in her face, energy in her step. The flu did not disappear, but simply dissipated into an endless tiredness: a creakiness of the joints, an occasional pain in the lower back.

The door swings open.

'Peace be upon you! You're going to dinner?'

'Just getting ready.'

'No, habibi. No dining hall for you today.'

'Huh?'

'Come with me.'

Maryam leads her down the corridor, up a stairwell and around a corner.

'This is my place.'

She seems inordinately proud of this door, dull as any of the others, as she pushes it in. Tuqa's nostrils twitch.

'Tuqa, this is my husband, Hakim.'

'Pleased to meet you.'

He is an older man, big and broad-shouldered, but with a gentleness in his eyes. A sadness there too.

'Quick, close the door.'

The room is smaller than hers, but with only two beds. They

have been dragged close together, a stool in between, cups perched on it. And their desk is cluttered.

Tuqa's nostrils twitch again; yes, that familiar aroma. On the desk sits a hotplate, some pots, spice jars, bags of rice and durum.

Maryam giggles at Tuqa's astonishment. She points at the ceiling. The smoke alarm is gleaming, wrapped wrinkly in cling film.

'I had to cook. I missed it too much.'

Tuqa closes her eyes and inhales. The past month dissolves in that warm aroma.

'Here, sit.'

Nothing is spoken for some minutes, just the clink of bowls, the slurping of soup.

'You like our lavish seating arrangement?' asks Hakim.

'It's very opulent,' laughs Tuqa. 'But isn't this the couples' section?'

Hakim sighs. 'It is, but you still get single beds. We push them together at night, apart for meals. The desk is our kitchen, so a stool must take the role of table.'

'Resourceful.'

'Algerians are like that.'

The door creaks open, and a hijab pops in.

'Peace be upon you!'

'Welcome, come, sit.'

A short woman enters, and then a man, who sits on the bed beside Hakim. They are young, thin. Their eyes are pouchy, their faces weathered, wrinkling early.

'Tuqa, this is Amena and Ziad.'

'Lovely to meet you.'

'They're from Syria,' Maryam explains. 'They just got here, like you. Tuqa is from Palestine.'

'I've never met Syrians before. It is good to meet you.'

Amena smiles. 'Well, our folks are from your neck of the woods. We are Palestinian too, really. We've been raised among Palestinians, as Palestinians.'

'Your accents are the same,' says Maryam.

'We've followed the news from there since childhood,' continues Amena. 'Grandmother would tell us of the oranges on her farm. How they burned in the Nakba.'

Tuqa nods and sighs.

'The Zionists marched into the neighbouring village. They started shooting all about them. Those who ran inside, they finished with grenades. A handful escaped. Unwitting messengers. The next nine or ten villages didn't wait around.'

'Easy real estate,' says Ziad.

Tuqa tells some of her family's histories, of their flight out of Jaffa. Then she steers the conversation away, into nostalgia: the ways of the old people, the food and the music, the weddings and feast days. The Syrians are familiar with most of it, and weave in their own additions, which Tuqa in turn recognises. The Algerians listen.

'So,' says Maryam, 'are you ready for some delicious couscous?'

Tuqa glances at the Syrians, they at her. They burst out laughing.

'You easterners are vulgar,' Maryam scowls, blushing.

'I'm sorry,' Tuqa laughs. 'We call it maftoul. Couscous, for us, is … something else.'

'I know what it means!' Maryam shakes her head, sinks into the bed, between Tuqa and Amena. 'Well, there it is: *maftoul*. Enjoy.'

They praise and thank her, and dig in.

Maryam refills Tuqa's bowl. 'You're getting too skinny,' she observes.

Tuqa has forgotten how it is to eat seconds, then thirds. How to stifle laughter with a full mouth, to sip tea before answering.

'So,' asks Tuqa. 'You came through Greece?'

'Yes,' says Amena. 'It was terrible. There were many locals who …'

Her eyes water up.

'There are neo-Nazis there,' says Ziad. 'They go about in gangs, search for Syrians.'

'Most Irish are nice,' says Tuqa.

Maryam scoffs. 'Only ones I've known are the staff here,' she says. 'Not too impressive.'

'This place is not normal,' says Tuqa. 'Believe me. It is better. Out there.'

The Syrians are staring at her, drinking in the hope.

Ziad takes his phone from his pocket. 'See, this is where they are sending us.' He points at a map on his phone, far to the rugged west of the country. 'Ball-Ag-Ha-Der-Reen.'

Ballaghaderreen.

'The names are so strange,' says Maryam.

'They are,' says Tuqa. 'It's a whole other language.'

Hakim chuckles.

'English is difficult enough!'

They all nod. Maryam serves them dessert: yoghurt and nuts.

'I hope you're right, Tuqa,' says Amena. 'About the Irish. You're the first person we've met who could tell us anything about this place. Our relatives knew about Germany and Sweden and those bigger places. But no one knows anyone who has come here.'

As compared to other EU countries, even allowing for population and economy, Ireland welcomes pitifully few displaced persons.

'Well,' says Tuqa, 'I've been to the west coast. The westerners are the most friendly of all. You will be good. I'll come visit you, when you are settled. You can show me around.'

'That would be nice,' smiles Amena.

'I'll come too,' says Maryam.

Tuqa goes for fresh air before bed. Wanders outside. There is not much to gaze at, only a bare yard and the perimeter gate, locked up since curfew. The moon peek-a-boos out at her, through cloud drifts. She passes the kitchen on the way back. A woman is rapping on its double doors, smiling in anticipation. Tuqa recognises her. She is an Arab, in her thirties; they have chattered once or twice in the hallway.

'Hey.'

'Tuqa, how are you?'

'Good. What's going on?'

'I'm getting a snack. You hungry?'

The doors part. It is the server, grinning broadly. He eyes both of the young women up and down.

'Ladies, good evening. How can I help you?'

The woman blinks her lashes.

'We were wondering, mister chef man, if, maybe, you could sort us out?'

'Hmmm,' says the server. 'That depends. What is it you need sorting?'

'We were hoping for some … *toast*.'

'Toast?' He laughs. 'For you lovely ladies, I can get anything.'

'I'm hungry,' says the woman. 'For toast.'

She stares at him, then bursts into giggles. He dips into the kitchen, returns with the toast.

But Tuqa is halfway up the staircase.

Tuqa brushes her teeth, begins to undo her shoes. Her roommate is still out. There is a knock on her bedroom door, it opens.

'Evening.'

It is the server.

'Eh, hello. What do you want?'

'I just wanted to make sure that everything is all right up here. That you have everything you need.'

'Yes, I'm fine.'

'You sure?'

He steps in, slouching in the door frame. 'You don't need anything in here? Maybe some company? You must be lonely?'

'No, I'm fine, really.'

'Don't you have a boyfriend? A pretty girl like you must have a boyfriend? No? You *must* be lonely up here.'

He seems tall, taller than she realised before, now that he is so close. She feels frail in comparison, miniscule. She can smell the kitchen in her room, the grease and the soap.

'Please get out.'

'You wanna come outside? For a chat? I'd love to get to know you better. You're so lovely.'

'Get out,' she growls, 'or there'll be trouble.' She breathes in deeply, filling her lungs, ready to scream.

'Okay, okay.'

He backs out, still grinning. The door eases shut.

Tuqa jams a chair under the doorknob. She sits for a long time on her bed, hugging her knees, staring at the gap under the door. Eventually, the shadow moves away and she hears footsteps padding downstairs.

Tuqa files it away, along with the bedsprings and the rumours, hearsay about garda raids, drugs and prostitution. It seems to confirm some of the gossip, though: this man has been seen late at night, kissing another woman in the corridor.

Expensive toast.

✦ ✦ ✦

Pains have seared through her for days now. Starting as throbbing, in under the ribcage. Now she is writhing in bed, sheets of agony roiling through her. Her sister had this before. She knows these symptoms. She has felt ill throughout these past weeks, has lost much weight. The evening meals with Maryam have been a recent development, and have not yet begun to take effect after the weeks of limp lettuce. Her eyes are ringed, her cheeks pointed for the first time in her life. She feels skeletal when she looks in the mirror, feeble when dressing, one sock at a time, one sleeve, a breath, then the other. She knows she has not been drinking enough water; the only source is in the dining hall, which she avoids as much as she can.

'You need an ambulance,' says Maryam, standing over her bed. Tuqa moans. 'Come, I'll help you get dressed. Then we'll get you an ambulance.'

'No. A taxi.'

'You are in agony, habibi, look at you! Your face is green. If you go by taxi, you will wait for hours. That's what happened with Hakim, the time he had that trouble with his pacemaker.'

'Taxi.'

Tuqa has one memory of ambulances. Their sirens: the shrieking that followed the silence after an air strike. The dusty rag dolls, dragged from ruins, dripping on the pavement, the slamming of doors. The inevitable funeral. The headlines. The keening women. The bitter mutterings.

Downstairs, she mumbles to the receptionist.

'I need a taxi.'

'Taxi?'

'To go to hospital. I'm not well.'

'Sorry?'

'The hospital, I … I'm sick.'

'You look fine.'

'Please.'

'The bus will be going soon. Get that. If you can wait for a taxi, you can wait for a bus.'

'But, please –'

'I don't know that you're sick. I'm not a nurse. Maybe you're making it up.'

'What do you mean?'

'You're making it up. You don't want to be transferred.'

A notice of transfer had been pinned on the wall yesterday, but Tuqa was so unwell she hardly noticed it.

'You think I don't want to leave this place?'

The receptionist shrugs. Tuqa gasps, wheels away from the desk and staggers over to a chair. Tears stream. She clutches the small of her back. The receptionist swivels away, swish of chestnut, goes back to thumbing her phone.

Vomit wells up and Tuqa is outside, hands and knees wet with dew, grass spattered in bile, again and again. She returns inside, sits in the chair, quivering.

'What's wrong with you?' asks the receptionist. 'Are you pregnant?'

'I'm a virgin!' screams Tuqa, eyes flaring up.

The receptionist raises an eyebrow, swivels away again.

Ten minutes later, Tuqa is struggling up the steps of the centre's private shuttle bus, squeezing her bottom rib, groaning. The driver looks at her, perplexed.

'I need to get to a hospital.'

'Yeah, there's one right down the road from the stop.'

'Can you drop me there? Please, Sir. I don't know the way.'

'Yeah,' says the driver, nodding. 'Of course.'

She sits behind him, folds double, straightens stiff, stands up, sits down again. She catches the driver's confused eyes in the mirror. The pain has become an inferno. At the next traffic lights she bursts past the driver.

'Let me out. Please. Now.'

The door slides and she stumbles out, crosses the street, to a pub. She fumbles for her phone, rings an ambulance. They know the pub, thankfully. She does not. She has no idea where she is. Should have listened to Maryam.

The ambulance streaks across the city. Tuqa squints in the brilliant light of the lamps above. She smells disinfectant, tastes bile. Two voices warble back to her, from the front. Her forehead is dotting with cold blobs of sweat.

'Where are ya from?'

'Palestine.'

'Palestine?'

'Yes.'

'Palestinians are very brave. You have to be brave now, okay?'

She gasps, nods faintly.

'You're very pretty.'

'Thanks.'

'And your English is really good.'

'Yeah,' says the other. 'Fair play.'

'I would hope so,' she thinks, 'after reading all that English literature.'

'I never met a Palestinian before,' one whispers to the other.

They jolt over a speed bump, round a corner.

'How are you doing back there? You still with us?'

'Yes.'

'Good. Be strong.'

'Palestinians are strong,' says the other.

'Tuqa, are you on any medication?'

'No.'

'Any allergies?'

'No.'

'Any recent operations we should know about?'

'No.'

'Do you smoke?'

'No.'

'Drink?'

'Not really.'

'Jaysis, you're very healthy altogether.'

'Fair play,' says the other.

'And where is it you're living, Tuqa?'

She says the name of the centre. There is a pause. After a moment one of them speaks.

'Is there any chance, Tuqa, that you could be pregnant?'

'I'm not pregnant,' she growls.

This is Tuqa's first experience of a hospital. She has never in her life required one. In the packed emergency room, a nurse scans her up and down.

'We'll get to you as soon as we can.'

'Wait, I have kidney stones, please, I know it, my sister had them before.'

But the nurse is gone. The agony comes in waves. For now, Tuqa is in a trough. But God knows for how long. Double doors whoosh, intercoms warble, drunkards bellow, security guards charge and a janitor's mop sploshes.

An old lady turns to Tuqa.

'Where're ya from, love?'

'Palestine.'

'Palestine? The Holy Land?'

Tuqa nods.

'I've always wanted to go!'

The stable at Bethlehem. The Sea of Galilee. The salt caves of Sodom and the Mount of Olives. Tuqa can picture the droves of tourists, the flashing cameras.

'There'd be so much to see,' says the lady, eyes sparkling.

'You'd be busy.'

The old lady smiles. For so many people, Palestine is an antique land, a biblical cabinet of curiosities. That or a crucible of unending violence, a nursery for foreign correspondents, a proving ground. Would this old lady ever wake up to the aroma of kaek, though? Of jasmine and olives? Of the freshness after rain has cleansed the dust? Hear the oud drift over a courtyard? Listen to the poet in a teahouse? Or see napkins twirling in the hands of dabka dancers? Would she ever know Tuqa's home as a place not for the long-dead or the soon-to-be-dead, but as a place for living, a place where life refuses to surrender, where it somehow sprouts up between cracks in the ferroconcrete?

The old lady talks a lot about Ireland and its history. She is keeping her mind off her sister, who was shuttled away on a trolley some time ago. It reminds Tuqa of her sisters. They would do the same for her. She for them. If only they knew.

'Ms Sarraj?'

A white coat arrives before her.

'Doctor, thank you, I think I have kidney stones. Can you check? Do a scan?'

The doctor asks a burst of questions: date of birth, medical history, whether she possesses a medical card, address.

'Direct provision?'

'Yes.'

'Mmhmm.'

She puts a hand on Tuqa's forehead, looks her up and down, scribbles on her pad.

'You're okay.'

'But, the pain, can't you do an X-ray or something?'

'You'll be fine. You just need to drink plenty of water and eat your fruit and veg.'

'No, but –'

In the taxi back to the centre, the agony begins swelling again. She cries in frustration at herself for not standing her ground, demanding a check-up. The night is endless. A sweaty hell.

Maryam takes her back to the hospital on the first bus. This time, they run an X-ray. Kidney stones. Maryam knows the nearest pharmacy, buys the three prescriptions. Soon the pain is gone. Tuqa has never used painkillers before. She feels high, glides out of her body, races with the clouds.

'Here, eat that.'

Tuqa props herself up, sagging into a pile of pillows. Steam hits her face from the bowl hovering in front of her. Maryam is nursing her. Bringing food, plenty of water and the news that her transfer has been deferred.

'Is it … chicken?'

'Eat. You are weak. Now is not the time for your ideas.'

She closes her eyes in acceptance, takes the soup.

'So,' asks Maryam. 'Where are you off to this morning?'

They are sitting at a table in the corner of the dining hall, sipping tea, munching toast.

'I'm just going to town.'

'Town? Why, though?'

'For a look around.'

'No, no. You shouldn't. Only go when it is absolutely necessary.'

'I want to see the city. I need to get out of here for a few hours. This place is driving me crazy.'

Maryam huffs.

'Well, where is it you're going?'

'I was thinking of looking at Trinity College, Dublin Castle, you know, up around Parliament Street.'

'Parliament Street?'

'Yes.'

'Parliament Street is too dangerous. You will be stabbed! Or …'

'What?'

'They could take your honour. If you're not careful. The way you strut around, Tuqa, no hijab. It's unseemly for a girl.'

Tuqa's eyes close. Not this again.

'Why don't we go shopping,' Maryam continues. 'I know a little place near here that does hijabs, the best of fabrics, just like –'

'Maryam. Don't go there. Please. We've been through this. I respect your beliefs, but I don't share them. I've never lived like that and I don't intend on starting now.'

'But it's just that you are unschooled. We'll read the Quran together, and you'll learn to see the depth of Islam. Then you'll understand, then you'll believe as I believe.'

'I'm familiar with the Quran, Maryam. I've read it.'

Maryam downs the dregs of her cup. Stands up. She begins to say something, but turns and storms off.

Tuqa sighs. She knows Maryam is trying to be helpful. She has no children to look after, sees Tuqa more as a daughter or a niece than a friend. Life in the centre has made her increasingly nervous, twitchy, and often irritable with her husband. The staff raided her room yesterday, uncovered the hotplate, ripped the cling film from the smoke detector.

'This is a serious breach of regulations,' they said. 'We may have to report this.'

Maryam wept all night. Her little evenings of hosting, of recreating a sliver of home, were over.

Asylum life takes its toll in different ways. It seeps into the mind and institutionalises. Keycards report every click to a centralised computer, observed at all times by the staff. CCTV cameras perch in every corner. Tuqa hates how Orwellian it is and hates even more that it does, at times, make her feel slightly safer. She has not had any more nocturnal visitors slouching in her door frame. Not so far.

The outer world becomes dangerous, the inner world paralysed, stagnant. There is a temporariness, an atmosphere that renders any endeavour futile. And yet this temporariness is non-temporary; it drags on. And on. And on. Sometimes for years. People shuffle about like pensioners. Or prisoners with invisible chains. Tuqa has existed here for over a month now. It seems more like a year. Time shrinks, stretches.

Tuqa picks a window seat in the cafe. She admires the columns of City Hall across the road, their florid capitals. It is a mild spring afternoon, the crowds bask in the hint of warmth, jackets unzipped. There is a Friday feeling in the air, youthful anticipation of the night lights. She buys herself a coffee, a rare, even overindulgent, treat. She pushes the change across the polished wood, ten cents and twenties, a yellow hoard.

'Would you like anything else?' asks the barista.

Yes, please, I would like the freedom to earn a dignified wage rather than a weekly gesture of twenty euro. I'd like to show this society what I'm capable of, what I can contribute. I'd like a driver's licence and a bank account. I'd like the chance to cook my own food, in private.

'No thanks,' says Tuqa.

She is reluctant to climb aboard the shuttle bus. But it is the last one of the day. The bustle drains away as they lumber out of the city. Back in the centre, a new list is pinned to the bulletin board.

Once again, Tuqa's name is on it. Transfer.

'Goodbye,' says Maryam. 'I'm sorry.'

Tears stream down her cheeks, plunge into the silkiness of her headscarf.

'Don't be sorry. You looked after me when I was sick. Cooked all that maftoul.'

Maryam rolls her eyes, but they are both smiling.

'Thank you, Maryam.'

'We will see you again someday, God willing.'

'I hope so. In happier times.'

'I'll pray for you.'

'Pray for us all.'

Tuqa is on the bus and it turns out of the driveway and the centre disappears behind the high hedge. The coach, with its five passengers, hurtles southward, into the unknown. Tuqa is on the move again, her suitcase below in the hold, her worldly possessions within.

She falls into a doze for a few hours. When she awakes, she looks out the window, where a squat round tower squints back at her through its arrow slit.

Townhouses and shop fronts pass by, a steeple juts above the rooftops and the lamps of the quayside are reflected in the river, yachts bobbing on the shimmer. Waterford, Ireland's oldest city. A baby compared to Jaffa or Jerusalem or Jericho.

This centre is smaller than the first one, but the reception is the same. A woman in a trouser suit, a staff member, approaches Tuqa.

'Hi. Do you speak English?'

'I do.'

'Oh thank God. I haven't got an Arabic translation for these forms.'

Tuqa is led down the corridor and up a staircase, to her room. The door swings open. It is spartan, impersonal. A bland dusty smell. But there is only one bed and only one wardrobe and no other door swinging open to reveal an angry towel-clad blonde. She parks her suitcase and collapses onto the sheets, spread-eagled. She closes her eyes. Smiles.

There are twenty other rooms on the floor, all occupied by single women. Above are single men, below families. At one end of the hallway is a bathroom: to the right, three shower stalls. To the left, three toilet cubicles. At the other end of the hallway is a kitchenette. A camera is perched up in one corner, lord of all it surveys.

The smell hits her like a jackboot in the stomach. The fridge is jammed: black bananas, mouldy yoghurts, butter blocks smudged with crumbs, several milk cartons: pink, red, green, blue, a stepladder of fat content. Some are worryingly bloated. She slams the door, grimaces. The kitchenette counter is greasy, the sink an assortment of browned mugs. On the hot water dispenser, over the button, is a sticky note: *out of order*. Brilliant.

Where is Maryam and her magical hotplate?

The dining hall is in a separate building, down a long footpath. The March mornings make it unappealing, but, even worse, the food is much the same as in the first centre. Limp lettuce and bland rice. Dribbly mysteries and over-cooked eggs. Tuqa is glad, however, that there is no leering server, with his broad grin and gifts of toast.

Where is mama and her falafels?

She has never thought of her mother as much as she does these lonely nights. How little she appreciated her. The blue glow of the phone, the static-filled lacunae, are scant connection.

Hekmat was eighteen when she married. He is from a big family, her mother said. A prosperous family. And such a nice house, overlooking the sea. What does it matter if he is a bit older? Hekmat left college, left her classmates studying towards their degrees, while she studied her new kitchen and the medicines needed by her ailing parents-in-law. She became pregnant. The Intifada erupted. She became pregnant again. And again. Then came the Oslo Accords and her Oslo baby, infant number four, Tuqa. First her mother-in-law passed away, then her father-in-law. Her brother-in-law lived upstairs, his children played with her daughters, but he and his wife did not have much to say to Hekmat. Her husband too, increasingly. She was curious, energetic, open-minded. It irked him.

When the children grew a bit older, she began attending classes again. Unfinished business. Journalism. She spread into that world, made contacts, friends, from all over the world. She was invited to a conference in the US in 2002. The distance brought her some clarity. Somewhere over the Atlantic she recognised how unhappy her marriage was. A divorce followed. At first she had barely been able to utter the words to herself, such was the tidal pull of the taboo. It was practically unheard of. But she worked up the courage, faced the onslaught.

Hekmat and the girls moved into their own apartment, across town. She bought her own car. She was a female journalist and a single mother. She was Wonder Woman.

From the very first doodles, Hekmat encouraged Tuqa's artistic spark, fanned the flames, threw in paper and crayons and canvas and brushes. She did not think her daughter mad when she did not clutch at college, any college, the moment school finished. She understood Tuqa's decision to volunteer instead at an art gallery, to take a year to expand her mind, learn from practising artists, to make contacts and grow autonomously. Tuqa took French lessons, studied watercolour painting under a US artist. She read a lot, in Arabic, in English, bombarded with recommendations from new friends and mentors. As a volunteer she set up exhibitions, saw the practical ins and outs of the scene. Her new friends discussed how art interwove with the struggle for freedom, how the spray can is mightier than the mortar. They adhered to Orwell's maxim: 'The opinion that art should have nothing to do with politics is itself a political attitude.'

Besides, the course Tuqa wanted to enrol in was offered only every second year, so it made perfect sense to accumulate knowledge while she waited.

No one celebrated louder than Hekmat when Tuqa was accepted into the International Academy of Art, Palestine. No one showed more interest in her projects.

Her first was devoted to the bin men of Ramallah, who cleaned up the wealthy district every dawn, before melting away, back to their poverty and the tears of their children, out of sight of the Palestinian Authority elites, out of mind of those who were doing rather well as neo-colonial middlemen.

It was not until the offer of the workshop in Ireland that Hekmat displayed doubts.

'Mama, only five of us were chosen. I did well. This is such an opportunity.'

'It scares me, Tuqa.'

She hears of the Palestinian hunger strike in April. It takes place simultaneously in jails across Israel. Prisoners range from stone-throwing children to people charged with weapons possession and some, a minority, are linked to terrorist attacks. They demand visitation rights, two days per month, and to be allowed to telephone family members. A right-wing Israeli youth group organises a big barbecue just outside the cell windows, close enough for the kebab smoke to curl in around the bars.

In Waterford, Tuqa stands out by the quays with a sign: *Freedom and Dignity for Palestinian Political Prisoners*. She wears a black and white keffiyeh around her shoulders. Some cars beep. Most just zoom past. A local artist joins her. They become friends. Tuqa is introduced to others and soon a web of friendship is spreading across Munster. She visits Limerick often, connects with still more artists and activists.

She gets to know the people in the centre. They are from all over. There are some Arabs, but mostly it is Africans, a jigsaw of the continent: Somalia, Benin, Zimbabwe, Kenya, Uganda, South Africa. Most are from Nigeria and the Congo. Some are dipping their toes in the waters of activism. Perhaps by coming together, in solidarity, their voices will be heard. They meet with activists on the outside. There are long discussions, strolling the grounds, seated around dining tables, chatting in the kitchenette until all hours.

They compare and contrast the treatment of Congolese and Nigerians here with Syrians, or indeed, Palestinians. They have never heard: 'There is a lot of solidarity here. In Ireland. With Kinshasa.' Or, 'with the Niger Delta'. And yet there are swathes of these regions that are often far more dangerous than even Gaza.

A small group of them meet a local historian, a pensioner, at a nearby cafe. He has thick glasses, magnified eyes, watery. He wears a ragged cardigan, a badge with a Co. Waterford crest on it. Taught science and history for decades.

'Have ye heard of Roger Casement? No? A great man. An

Irish hero. He investigated the oppression in the Belgian colonies. He stood up for the people of the Congo.'

He sips his coffee.

'Then there was the Irish peacekeepers. They fought for the people of the Congo too, at Jadotville. 1961. Fought like lions. It was a brave fight, but it was a drop in the ocean, I'm afraid. Same blackguards are there to this day, extractin' and exploitin' away, so they are. Coltan is what they're after now, instead of rubber. A disaster altogether. I read somewhere that the wars over them minerals have been the most deadly since the Second World War.'

'Yes,' says one woman. 'Millions dead.'

'We've had some stuff like that too,' says another. 'In Nigeria. The Niger Delta. The oil men arm militias, send them in wherever there is resistance. Nobody calls the police; the government are in on it too.'

'Oh I know them,' says the pensioner. 'The same boys are at it here too, only without the bloodbath. That'd be bad publicity, if they were butcherin' whites. They've found other ways, though, other deals. They're suckin' millions each year from our teat, billions probably, from that tidy little operation up in Mayo.'

'And yet we Nigerians are the criminals. We asylum seekers.'

The pensioner nods, frowning.

'You escape our mutual tormentor, and we – some of us – torment *you*. And what does the tormentor get? Tax breaks.'

'That stuff should stay in the earth,' says another man. 'My home, my birthplace, is a ghost village today. The desert swallowed it up. Because of drought. Because of climate change.'

They ask questions: why are there so many of us, so many of the displaced, knocking on Europe's door? Seeking a life in the US or Australia? We are the symptoms, but what is the cause? Why such misery and poverty at home? Why such instability? What could push people to risk everything, to leave everyone and to step aboard a dinghy or clamber into a container?

The pensioner drops a sugar lump into his cup, stirs it in.

'Perhaps,' he says, 'we need to ask who's orderin' thousands of African children down mines on a daily basis. Dickensian conditions. Barbaric. Or who orders the orderers. Who's butterin' whose bread? And then there's the intelligence agencies. Every time an African leader tries to claim his country's resources for his country's people – bang! Coup. Then there's the lobbyists scurryin' about to cover up climate change. Shower of scuts.'

He clinks his spoon, slips it onto the saucer.

'But, I suppose, to be fair, worst of all is ourselves. Us. The affluent West. Always diggin' in our wallets for that dream diamond or the latest smartphone; always needin' some new-fangled necessity, upgrade, gizmo. And coltan, precious coltan, fizzlin' away inside, in our hands, in our sitting rooms, a long way away from the dark tunnel that coughed it up. Should we really be buyin' couscous harvested on illegal settlements? Or laughin' at electric cars? Or, God forgive me for sayin' it, because I love the rashers, but maybe we shouldn't be eatin' so much meat?'

He chuckles.

'Sure what do I know?'

But his jowls are wobbly, his brow furrowed and his eyes have somehow become even more watery.

'Funny thing is: it's those who don't like the idea of foreigners landin' here that need to get stuck into these questions, more than anyone. There's sixty-five million displaced people in the world now. Sixty-five *million*. Zero, zero, zero, zero, zero, zero. More than any other time. Ever. And no sign of it stoppin' either, the way things are goin'. A vast tide of misery. Hopelessness. Despair. Utter despair. Thing is, whether ye know or not, these people are simply followin' their resources. Call it colonialism or neo-colonialism or whatever ya like. All this shiny stuff, these brand new SUVs, flat-screen TVs, gleamin' skyscrapers; devices for puttin' on socks, electric toothbrushes, overpriced cocktails. We don't let the youngsters climb trees any more but we fill their rooms to brimmin' with plastic gimmicks. Trillions of straws, billions of cups, millions of kettles. Gold, rubber, oil – it's the greatest heist in human history.'

Pop music from the radio fills the cafe, the till rattles, a steamer hisses.

Some of the asylum seekers are wise, well-read; graduates or autodidacts or simply street-smart. Others are less sure of these topics, these murky waters, sure only that they have endured their own lives, hewn their own stories and journeys. For some, even this is not so sure. Memories sift underfoot like sands.

One of Hekmat's friends, who once stayed with them in Ramallah, has a cousin in Ireland.

'I'll link you on social media,' says Hekmat.

Marina arrives some days later. A nest of curls, grey and black, piercing blue eyes, warm smile.

'You look so much like your cousin,' Tuqa says.

She has brought a bicycle, wheels it around, hands it over.

'Thank you. So much.'

'Nah, it's nothing. It was lying around, gathering cobwebs. Now you can use it – it'll get you out and about, so you can be part of the town. You'll have to try the greenway, the cycle route. It's lovely.' Tuqa wobbles on the saddle, does a circle around Marina. 'And you'll come stay with us some weekend?'

'Really?'

'Of course, we'd be delighted to have you.'

Tuqa smiles. She must inform the staff at her centre, but as long as she does so, she may go on trips.

A few short weeks later, she is being driven up a driveway under a colonnade of chestnuts. Fields on either side, horses following alongside the car. Through hedges, between buzzing flowerbeds and a crisp lawn, the tyres crunch to a halt. It is an old farmhouse, bearded in ivy, out of which sprout a gable and clustered chimney pots. It is a hive: Marina's son farms chickens, there is a singer-songwriter living in one of the outhouses and a woodworker carving antique caravans in the stable. Other artists come and go, for dinners, for walks, for cups of tea and chats. The interior is a museum: classical busts, ancient maps, a knight in armour. Greyhounds slink about, looking for rubs. Amid the artefacts she has her own room for her stay. Tuqa is sorry to leave on the Sunday.

Back to the centre. Another artefact entirely.

With the help of her mother and some friends, Tuqa manages to cobble together enough money to buy herself a mini-fridge and some art materials. She holes up in her room, paints furiously, canvas after canvas, snacking on cereal. A dam bursting, a deluge of hue and shade. Too long without brush in hand. It feels good. By day three she is exhausted and wanders back out into the world, surprised to see it still exists.

Spring gives way to summer in a cycle of visits to friends and painting days and centre life. Tuqa learns that she is lucky, that this centre, for all its shortcomings, is one of the better run in the whole country. It is certainly nicer than the first place. Things have improved, but always, unmoved by friendships or welcomes or collaborations, a sword dangles over her head. The interview. It will decide her life, determine whether she will be allowed to stay, to contribute to a new home, or be pushed back into the arms of an occupation, into the wreckage of a toxic slum. She receives a date. August. As the summer wanes, so does her sleep.

The interview is postponed.

'We'll be back to you soon, Ms Sarraj, with a new date.'

A stay of execution.

Eleven months pass. She visits Marina again, several times. Marina rings her after the latest visit.

'It's yours if you want it,' she says. 'The room.'

'No. I can't.'

'Of course you can.'

'I would love to …'

'But?'

'I have to be sure it's allowed. I have to check with the IPO.'[11]

'Then find out.'

It is allowed – though many of the same old rules will remain. Again Tuqa packs her suitcase. Again she unpacks it, in a new place. The room is cosy, with a window gazing out at a forest. There is a studio downstairs, where she paints most days, sometimes joined by jamming musicians. Tuqa bakes cakes, old recipes, chocolate or semolina, shares them out and in them smells home.

'Tell us how ye slew,' sings the woodcarver, 'them poor Arabs two by two.'

Her activism increases, both for Palestine and for asylum seekers. She joins the Movement of Asylum Seekers in Ireland (MASI) and Refugee and Migrant Solidarity Ireland (RAMSI). She learns how most of the centres in the country are outsourced, privatised, making tidy profits while the state pumps, by some accounts, over a million a month into the system. Many of these direct provision firms have registered as unlimited companies, thereby pulling a shroud over their annual accounts.

Tuqa makes friends in Dublin now too, and all over the

---

11 International Protection Office.

country, all throughout the arts. Already she has more 'mates' and 'pals' and 'buddies' here than most Irish people do in a lifetime.

But, at night, she lies awake and stares up at the sword dangling overhead, the pendulum, the pen that will stroke, one way or another.

Summer 2018. Almost a year has passed since the interview was postponed. Tuqa is perched on a chair, at the end of a row, which is bolted to a linoleum floor. She is hollow-bellied, dry-mouthed.

'Tuqa al-Sarraj?'

A tremor passes through her, like the faint earthquakes at home that sometimes tip cups off tables, or tilt picture frames.

'Yes, that's me.'

The hand she raises is quivering. But she stands straight and walks into the interview.

It has been a turbulent year back in Palestine. Protesters along the Gaza perimeter were met with bullets, rubber and steel, throughout April, arousing worldwide indignation. Medics are shot with alarming frequency. Footage leaks of laughing snipers. In the middle of it all, the Trump administration relocates the US embassy to Jerusalem.[12] By mid-May, over a hundred Palestinians have been killed, over ten thousand wounded.

There are air strikes and rocket attacks back and forth. Dust clouds boiling in the summer sky. Tuqa has been accepted into a scholarship at the National College of Art and Design. Gold dust. But it will be for nothing if she is deported, if she is forced back to a place where the last remaining cultural centre has just been bombed into oblivion.

---

12 Israel's sovereignty over the city has never been recognised internationally. Prior to this, all embassies were located in Tel Aviv. Most Palestinians consider East Jerusalem to be the capital of a future Palestinian state.

Tuqa leaves the interview. She is drained, relieved to be out. A relief that soon gives way to a dull, deep ache. The verdict awaits.

Three weeks later, Tuqa strolls out of the farmhouse, down the chestnut colonnade. The horses' flanks are shiny in the heat, tails flicking at flies. At the gate she fishes in the post box. An envelope.

Accepted.

Tuqa is hopeful now. And supremely privileged, she knows. She has been luckier than most. Most Gazans, most asylum seekers. But her art and her activism will struggle on now from a newfound platform, a newfound shelter. She may never be allowed to return home. Or even visit. But she will never forget it. Never forget her people.

Palestine may be an antique land, but it is not, as is so often bemoaned, an antique conflict, timeless and intractable. It is a most modern conflict. There has been a solution available, on which most of the world agrees: two states, built along the 1967 Green Line. Israel and the US alone have prevented it. Some say that this solution has been undermined by the continuing expansion of illegal Israeli settlements into Palestinian territory, that there is no viable area left on which to build a nation, only a jagged checkerboard. In that case, perhaps a single state built on equal civil rights is the only option left. That or apartheid.

But the illegal settlements, the ever-expanding annexation wall, the quasi-apartheid are only as sturdy as the White House support. In one respect it is no different than the South African apartheid: a seemingly immutable system that collapsed overnight as soon as Washington washed its hands. And why did it wash its hands?

Privilege has responsibilities attached. Duties.

Tuqa has a ghastly dream. She is standing in a vast desert, baking under the blue. Jutting out of the sands, leaning into its long shadow, is the rusted skeleton of a watchtower. The glass is long gone, the flagpole bare, its rags far-flung dust. A buckled panel, loose, creaks in the wind. Graffiti is sprayed across it, red, dripping:

My name is Ozymandias, King of Kings;
Look on my Works, ye Mighty, and despair!

WAITING

Iraqi Kurdistan

WAR CAME IN AN EGG. In the low stone hovel, a nine-year-old boy peered past his mother as she stooped over the stove. She swirled a steaming pot with a spoon, twirling the lumps bobbing in the broth. One of the lumps rolled over, and a goat's face leered out, furless. The boy grimaced.

'I want an egg,' he said.

'An egg?' said his mother. 'We're having sarupe, Hawraz.'[1]

She turned to him and put her hands on her hips, the forearms bulging where they met her rolled-up sleeves. Her hair was a wavy black cascade, parted by her face: cheeks high and hard, but with eyes capable of a kindly crinkle.

'I don't like sarupe.'

'Don't like sarupe? Everybody likes sarupe.'

The boy glared at the goat skull, its lolling tongue and bared teeth. He pouted. His grandmother shuffled in the doorway, carrying a basket of rice. Her grey fringe tufted out from her headscarf and her emerald eyes glimmered under bushy eyebrows. Close behind was a little girl, Hawraz's younger sister.

---

1 Sarupe is a type of Kurdish stew, containing offal and inexpensive cuts of meat.

'No,' said the old woman, 'it's true. He really doesn't.'

'He should eat what he gets,' said his mother. 'This is what city living does to a child.'

She turned back to the stove with a wry expression. Hawraz wondered at this. Was there a certain guilt gnawing at her? The children were living in the city, being raised by their grandmother because of her choices. She chose to stick by her husband, the captain. This was a rare visit; a couple of summer weeks and they would be gone again.

'He's young, dear,' said his grandmother. 'Here, Hawraz, take this and get an egg for yourself.'

She dropped a coin into Hawraz's hand and bent down closer to his little sister.

'Hello, petal. Would you like an egg?'

The little girl nodded, pulling at one of her knotty pigtails, her eyes huge and watery as she looked up at her grandmother.

'So,' said the grandmother, 'get one for you and one for your sister.' She glanced at Hawraz's mother, turned back to him and winked. 'And one for me too,' she whispered.

Hawraz and his sister went out into the dusk. He marched along the narrow street crowded with other stone hovels, his sister jogging to keep up with him. This was the main thoroughfare of the isolated village, the only one, in fact – and it was crooked like an elbow and steep, nestled at the foot of an overshadowing summit that held the villagers under constant scrutiny. The dwellings, with flat roofs of baked mud, were all among and atop of each other; a bundle of cubes glued together. Cooking smoke drifted from several. They were not merely on the mountains, but *of* the mountains. Their windows – few, narrow and dark – squinted across at distant brown ranges: golden peaks shrinking upwards as the sun set.

The lone farmhouse, known for its bountiful hens, was a short way away from the village. It was stone-built, like all else. The children rounded an outcrop, which hid the village and opened out the vista of the valley, spread far below them; fields of rustling bronze. A wind stirred the dust at their feet as they walked.

'Let's go back,' said his sister.

'What? Why?'

'Something is coming.'

'No it isn't. Don't be such a baby.'

'I can hear it. I'm scared.'

A scrunching of many boots and tired chatter ascended towards them on the track. The men appeared around a large boulder: rifles slung on their shoulders, in drab browns, greys, olives; baggy pants and shirts, waistcoats and patterned sashes. Their moustachioed faces were like leather beneath their flat turbans: the traditional black and white jamadani. One had a dagger, another a radio set. They smelt of sweat and tobacco. Some whistled. These were Peshmerga, Kurdish rebels, returning from a long patrol.

'Hey,' said one, with ashen hair. 'It's the captain's kids.'

'Where are you going?' asked another, with a narrow, lumpy face thatched by a black monobrow.

'Getting eggs,' said Hawraz. 'Did you catch any Iraqis?'

The rebels laughed and swept their arms as if to say: do you see any?

'How is your father?' asked the ashen one.

'He is resting in the house,' said Hawraz.

'Yes, let him rest,' said the ashen one. 'Later, I will beat him at chequers.'

He chuckled and continued towards the village with his comrades.

'You see?' said Hawraz, turning to his sister. 'It was just the men.'

'No,' she replied. 'There is something else.'

Hawraz rolled his eyes and stomped away.

The children arrived at the farm and got their eggs. Hawraz wished to stay, to watch the chickens strutting about, maybe even chase them, but his sister kept tugging at him, eager to get home.

'Okay,' he barked. 'We'll go.'

They began to walk back.

'What's wrong with you?' he scowled.

'It is getting closer.'

'You're hearing things.'

She scanned the amber sky. 'There,' she whispered, pointing.

There was a glint, a row of glints, and then Hawraz too could hear it – a whispering or whipping, like a thousand metallic crickets. The sound grew louder, then thunderous.

Three dots grew into helicopters, zooming towards him, dipping snouts, which blazed suddenly. Showers of grit exploded all around Hawraz as the craft zipped overhead. They continued out beyond the village, before twirling about to face it. Hawraz crouched and clenched every muscle, dust filling his hair, thickening his tears. The three monstrous bugs hovered for a moment, then puffed out cloud after cloud of smoke, which seared, shrieked, earthward. Behind the outcrop, where the village stood, there was an eruption of blasts.

Directly above Hawraz, high on the outcrop, there was a nest of sandbags, webbed in camouflage, which suddenly poured out a fountain of fireflies towards one of the helicopters, causing its flank to sparkle and clatter. The three great bugs swivelled around towards the outcrop and the clouds puffed out again, towards their new target.

Hawraz shielded his head and screamed a soundless scream as pebbles and shards and boulders tumbled past him on either side. Above him, the rebels' nest was wreathed with roiling smoke, but the stream of tracers from it did not relent, and then one of the helicopters was belching black fumes. The damaged craft, along with the two other helicopters, lifted their snouts, soared up over the mountain and were gone. Their whomp, whomp, whomp diminished into the tack, tack, tack of cooling gun metal up among the sandbags.

Hawraz turned to where his sister had stood. The world rang sharply, unbearably. The air carried a smoky tang, like the smell of some sort of chemical incense. She was like him: crouched, quivering, but alive. Both of them, ghost-like in their dusting, ran around the corner. There was no village, only scattered stones and smoke billowing up into the gathering night. A cooking pot rolled past. Behind them, the eggs lay dashed in the scree.

Hawraz stares at the egg. It is fried, centred perfectly on the plate, its edges crispy. Its yellow yolk stares back, unblinking. Hawraz is thirty-eight and without appetite. Since long before dawn, he has been sitting at the desk – the capitulation to another sleepless night. His world is bound by four walls, not snow-capped ranges. He has a ceiling of plaster, not stars. As it was yesterday, and the day before, and the day before that, et cetera, et cetera, ad nauseam. A bed, desk and wardrobe permit only narrow awkward passages among them in this tight little room. Or cell, as he has come to regard it, for he cannot leave. He is a fugitive and this is his safe house.

'Tchak, tchak, tchak,' says the gecko, high up in the far corner.

'I could be bounded in a nutshell and count myself a king of infinite space,' says Hawraz, 'were it not that I have bad dreams.'

'What nonsense,' says the gecko. He flickers his tongue, scurries in a circle, and is still again.

Hawraz pushes the egg aside, opens his notebook. It has more cross-outs and blots than actual text. 'That was my first taste of war,' he writes. 'Those three rotary dragons, spewing shells and rockets, those angels of death, Saddam's wrath, sent not to …' he stops, rubs his chin. It is stubbly. Then he crosses out 'angels of death'. A bit baroque, he thinks. Besides, there had been no casualties that evening: the villagers had fled just in time, sheltering in the caves nearby. They later emerged to find him and his sister wandering among the ruins. He pauses, then scratches a vicious zigzag through the lot.

'Who are you to write a memoir?' asks the gecko.

'But what else is there to do in this damned cell?'

'Wait,' says the gecko. 'We are waiting.'

'Nothing to be done.'

'Indeed. I'm glad you're coming around to that opinion.'

The gecko winks.

'Enough,' says Hawraz.

He stands up, edges around the chair, shuffles over to the window. In the corner of his eye, the gecko follows. Hawraz does not part the curtains. They are brown, slightly silky; sunlight is glowing through their weave. He rubs them, feels the texture. They remind him of his father's waistcoat, one of his earliest memories from when he was about five. Hawraz can still remember that garment on the back of a chair, blackened with blood, three blossoms of it; still hear the hurried whispers of the adults in the hallway, their talk of pulse and penicillin. The rebels had raided a Baathist barracks, searching for weapons and ammunition.[2] His father had been successful in as much as he had found bullets: three of them.

Behind the curtain he imagines a scene of astounding beauty: a gurgling brook, meadows rolling up to a tree-line; a pine forest rising in undulations to a remote, snow-capped pinnacle, surrounded by a court of lesser peaks. Nearby, a shepherd plays

---

2   The Baath Party, led by Saddam Hussein, governed Iraq from 1968 to 2003.

the flute to his flock; further off, a village is lighting torches and bonfires, preparing for the New Year. Birds are singing.

But birds are not singing out there, brooks are not gurgling. Not really.

Hawraz rips the curtains apart and a limitless metropolis appears, glittering, shimmering, and stretches out, fading into the fumes of rush hour. He presses his forehead against one of the horizontal bars placed in front of the window, curls both sets of fingers around it, and peers down twenty dizzying stories to asphalt choked with traffic: humming, buzzing, reverberating in his skull. It is Kuala Lumpur, not Kurdistan.

'The sun shone, having no alternative, on the nothing new,' says Hawraz.

'Ah,' sighs the gecko. 'Beckett.' He wriggles with delight.

Beyond the window, to either side, the wings of the building jut out: dark glass and pale concrete, floor upon floor, row upon row of windows, just like his one – numbing in their uniformity. On one of these wings, far below him, he can see the cuboid skull of a camera, scanning the streets with a cyclopean stare.

'Big Brother is watching,' says the gecko.

'Nonsense. Nobody is watching. Not for refugees.'

'Don't be so sure.'

'Why would they install such an expensive piece of equipment, just on the slight chance –'

'Anyways,' says the gecko, 'there are no refugees in Malaysia, you know that. They recognise no such term. You are an illegal immigrant. Do you really think they care about the International Organisation for Migration?[3] They don't give a flying fedora for

---

3 The International Organisation for Migration (IOM) is an inter-governmental organisation that provides services and advice to displaced persons, often assisting in refugee resettlement. It has 166 member states throughout the world.

the IOM, or that you applied for status with them when you arrived. All that matters, now, is that your tourist visa has expired. Long expired. You came, you saw, you stayed. There are two places the Malaysians will send you: into the jailhouse or back to the brink of the caliphate.'

'You're just a lizard, what would you know?'

The gecko shrugs.

Hawraz gazes back out the window. Across the boulevard is an enormous shopping mall. He pictures its interior, its churning crowds and flashy signs, the ice-cream stalls and fashion outlets. He had been there once before his tourist visa had expired, wandering about, trying on expensive suits in dressing rooms, riding escalators, gazing at bright rows of widescreen televisions, all showing the same scene: a snow-capped mountain wreathed in clouds. He bought pizza and ate it in the food court, watching the world drift by as he slurped cola. But that was months ago, in a time of relative freedom.

'When will I see it again?' mutters Hawraz.

'Nevermore,' quotes the gecko.

Hawraz kneads his eyes, allowing the curtains to fall again. He looks back at his notebook with distaste, steps over, shuts it. His hands reach out for the pile of books on the desk, shuffling them about without purpose. Samuel Beckett, silver and wizened, peeks out over the edge of the Quran. Hawraz has few books – books take up space – but the few he retains allow him, occasionally, to bask in the recollections of a now-ruined career. Even now, he starts reminiscing and, absent-mindedly, takes up the pen and opens his notebook.

'Tchak,' says the gecko.

Hawraz ignores him and puts the ballpoint rolling.

'An academic is a rare creature in Kurdistan. He – for it is almost always a he – may be considered an eccentric but always an eccentric with lofty stature, a man to be respected, to be listened to. It took my young self a long time to realise this. As a child I was constantly switching schools, whether because of disciplinary transgressions or because the turmoil of the times required it. There were vast pauses where I was simply surviving. By the time I finished secondary education, I had attended seventeen different institutions across a dizzying spectrum of quality, throughout Erbil and beyond.[4] Perhaps it was inevitable, with no parents in the home. It was my grandmother who raised me, in a charming little townhouse in the middle of Erbil, a neighbourhood that was both ... both ... what is the word?'

'Salubrious?'

'Yes! Salubrious. Salubrious and ... and ...'

'Industrious?'

Hawraz grins but quickly frowns on seeing the gecko's smugness. He continues writing.

'... a neighbourhood that was both salubrious and ... *vibrant*, and it apparently remains so, or tries to, despite all that has befallen our homeland. I remember the tiny courtyard, its hanging pots spilling greenery and pink petals, its gurgling fountain, and, just around the block, the bustling strip of cafes, kebab shops and boutiques: an endless supply of amusement for a whippersnapper such as I was.

'And yet, I longed for the summers, when school would finish and grandmother would take my sister and I to the mountains, to be close to our parents for a few weeks. This may seem reckless to you, reader, especially given the incident of the eggs, but in truth it was far from the front. It was a peaceful place for weary rebels to recuperate. So went the thinking, at least.

'It was within this alpine settlement, this mud-roofed

---

4   Erbil is the capital city of the autonomous Kurdish region of northern Iraq.

Olympus, that I could lay eyes on the hero, the warrior, the legend, who was fighting for our freedom: my father. This man, with his rifle and his scars and his obedient comrades, was a god to me. Why study in the city, I reasoned, when there was glory to be found in the wilderness?'

'So compelling.'

'Silence!'

Hawraz proceeds with the pen.

'The struggle continued for over a decade, until the Americans suddenly renounced their friendship with Saddam and obliterated his tank battalions from on high. I have often wondered how those three helicopters – the ones that destroyed the village – fared. Were they like petty schoolyard tyrants suddenly faced with hardened street heavies? Who knows.

'In the chaos, the Peshmerga swept down from the mountains and chased their enemies out of the north. The Yankees did not topple that butcher, Hussein, but did tell him to keep out of Kurdistan. And so, a certain autonomy developed. My father's rebellion, it appeared, had won.

'But the jubilation soon faded. Factions polarised, stockpiled, drew lines in the sand, spitting insults back and forth. The insults became bullets and the bullets became civil war – Kurd against Kurd. Victory was a corpse, fast rotting. Deals were cut with Iranians, with Turks, with Iraqis, who stoked the flames to their own advantage. They certainly did not weep for dead Kurds.

'Leaders of both Kurdish factions, the once-gaunt heroes of the wilderness, grew paunches in the cities. They sipped from cut glass instead of waterskins. Corruption flourished. My father survived those three bullet wounds, just about. My mother nursed him back to health, stood by him and the cause, through hunger, through battles, even through prison. When the guards offered her freedom for information, she gave them nothing.

'And yet, after all that, when success finally arrived, my father took for himself another wife, a younger woman, pretty and pampered. He bought her a house, a mansion in comparison to our apartment, and promptly moved in with her. His visits to us trickled off into a rarity. My mother never stopped idolising him, even as the neglect ate away at her health. When she died, several years later, she was still very much in love. I have never witnessed such unbending loyalty.

'For myself, the gilt had long ago flaked off to reveal a statue of mud. Worship gave way to disgust. And so, at the brink of adulthood, I turned my back on adventurism and stuck my snout into schoolbooks. The civil war raged on for two years before petering out, with little achieved beyond several thousand corpses.'

'Good,' says the gecko. 'Poignant.'

Hawraz huffs, calms, continues:

'There was much disruption, including that minor affair of 2003, when the US invasion finally put the butcher into hiding. Saddam was a butcher to the Americans too, by then – though, I might add, he had enjoyed their friendship and support well enough when it suited them. At any rate, all of this upheaval was not conducive to a young fellow's education.

'Finally, however, I got my chance. The year after the statues toppled, I enrolled in Koya University, about an hour's drive outside of Erbil, and began a degree in translation. It focused on Kurdish, Arabic and English. I embraced academia with open arms, drawing energy from my growing competence, taking pleasure in becoming a translator, a member of an esoteric brotherhood, a keeper of keys, a conduit for diplomacy and business and philanthropy. I married my wife, Sakar, before second year began and by the middle of third year we had a firstborn, our beautiful daughter, Eva. Graduation came after four years of study and I was soon working as an assistant translator.

'I was almost content to be studying, teaching, providing for my family. Almost. I felt the remunerations of my position would not be sufficient in the long term and so I devised myself a plot. After a year of saving, I set out for India with my wife and child. We landed in Mumbai and from there travelled inland to the smaller, though not inconsiderable, city of Pune. England was too expensive, I had decided, but here, in this sultry sub-continent, my plot was plausible. A master's in English literature was just the ticket to bolster my degree whenever I applied for a promotion, I reasoned. So we endured fifty weeks of homesick-ness among the locals, a curious though amiable people. They were happy without wealth, I noted. What was their secret? I left without fully discovering it, but with a master's and another child, according to my apparent custom of accumulating an offspring per parchment. 'Ara,' we named him, which of course means *joy*.

'My plot came to fruition when I returned home and be-came a tutor at Koya University: conducting research, spouting seminars, supervising theses. It was a dream job with much op-portunity for advancement. To compound my fortune, there was much side-work on offer, in translation and interpretation. Many foreigners – diplomats especially – came looking for my servi-ces. It was the best of times – for my family and for Kurdistan. The civil war tensions remained, but they were now being waged in parliament, with skirmishes of sarcasm, volleys of vitriol and battles of ballots. Stability was a fertiliser whence prosperity was starting to sprout.'

'But that is all over now,' says the gecko.

Hawraz rubs his temples. He recalls the airy living room of his villa in Koya: the yawning couch, polished tiles, thick rugs. A beautiful bookcase had stood against one wall, a grand old thing, full of intricate carvings, hewn of cedar wood, painted brightly.

It had been densely populated – as densely as the city that now constricts him. Such a repository, such a panoply: dozens of tomes in Kurdish, Arabic, English. And now this: he jostles the assortment of books on his desk again.

'How many?' says the gecko.

'I dunno. Nine. Ten.'

'Pathetic.'

Terror came in an envelope. It was a lazy August afternoon, the time of year and day when most sane people are seeking to relax beneath a tree or an awning, to sip and to chat. Those in academia, however, were rushing about, finalising preparations for a new year. Hawraz was no different. Having devoured his lunch, he strode out of his porch and into the leafy avenue, a dishevelled sheaf in one hand, a briefcase in the other, humming his way towards the curb where his car was parked. A rustling paper, trapped beneath the windscreen wiper, caught his attention, silenced him, dragged his heart down to his bowels.

Traitor,

We know everything. Do not waste your time in useless denials or appeals. You have been collaborating with the infidels and supporting their occupation. We know of your work with the American consulate. It was wicked enough to teach their faithless Western tongue, but now you have gone too far. You have betrayed your brothers, your Prophet and your God. The punishment for all traitors is death. Your family will be taught your shame. They will learn our discipline.

Sincerely,
Those who are coming

This was 2013. The letter could have been from any number of splintered – but steadily strengthening – fundamentalist organisations in the region. Hawraz did not know it then, but one group was soon to rise above all the others.

A death threat. All for a smattering of translation projects here and there, vaguely connected to the US consulate. The minor level of the so-called collaboration did not matter, though; he knew in his heart that this was enough, that these people were quite serious.

He and his family packed their bags and left Koya that evening. They stayed with his mother in Erbil until the spring and then left the city, renting a small house by a remote village in a valley of anonymity. Eva, now seven and increasingly loquacious, had to move school. She was miserable; frustrated at the inferior level of English in the rural classroom. The pumpkins that grew there in abundance, with their alien bumps and tendrils, were a novelty that soon wore off, even for little Ara.

That March Hawraz attended an interview with the IOM in Baghdad, applying for refugee status. With nothing to do but wait, he plunged into his own pumpkin patch, relishing the tenure, absorbing first the villagers' knowledge, then whatever books he could borrow on the subject. After several months, however, he had squeezed *Cucurbitaceae* of every drop of intellectual stimulation they had to offer. Mere toil was all that was left.

His savings, drip-dripping away by the week, were at a precarious nadir. It was time, with due caution, to return to Erbil. He applied at the Ministry of Education and was hired to do some translating. A routine developed, commuting from his colleagues in Erbil every evening back home to his oasis of family in the heart of the valley of anonymity.

One morning, in June, Hawraz slumped into his car seat and turned the ignition while coffee and sunlight were flittering away

his sleepiness. It was a week before his final meeting with the
IOM in Baghdad, a week before resettlement, before his family
would be safe. What possibilities would emerge in his new world?
What challenges? He was both daunted and excited.

Hawraz was twenty minutes down the road before it dawned
on him how much traffic was trundling past him in the opposite direction. It was unusually busy, the dust hung thick. He
shrugged and passed it off until he reached the next petrol station. All the pumps were taken, every car facing south. People
were rushing into the shop, emerging with arms full of water
bottles, snacks, tobacco. A baby was screaming. The vehicles were
jammed, crowned, strapped with suitcases, boxes, silver orna-
ments. A man snapped his fuel cap shut, jumped in and revved
off; immediately a minibus replaced him and began guzzling
from the nozzle.

'What's happening?' he asked a passing woman.

Panic was etched in her face, blonde hair streaming from
her hijab. She was clutching tins of fruit to her chest, her chin
clamped down on the uppermost.

'They are coming,' she said.

'Who?'

'They took Mosul.'

'Who?'

She pushed past and hopped into a shiny saloon, which spun
dust and shot off.

'Daesh,' said a gravelly voice.

Hawraz turned around to face an old woman, sitting in the
shade at the front of the shop.

'Those Islamic State lunatics?' asked Hawraz.

She nodded.

'But how? What about the army? There are two whole
divisions in Mosul. Must be, what, about thirty thousand troops?'

'Not any more. They have collapsed. The radio said it. They are fleeing to the east; the militants will soon take Erbil.'

Hawraz queued, filled his tank, and raced back home.

The IS horde surged forward: capturing, raping, beheading. An army crumbled before them, soldiers discarding weapons, equipment, vehicles, swapping uniforms for plain clothes and joining the thousands of civilians clogging the highway. There was hysteria in the streets: consulates burning papers, grocery stores gutted, mosques swamped. Daily life disintegrated. The enemy blitzed towards them: forty kilometres away, thirty, twenty, then slowed, halted, and, after a few days of held breath, withdrew. Erbil was spared. Nobody seemed to know why, least of all Hawraz. A front line materialised roughly fifty kilometres away and was reinforced, fortified. Stability grew, and with it, knowledge, determination, normalcy. The offices and classrooms and markets began, cautiously, to buzz again.

And yet, all was not normal. Far from it. An old friend of Hawraz, an army officer, had the top of his skull blown off by a revolver at point-blank range: a lone assassin had infiltrated his headquarters while he was organising a counter-attack. Erbil had escaped outright cataclysm but went on to endure sporadic acts: shootings, car bombs, reams of casualty lists from the front. Blood or tears flowed daily. If Hawraz had doubted it before, he was now sure that this country was no place for his family. The death threat rustled in his dreams nightly.

The road to Baghdad, however, had been severed. The IOM postponed his final meeting until the situation could be stabilised. How long his case would be put on hold was a mystery. Hawraz could not afford mystery in a world of mutilation and murder. He continued working in Erbil, saving as much as possible, while researching frantically in the evenings. Turkey, a swirling, sucking drain for many refugees, was no place for Kurds. He studied other destinations, leaning towards Georgia at one point, before finally choosing his sanctuary. They sold their property, booked their flights, said their goodbyes.

In November 2014, the family of four stepped off a plane and into Malaysia, where Hawraz immediately found an IOM office in Kuala Lumpur and reapplied for refugee status. They settled in to await their answer.

'What was that?' says the gecko. 'Ten, eleven months ago? A year?'

'Yes,' says Hawraz. 'A little over a year.'

'How time flies, ey?'

'How time crawls.'

'Hey,' says the gecko, thoughtfully. 'What if your money runs out?'

'Why are you such a damned nuisance? You folk are supposed to be auspicious.'

'Who says?'

'The Indians.'

'Indians?'

'They told me in Pune.'

'Sorry to disappoint, old sport.'

The gecko waggles its tail, then stops. Silence settles in.

'What about your wife?' asks the gecko. 'What if she ends up in jail? Like your mother did?'

Hawraz remembers the one visit they were permitted to the prisoner-of-war camp, in the middle of the desert, where his pregnant mother had been crowded with all the other villagers. He had been no more than four years old and had cried the whole way back to the city. She had given birth to his sister long before she had been released.

'Or, what if –'

'Stop,' says Hawraz. 'Please.'

He knows the memory that the lizard is probing for. He was eleven, doing, or pretending to do, his homework one night, when there was a knock at the door, which his grandmother answered. There stood his mother in the drizzle: haggard, pale, barely recognisable, with a tiny bundle of rags in her quivering arms.

'He's so sick,' she cried. 'It's from the caves. They're too damp.'

His grandmother brought mother and baby to the hospital immediately. A week later the two women returned. The infant did not.

'What if,' says the gecko, 'your children die? Like your little brother?'

Hawraz grabs a thick tome and launches it at the wall, but the gecko dashes away behind the wardrobe, bursting into tchakles.

The door opens.

'Who are you shouting at?' says his wife.

'Oh … nothing. Just that damned lizard.' He turns to her. 'What are we going to do, Sakar?'

She stands beside his chair, pulls him against her waist.

'It's been so long since the interview,' he says, 'all this waiting and waiting, hiding like hunted animals, trapped inside all day. What if the IOM have forgotten us? What if they lost our file, or the case worker made a mistake, or –'

'They haven't forgotten, Hawraz. Hold on. Tomorrow could be the day.'

She smiles down at him. After a pause, his furrowed forehead softens and he smiles back.

'You're right,' he says.

'Oh, I see it!' Sakar leaps over to the window, slamming it shut. 'Gotcha.'

A tail squirms, weakens, stills, on the sill. Hawraz bounds across and peers out. There is no sign of the rest of the gecko.

'He must've fallen,' she says.

A grin spreads across Hawraz's face.

'No more tchak tchak,' he whispers to himself.

'You didn't eat your egg,' says Sakar.

'Sorry,' he says. 'I forgot.'

'How is the writing?'

'Painful, torturous, excruciating.'

'Won't you come into the living room? I made baklava.'

'Really?'

'Come in, tell the kids a story.'

He shuffles out of the cell, into the sweet aroma of pastries. After the family has eaten, he sits the children down and recounts for them the tale of *Rita Hayworth and Shawshank Redemption*. They hang on every word: horror at the unjust sentence, disgust at the prison conditions, fear of the cruel warden and, finally, wide-eyed wonderment at the escape.

Later, Sakar and Hawraz undress and rustle in under the bedsheet. She kisses him goodnight and achieves sleep like the flicking of a switch. He envies her.

Oblivion comes in a trench. The sun is setting on the desert when gunshots rattle, echoing out across the rocks. The trench is long. At one end several silhouettes are shovelling sand. At the other end is a cluster of parked trucks. A pair of silhouettes emerge from behind the trucks, dragging something limp, sack-like. They dump it into the trench and plod back behind the trucks. Another pair follow, dumping their burden, then another pair and another. More shots ring out, there is further dragging and dumping.

It is difficult to see into the trench: its depths are not warmed by the last rays of day. But then the throbbing dark stills, acquires texture, dimensions. A tangle of limbs can be discerned: the black-blossomed waistcoats, the sashes, the jamadani – worn to the last. There are lifeless hands reaching skyward in claw-like contortions, bloodless faces and fastened eyelids or, occasionally, opened eyelids, revealing faint gleams, tiny convex mirrors reflecting the silhouettes as they approach the precipice again and release another broken body.

A shaft of light hits the silhouettes: they wear berets, laced boots, uniforms; their assault rifles have curved magazines. They are clean-shaven apart from their clipped moustaches. The scene shimmers, turns to static, wavers and is back. The trench is still being emptied of earth at one end, filled with death at the other. Only the silhouettes are different now. Their faces are wrapped or bearded and they are not dressed uniformly: they sport ballistic vests, bullet belts, grenades, swords, smartphones. There are no more gunshots, but the bodies still appear, headless now, and topple into the depths. Some shaggy footballs are tossed in as an afterthought. Both sets of silhouettes have been equipped, via proxies, by far-flung chess masters. The trucks rev up, roar off and diminish into the night, leaving the trench to silence. All is black.

Hawraz wakes. Still, all is black. He is not in bed but, as his eyes adjust and faint outlines appear here and there, he discerns that he is in an overgrown clearing or square in the middle of a junkyard, surrounded by rows of scrap stacks. He is cowering among weeds. He is prey. There are Malaysian policemen prowling all around him, searching the surrounding structures, circling like sharks. He hears a radio crackle and a martial 'affirmative'. There is a metallic click, like a bolt sliding back. He crouches further against the ground. His forehead is oozing a cold syrupy sweat. It is a cemetery, he realises, not a junkyard, with rows of sepulchres, not scrap.

Suddenly, the moon penetrates, beaming a spotlight down on him. There are shouts and boots scrunch across stones. He tries to make a break for it but his feet are inert: clamped in thick iron casts. The figures swarm towards him. Nothing to be done. But suddenly there is a great flutter and drafts are pumping against him as if from giant wing beats. There is a flash, the iron casts shatter and he is away!

He sprints between the structures, past row after row, then he is in the open, a vastness, running, running, still running, though the pursuing voices have faded far behind and the night is lifting. The ground rises, no longer hard pavement but soft meadows leading up and away from that deathly hallow, towards woods. The sun also rises – twenty-one golden rays in blood-red sky – and lights up a green mountain in the distance, bright clouds haloing its pure white pinnacle.

Hawraz jolts up from his pillow, opening his eyes to blackness. He feels about frantically – sheets, lamp, wife. He sighs, but he does not fall back to sleep. After a few minutes, he lowers his feet to the cool tiles and stands upright, swaying. He feels nauseous, in the way that often accompanies poor slumber and troubled dreams. His tongue is arid. He shuffles to the curtains, rubs their silky weave. Slowly, almost imperceptibly, they begin to blush: a glacial, unseductive pallor.

'Tchak, tchak,' says the gecko.

'Morning,' says Hawraz.

KEY

Bosnia

MAY 1980. A BLUE TRAIN is racing across Yugoslavia. It sweeps past cities and forests and mountains, plunges into tunnels and out again into sunlight, passing onlookers in twos and threes, in clusters and crowds, in streets and in fields, farmers and miners and nurses and seamstresses, schoolchildren and old folks. Some wave, some salute, while others stand mutely, wiping tears away. It trundles on, past the people of the nation, under crosses and crescents, heading straight towards the nerve-centre: Belgrade.

Inside its foremost carriage, between six honour guards in impeccable azure uniforms, lies a coffin, draped in the flag of the republic.

Marshall Tito is dead. Partisan hero, vanquisher of the Nazis, leader and locus of the Yugoslav nation for over three decades. Gone. The train thunders past, diminishing into the distance, and, as the rattling tracks settle back into silence, Tito's ghostly refrain – *Brotherhood and Unity* – drifts away on a breeze.

A baby girl is born, five months later, in Ključ. It is a sleepy town in the northwest of the Socialist Republic of Bosnia and Herzegovina, one of the six republics that make up Yugoslavia.

The parents, a welder and a bookkeeper, name her Bojana.

September 1995. An explosion jolts Bojana awake. She sits up in bed as the echo thunders out across the heavens. She scrambles out of the sheets, rubbing sleep from her eyes before tugging apart her bedroom curtains. The town stretches out before her, ghostly in the twilight, meandering along the valley, an expanse of old townhouses and modernist apartment blocks, like the one she is in. Dark hills rise up on either side towards the grey sky. The streets are deserted, as they should be at such an hour. Perhaps it *was* just thunder, she thinks. But then she spots it: a roiling blossom of smoke on the edge of town. There is a flash and another blossom erupts near the first. Then the sound arrives: an almighty clap followed by the sickening crumble of masonry.

There have been rumours all week of battles to the west, of advancing Bosniaks and Croats, and of NATO air strikes, but normal life has continued uninterrupted, a wartime routine, well-established these three years past: power outages and rationing, tilling the vegetable patch and hoarding water at every opportunity. There have been no ripples lapping against Ključ in recent days, no signal of the coming tsunami.

Her brother, younger by a year, bursts in the door.

'Quick,' he says. 'We have to get ready. Mum said –'

He sees what she is staring at and is drawn to the window. A siren is wailing now and flames are streaking up out of the stricken neighbourhood. Then another flash – *boom* – and more smoke is churning. It must be a dream, Bojana thinks; it is too ridiculous to be true. But she does not wake.

A whistling noise comes plunging, seemingly directly towards her, rising into an ear-splitting shriek, and just down the street a rooftop disappears, and the whole world is roaring, rocking, reverberating. The light bulb flickers, and outside they can hear screaming and the rumble of collapse.

Bojana's parents rush into the bedroom, her father grabs the boy and drags him out to get dressed, and her mother flings open the wardrobe and starts hurling clothes at her. Bojana pulls on an outfit, stuffs some spare socks, underwear and a toothbrush into a bag and grabs her jacket. She pauses, then snatches her photo album from the bedside locker and runs out into the living room. Her father is holding the front door open, urging them out, her brother is tying his shoelaces and her mother is shuffling frantically through a stack of papers: bills, postcards, notices – there! She plucks out the birth certificates, jams them into her coat pocket, and the family of four are bundling down the corridor, among a torrent of neighbours, before spilling out the front entrance as the sun rises over the shaggy crest of the valley.

The main street is swamped now: vehicles lurch forward through the desperate crowd, women clutch babies and shout at children to stay close, old folks refuse to leave and are dragged away weeping, as drivers bellow at each other or honk horns. With every incoming shriek the multitude dive for cover, emerging again to pick up their possessions and push onwards.

'Where are our troops?' cries an old man.

'They've retreated,' cries another.

'Abandoned us?'

Bojana stares about at the hysteria and wonders how it is that people can hammer such terror into each other. How and why? Because we are Serbs and they are Bosniaks? Because we are Orthodox and they are Muslim? She recalls, vaguely, a time when such distinctions were not taught. Now they seem terribly significant.

Bojana and her family manage to get aboard a van with a family friend and join the tail of traffic streaming to the southeast, where a road accompanies the River Sana along the valley bottom deeper into Serbian territory. There is no military presence to instil calm: only a few stragglers as panicked as the populace.

At a bend in the road, Bojana strains in her seat to look back at where she has spent her whole life. She sees a raggle-taggle caravan, a column of pale faces under flat caps or kerchiefs, while pillars of smoke coil up from the town like so many charmed snakes. There is a glimpse of the glittering river and the red rooftops, and then it is gone.

They would head for their ancestral home, a farmhouse in the mountains, had it not been trampled already under the hooves of war. Instead they are a drop in a swelling stream of refugees, which merges with other tributaries, a vast flood of human misery, surging by foot, truck and donkey towards the capital of Serbian Bosnia: Banja Luka.

Once famous throughout the Balkans for its charming squares, boulevards and architecture, the city of Banja Luka has become inundated with those who have nothing.

Bojana and her family spend the next few weeks living with family friends in various districts, sleeping in spare rooms or, more frequently, basements, with just a few rugs and rags between themselves and the cold concrete floor. They are the lucky ones. Most are forced to the outskirts, crammed into windswept camps where tents float on a sea of footstepped mud.

The displaced, Bojana included, line up every morning in the cold, each in turn holding up a tin while the volunteer ladles thin soup from bubbling vats. The vessel warms hands then, the steam warms faces, but the liquid within is bland beyond belief. It is a sort of diluted tomato paste, having the appearance of rusty pond water, with a few token cabbage leaves troubling the surface like withered water lilies. Every time Bojana stands in this queue – glacial in its progress and in its soundscape: silent but for the odd groan or rumble – she imagines that today will be the day they will serve her a plate of ćevapi: succulent minced meat, grilled on a skewer, chopped onions, red pepper paste and sour cream stuffed into toasty flatbread. Her mouth waters at the prospect. But always, on reaching the front of the queue, it is the pond water.

'I'm sick of this,' her brother says. 'It's like food for homeless people.'

Bojana looks at him, shaking her head.

'We *are* homeless,' she says.

He is quiet for a long time after that.

Everything is grey that October in Banja Luka: the imperial facades, the supposedly autumnal boulevards, even the golden domes of the cathedral are somehow just a glinting shade of grey, like faded foil.

Bojana sees colour only in the pages of her album. In one picture Bojana and her friends, a troop of grinning ten-year-olds, cling to the branches of a tree like little monkeys. In the background is a cloudless sky above Ključ: pure azure dipping down to the green meadows, bright white walls and scarlet tiles. There is another of a vacation: the Adriatic a rippling turquoise, its brilliant beach covered in a kaleidoscope of towels, parasols and bathing suits. A third image: Bojana and her brother are decked out in crisp karate garb: poised, confident. Now they are hunched in a damp cellar, peering myopically at their childhoods through the candlelight. She sheds a tear for those summers.

Hunger and boredom fight a see-saw battle for the territory of her soul, much like the clashing armies to the west. It is dire hunger before breakfast, then, soon after the tin has been sucked dry, boredom settles in, until, as the sun sets, hunger creeps back, advancing throughout the night.

After the soup, they receive their daily ration of rumour every morning. There is constant talk of the front line, of titanic tank battles and apocalyptic artillery duels. On clear days they point up at the vapour trails in the depths of heaven. The spectre of cleansing lurks constantly on the edges of conversation: descriptions in detail of derelict villages or roadways strewn with baggage.

Bojana watches her proud parents – their shoulders sagging lower and lower, their cheekbones rising day by day – and is privately horrified. Her brother is no longer the chirpy chap he once was. She is startled when the mirror reveals that she too, like all the world, has greyed: her rosy glow is gone. This vibrant city has come to feel like a necropolis, its ornate buildings like sepulchres, where hopes are extinguished one by one. She can see no future in these avenues of want.

November. At an airbase on the far side of the world, outside Dayton, Ohio, many old men in suits have gathered to discuss Bosnia. Alija Izetbegović is there for the Bosniaks, Franjo Tuđman for the Croats and Slobodan Milošević for the Serbs.

They are stirred together for three weeks; whisked in a mixture of wrangling, refusal, fist-shaking, flattery and curses. Added to this brew are pyramids of coffee beans, boxloads of tobacco and, towards the finish, several bottles of alcohol. A sprinkling of ink completes the recipe. It is a volatile fermentation process, at times furious, but in the end they emerge with a smooth product: peace. They sign their agreement in Paris, on 14 December. The world applauds.

By the time the news reaches Banja Luka, Bojana and her family have left.

April 1999. An explosion jolts Bojana awake. She sits up in bed as the echo thunders out across the heavens. She scrambles out of the sheets, rubbing sleep from her eyes before tugging apart her bedroom curtains. She knows it is not thunder; the NATO bombs have been falling for over three weeks. The town of Pančevo stretches out before her, a black muddle of roofs and chimneys, edges lit a glowing orange. On the outskirts she can see fireballs belching up into the night. There is a flash there, which illuminates the petrochemical complex for an instant – giant glinting spheres, cylinders, prehensile pipes – and then the stupendous snap reaches her ears.

Bojana is in an apartment similar to her childhood home. She and her family are staying with her aunt, who took them in when they were at their most vulnerable. Bojana and her brother have been attending school and attempting to eke out a liveable normality. But now, after almost four years of relying on the hospitality of others, they are preparing to leave again.

When they first arrived they had been merely awaiting the opportunity to return to Ključ. A year passed, then two. When it became clear that they could never go home, they applied for refugee status with the IOM, who accepted them, and they have been waiting ever since, until a few weeks ago, when they were accepted for resettlement in the US. But their flight itinerary has been postponed twice in the upheaval. They are hoping that the third time is lucky.

'You are running to the enemy,' a neighbour shouted last week. 'They are bombing us and you are going to them. Shame!'

But her family have decided on their plan, and they stick to it.

Packing is neither a long nor a complicated task.

To the west of the inferno flows the dark Danube, flame-rippled, and beyond that is Belgrade, blacked out, but spurting streams of pyrotechnics up into the guessed flight paths of the enemy. It is now the capital of a much-reduced Yugoslavia. Only two republics, Serbia and Montenegro, remain to be pounded by NATO.

Bojana watches the fireworks a little longer and then returns to bed and an uneasy sleep.

In the morning, the petrochemical complex is a charred junk-yard of twisted metal, still vomiting flames, random explosions and an enormous noxious cloud: some parts black, other parts white, like some nebulous skunk drifting through the town. In the street children and pregnant women are being helped into evacuation buses; everyone else wraps rags about their faces and tries to go about their day with some semblance of normality. Few of the townsfolk support the government, but the bombs fall on them, regardless.

The blaze in the complex continues all week, the river is slick and the rain slimy. Fish and vegetables still come to the market but are tainted unmistakably. People vomit and break out in rashes. There are miscarriages. Bojana is glad to be leaving.

The day before departure, she takes a final stroll. The streets are deserted for the most part, with people scurrying here and there. The market is a sorrowful sight, with hushed and hurried transactions. In the fowl-abandoned park two old men are hunched over a chequerboard. Bojana sits near them, gazing up through tree branches at the traces of blue beyond the grey.

'Another bridge last night,' says one of the old men.

'My God, is there no end to these bombs?' asks the other.

The next day, Bojana and her family climb aboard a bus headed northward, towards the Hungarian border. They each have a suitcase and a plane ticket: Budapest–Amsterdam–Chicago. As they roll out of town, a meadow of blood-red peonies blurs by. A sticky black rain begins to patter their petals, coating them. It is May Day.

August 2016. A blue saloon is touring across Yugoslavia. Or what was once Yugoslavia. It sweeps past cities and forests and mountains, plunges into tunnels and out again into the sunlight. There is not a cloud in sight.

In this rented car is a thirty-six-year-old woman: US citizen, refugee, Serb. Bojana has returned.

She passes combine harvesters and tour buses, smokestacks and skyscrapers, houses of God and houses for sale. She passes scars too: the occasional pockmarked ruin or rusted tank carcass, sometimes a memorial engraved with the details of some atrocity.

But, for the most part, the sun shines and the people smile.

The blue saloon emerges from winding hills upon a vista of the sparkling Adriatic. It descends into a resort town by the beach, all white masonry and red tiling. Bojana has journeyed to the far south of Montenegro, right on the Albanian border. She has misgivings about stopping here, as her Serbian number plate is drawing some scowls, but she has travelled far for this rendezvous and is hungry. She parks in a side street and strolls down the cobbled strip, passing hotels, restaurants, night clubs. There are tourists in trendy western fashions and youthful locals dressed indistinguishably, though the old folks remain unchanged, obstinate in their caps and kerchiefs.

Bojana wanders along until she finds the arranged meeting place, a little bistro. She scans the interior, then walks out through double doors onto a westward terrace. There are iron tables and chairs, a balustrade, and far below is the crash, splash and wash of the sea. There are yachts and jet skis skimming about on the shimmering turquoise.

A voice hails her, a woman. 'Bojana?'

She turns and grins.

'My God, Ana, you haven't changed,' she says, striding up to the woman and hugging her.

Ana is Bojana's best friend from childhood. They had met as refugees in Banja Luka. Her friend had never left the country.

'I love your necklace,' says Ana.

It is a chain with a bejewelled key for a pendant.

'To remind me,' says Bojana.

Ključ means *key*. They both smile, but a sadness too is in their eyes. The waiter arrives with the menu, so they take a seat by the balustrade and order. Bojana knows exactly what she wants.

'Your parents,' asks Ana, 'they're still – '

'Yes, they're good,' says Bojana hurriedly. 'The whole family is doing well. We're all working, all contributing.'

A tray arrives: two plates of ćevapi. The meat is grilled perfectly, the peppers with just the right sweetness. After eating, they sip coffee.

'So,' says Ana, 'you've mastered the English, I take it?'

'I suppose so,' laughs Bojana. 'Although I hadn't a word when I arrived. It took *a lot* of work. So different from our language. But I love it now. I picked up enough to start my degree, in 2001. I was twenty then. They made me editor of the school newspaper.'

'Do you know, I'm not one bit surprised.'

Bojana shrugs, takes a drink.

'What about you?' she asks.

'We'll get to me in a minute. What have you been up to, all this time? What was it like at the beginning?'

'Well … not easy. My first work was cleaning: hotels during the day, offices at night. Then I worked in a bakery. That was not so fun. But, since that I've been in social service, real estate, mortgages, health administration, class action, retail.'

'And studied a master's, I hear.'

'My brother is the smart one. He's an aeronautical engineer!'

'Shush,' says Ana. 'What did *you* study, in the master's?'

'Science and management,' says Bojana. 'And now I'm back in health administration again.'

'Very nice. Must be satisfying?'

'I like it.'

'I saw those pictures of the wedding. My God, your dress …'

The pair laugh and chatter away as the sun dips into the sea.

Bojana does not know it yet, but back in the US, in a matter of months, she will be hired by a nearby state government to a highly influential administrative posting, where she will deal with refugee issues on a daily basis. It is not something she could have envisioned as she fled Ključ twenty-one years earlier, with nothing but a backpack and an album full of memories. Perhaps this is what makes her the ideal candidate.

There will be other news, too: she will be pregnant with her first child in time to start the new job. She has an education, a fine house and the beginnings of her own family. It is a good life.

Still, there are stormy nights when her mind drifts and her skin crawls; nights when the lightning flashes and, in that split second before thunder erupts, she is back in Bosnia, watching the explosions devour her childhood.

THE HONEY FLOWER TREE

Laos

'Hmong are too tough to weep.'[1]

– Laotian proverb

TWO RENTAL CARS WIND UP the bumpy mountain track. Inside are Chue Vang Xiong, his wife, his two sisters, an uncle, an aunt and a nephew with his wife. They are surrounded by cool forest: gnarled colonnades, leafy rafters. They have long since switched off the air conditioner, the sweaty lowlands are far behind them. Above is the summit, from which they will be able to gaze down into the valley where Chue Vang spent his childhood. He has not laid eyes on it in four decades.

He savours the recollection: the verdant slopes, two glinting rivers forking together, fish leaping in abundance, small hamlets dotted about like mushrooms, terraced paddies shimmering in a breeze and meadows blooming with wildflowers. He can hear the buffalo lowing, the creak of their harnesses and the calls of farmers

---

1 Hmong are an ethnic group found throughout east and southeast Asia. As in every other country, in Laos they are a minority.

as they set out home for the evening. He remembers the paaj zib, the honey flower tree. Its purple blossoms could be snapped off to reveal a delicious treacle within. Most distinctive for him is the ring of dawn peeping over the range, and how he would rush with the other children to get at the viscous gold of the paaj zib before the honey bird could begin its flittering harvest.

Life in the village of Nam Kama had not been easy, but it had been simpler, even purer, to Chue Vang's mind. His boyhood lungs were strangers to exhaust fumes, his boyhood thirst was quenched by pristine water. He has always missed the scents of the valley, its almost nutritional air, laced with flowers, forests and the sweet paaj zib.

Every May black-bellied clouds gathered along the horizon and rolled out across the valley. They grumbled and rumbled, then exploded: fat raindrops bombarding the earth. Within hours the tracks and fields turned molten, isolating the valley even more than usual. Dark day was rent by lightning. Whole hillsides could subside in an instant, gushing mire over anything unlucky enough to be in their path. Monsoon season lasts four months.

There was no temple or monks in the village. Instead the elders – in other words, grandparents – would impart their regional variation of Buddhism along with their folklore and music. Neither was there a school or teachers. Formal education required a lengthy commute, by foot, to a town several hours away. Most children worked in the fields alongside their parents. Chue Vang was one of the lucky few who did attend. Every Sunday he and a few others would trek off in a little convoy, laden with packs. This was their food for the week. They took their staples: rice, corn, tomato, cucumber, beans, potato, banana or strips of smoked meat might be on the menu, depending on the season.

In the town they stayed with relatives. The school was constructed no differently than their own abodes: packed earth floor, bamboo walls and a roof of wooden shingles. Inside there were rows of desks, the teacher's table, the blackboard and little else. The national curriculum in Laos was modelled, as closely as resources would permit, on the French system: residue of the very recent colonialism. Subjects included mathematics, French, Lao (including poetry), geography, history, science and art. Religious instruction was a private affair. There was not much by way of materials: they would copy the teacher's notes from the board onto paper.

Throughout Chue Vang's childhood, the CIA had been busy recruiting and amassing a secret army from among the Hmong to help bolster the royal government against the Pathet Lao and their allies across the Annamite Mountains.[2] The Vietnam War soon surged over the border. In an effort to disrupt North Vietnamese supply lines coming through Laos, the US Air Force unleashed a storm of ordnance, dropping as many explosives on Laos alone as they did throughout the entire Second World War. It is the most bombed country in history. People are still dying, at least fifty per year, from unexploded cluster munitions.

There had always been scraps of news, vapour trails in the deep blue skies, distant thunder without clouds, but for a long time Nam Kama, or *Hoof Print*, escaped the roughshod stomp of war. The gears of history had been wound, however, and were soon to drag all Laos into their maw. The CIA's Secret War intensified. A plateau just to the east of the village, The Plain of Jars, became the arena for a colossal bloody wrestling bout that threshed to and fro for the remainder of the conflict, tearing up tanks and trucks and men. And women and children. All the while, the bombers circled overhead.

In April 1975 the People's Army of Vietnam swept to victory

---

2   The Pathet Lao were the Laotian communist movement, closely allied with North Vietnam.

in Saigon and unified the country. At the same time, Cambodia fell to the Khmer Rouge.[3] In Laos the royal government capitulated, rather than wage a futile resistance. Pathet Lao troops marched into the capital, Vientiane, and established the Lao People's Democratic Republic. They first consolidated their hold on the cities and strategic points, then began to mop up any remaining resistance.

The Hmong, many of whom had been recruited by the CIA, found themselves left high and dry with the US departure from Indochina.[4] Searches for collaborators and weapons caches often degenerated into skirmishes and a spiral of violence swiftly seared through the countryside. A cousin of Chue Vang's was summarily executed. He was not the first or the last. Others were dragged away for re-education. Very soon, the vicinity was denuded of young men. Even twelve-year-olds like Chue Vang were not safe. They fled into the uplands, taking whatever weapons and supplies were available.

He can still recall the upland skirmishes in detail: ambush points, retreats, advances, casualties, ammunition expended, weapons procured – including his own Kalashnikov assault rifle, which had been taken from a fallen Vietnamese soldier. For three years he fled and hid and fought in the forests. To the outside world, it was not even a forgotten war, for it had never existed in the first place. But war it was, war without end.

Escape or death, they eventually concluded, were their options. Chue Vang's older brother went first, travelling by night

---

3   The Khmer Rouge, the party of Pol Pot, came to power on a wave of extremist rhetoric, fuelled by outrage and bitterness which was largely a product of the unprecedented brutality of the US bombing in Cambodia.

4   On 30 April 1975 the last US forces boarded helicopters at the US embassy in Saigon, ending the Vietnam War which had lasted two decades. This war had spilled over the borders of Vietnam into other parts of the Indochina region, namely Laos and Cambodia.

through thickest jungle and slipping across the border into Thailand. He made contact with the Thai authorities and also with the US embassy, asking them to help his family and his people. But they told him they could do nothing, unless they themselves made it to Thailand. He returned – across rivers, around outposts and through wilderness – to tell his tribe what was required.

The family, along with dozens of fellow Hmong, gathered secretly at a quiet cranny by the Mekong River. They needed ferries to come from the Thai side quickly, before a Pathet Lao patrol could stumble upon them. Someone had to swim to the far bank.

Fifteen-year-old Chue Vang stepped forward. He had to swim the breadth of the torrent with his old Kalashnikov strapped to his back. He had always enjoyed splashing about in the river at home, and had been good at it too, but he had never had to do it while carrying a hunk of steel and wood almost a metre long, weighing about ten pounds, with its awkward curved magazine digging into his shoulder blade at each stroke. On the far side, dripping and exhausted, he was welcomed by Thai soldiers not with open arms but with small arms. They seized him for a rigorous interrogation – after all, he could have been a drug dealer or a spy.

'If you are indeed Hmong, then who is the chief of such a village? … If you are a guerrilla, as you claim, then who is the commander for such a region? … Perhaps, then, you can tell us what mountain was the headquarters during such an offensive?'

They had done their research, but Chue Vang replied to the barrage satisfactorily. Other evidence, such as his low body fat and his rusty Kalashnikov, proved for them that he was indeed a guerrilla, and not some opium merchant who might have the money for rich food and shiny weaponry. His traditional clothes, loose black trousers and tunic, along with his lack of urban mannerism, sealed the case for them. The ferries were arranged.

At the refugee camp, the group was granted refugee status, due to their being recognised, finally, as foot-soldiers of the US. There followed nine dreary months while they waited to be processed for resettlement. The inhabitants of the camp lived an existence that would not have provoked much envy from a convict. The conditions were spartan, the rules regimented. Not a fan was to be found to dissipate the heavy heat that draped over everything like a suffocating blanket. Guards were harsh and exploitative. Within the fence they would extort the refugees whenever the opportunity arose. Beyond the fence they would beat or even kill those found to have strayed without permission. Chue Vang spent his time attending English lessons, taught by other inmates of the camp. He learned quickly and then taught a bit too. There was little else to do there, anyway, besides waiting. Waiting and dreaming.

One day, in December 1979, a bus came and took them. They had been approved. Before they said their tear-stained goodbyes, a shaman had blessed them, invoking the ancestors for protection. Strings had been tied around their wrists, to keep the spirits alongside.

Night fell as they arrived at the airport on the outskirts of Bangkok. The sprawling metropolis lurked dim-lit on the horizon, humming faintly while Chue Vang slept in a United Nations tent. What is a city like? he wondered. Smoky? Smelly? Crowded and concrete and cornered?

The next day they boarded the plane: vast and sleek, with swept wings and bulging engines. A giant compared to the tiny toys they had seen inching across the heavens. They soared and landed and soared again: Bangkok, Hong Kong, Tokyo, San Francisco, Chicago.

Crisp white Wisconsin was bewildering for the newcomers. There were nine of them: Chue Vang, his parents, his two sisters, along with his brother, his brother's wife and their two children. Not one had seen a snowflake before, let alone a snowstorm.

'Strange,' said Chue Vang's father. 'The trees are all dead wood. Everything is so white and so cold. It must be the clouds falling down.'

They were not left to forage and freeze in the wilderness, however. In the village of Mishicot, a home had been arranged for them by the local people: snug and clean and warm, stocked amply for the winter. A cold white closet was jammed with odd food. The house was a repository of curiosities: locks, glass and a uniform pelt that covered the floor, water that flowed with a turn and lanterns that lit with a flick. There was a box that buzzed with moving pictures.

Some natives had opposed the welcome. There have always been, it seems, Americans who misremember their own outlandish forebears. But most of Mishicot had risen to the challenge. Father Brouchoud addressed his flock from the pulpit: 'This has forced us all to open our hearts as we've never done before. And we found love.'

As he rested under the quilt that night, a weight drifted out of Chue Vang: the fear of the hunted. He slept, for the first time in years, with both eyes closed.

Chue Vang's breath rasped. Each lungful was a struggle, like honey through a straw, his chest tight, his body weak. In fifty-two years he had never felt so feeble. Something was up. At the hospital they agreed, promptly sending him through a series of scans and tests. A clot was lodged in an artery, not far from his heart. Surgery was an urgent necessity, life or death. Nothing was guaranteed, even waking up.

Chue Vang insisted on a delay, a stay, some days to inform those who populated his life. He wished to say goodbye. Just another set of farewells: as at the village, as at the camp, as with his wizened parents and his brother.

There were his colleagues: he had worked twenty years at a refugee resettlement agency in Milwaukee, where he had been able to use his experience and, most importantly, his empathy to work with newly arrived refugees and immigrants. He had risen to the position of director of immigration and refugee services. Many, many stories were recounted to him during this tenure, from all over the globe, wherever misery and violence drove people from their homes. Many were sorrowful, but many ended hopefully, due, in no small part, to his own efforts.

There were also his fellow Hmong: a wave of them had sought shelter in Wisconsin during the eighties, building burgeoning communities centred on families and wider clans. His family was no different, moving from Mishicot to Manitowoc to be closer to cousins. Many of the Hmong found themselves in agriculture, having carried their knowledge from the paddies of Indochina. For years they have gathered annually at State Fair Park, a grand hall, to celebrate their culture: music, dance, food, crafts and clothing. Old friends and relatives come from all over the Midwest and beyond.

There was his brother's family: a wife and seven children. They had all struggled after he passed the previous year, but they had struggled together as a big family, as a tribe.

There were his children: four daughters, Yee, Yeeb, Noogsi and Baujci, and two sons, Yag and Noushelong, all grown and successful in their own rights.

There was his wife, La. They met in Manitowoc and were courting by the end of high school. She too was Hmong, from the same valley in fact, and their fathers' families had known each other well. La and Chue Vang had even met briefly among the drab humid huts of the refugee camp. She understood.

He lay on his back while orderlies wheeled him to his fate, ceiling lights glaring. They manoeuvred him and a mask was placed on his face. He heard a dawn breeze rustling the leaves of the paaj zib, children's laughter, the gas was flowing and he was out.

He did wake up.

A long recovery was forecast, with plenty of rest. Stress was strictly forbidden. Soon though, despite the hesitancy of those around him, he was back in the office, carrying his clunky heart monitor everywhere, its wires snaking under his shirt to the little pads on his chest. The incision was sore and it itched all the time. They had sawn open his breastbone, then clamped his ribs asunder to reveal his beating heart.

Bit by bit, he healed up, was able to discard the monitor, remove the stitches. He was grateful. Life is precious. And yet in the office, amid the buzz of the printer and the bleat of the phone, walking past conferences or banter at the coffee pot, he could see sunlight glinting through branches, purple blossoms swaying, whispering. The honey flower tree was calling.

A few months later, in December 2016, he was in Hanoi with La. Scooters whisked about, skimming rainwater off the shiny streets, which were narrow and cluttered with stalls festooned with red flags and banners.

It is never quiet here: always there is business or music. Even by night it stays bright, the bustle unabating around glimmering lakes and ancient temples, crumbling colonial mansions and sprouting skyscrapers. So this was the nerve centre, he thought. Where generals had pored over maps and equipment had been churned out, and from where reinforcements had tramped to the front. Perhaps that rusted old Kalashnikov had met with its previous owner somewhere in this city, in the yard of some ochre-painted barracks under the gaze of a bust of Lenin. Not far away, deep within a sprawling ceremonial complex, Ho Chi Minh lay sleeping in his glass box, forever.[5]

Chue Vang and La stayed just a few days in Hanoi, before driving north to the Chinese border. Here they climbed a lonesome and windswept summit, infamous in Hmong myth. Roughly translated, their name for it means: Place Where You Die of Hunger or Cold. Tradition claims that this was the point where the ancestors escaped from Qing armies sent to exterminate them. But at a terrible cost. From this cruel peak they had fled into Vietnam and Laos.

Afterwards, the couple descended to the more hospitable, though still quite elevated, farmland around Sa Pa. They visited some Hmong villages in the area, revelling in the familiar 'flower' textiles of the locals, before returning to Hanoi. From Hanoi they took a quick trip to Ha Long Bay, then flew into Wattay International Airport, Vientiane, in the Lao People's Democratic Republic.

They were just in time for the Hmong New Year, for which they travelled to the town of Phonsavan, capital of the Xiang-khouang Province. The population was swollen with brethren. Exiles from across the globe could be found amid festivities that completely overwhelmed the streets for a week. The full canon

---

5   Ho Chi Minh was a Vietnamese revolutionary leader from the Second World War until his death in 1969. Saigon, the capital of South Vietnam, was renamed in his honour after reunification with the North.

of the Hmong panoply was visible in every imaginable variation and accent: floral patterns on black bases, riotous pinks and blues, gaudy headdresses, skirts and leggings. Hmong cowboys strutted about in their brown and violet hats, winking at embroiderers in the bazaars, and street vendors sizzled sour sparrows, a local delicacy. There was bullfighting, matchmaking and feasting, and everywhere the meeting of old friends or the making of new.

When the revelry simmered down, and rubbish swirled in the hush, the Xiongs set out into the surrounding prairie. Browned by the dry season, humpbacked hills speckled yellow with sunflowers, it was scattered throughout with ancient stone vessels, thousands of them, often taller than a person. There are many theories as to their creation, but mystery abides. Craters too, less ancient, dotted the landscape. This was The Plain of Jars. The couple had to walk in strict linearity: the space beyond the flagged boundaries of their path was an immense lottery, where the silence of the grassland could be rent by an explosion at any instant. The backbreaking and perilous quest of the sweepers had been going on for decades, and would continue for decades more. In the earth, alongside the steel seeds of death, lay a harvest of bones, long flensed of ideology.

Chue Vang listened a moment to the birdsong over the old battlefield. Then he nodded to La, ever so faintly, and they turned around. It was time to return to the valley.

As the two rental cars approach the summit, the stately forest thins, shrinking into groves of bamboo and banana. Suddenly, the whole arch of heaven opens out before them: rarefied, blue, a hawk skimming past at eye-level. Below them is the valley. Or it should be. Instead, a vast sheet of water extends to the peaks opposite and off to the distance on either side. The verdant slopes are truncated, the paddies and meadows and buffalo have vanished. And the paaj zib, the sweet paaj zib, unknown beyond the valley floor, has drowned. The lake has made an Atlantis of Chue Vang's childhood.

He stands out of the car and stares. He pictures the honey flower tree in the shadowy depths, rotted branches hoary with weed, sinking beneath the sludge. He weeps.

'This dam will make us "The Battery of Southeast Asia",' said the politicians in the city, with their cigars and their scotch. Chue Vang had hoped against hope that the rising waters would spare Nam Kama. The construction was, after all, many miles away. He could never have imagined the birth of such a lake, such an abyss.

Chue Vang's relatives gather round him, hunched. There are sighs. Those who fled left everything behind them: they have lost not just their material shelters, but their customs, their rituals, their stories, their songs, the fresh waters, the bountiful fish, the clean air, and now this land that had been farmed and formed by generations. They have lost their *home*. None had wanted to leave, but there had been little choice. Such is the life of a refugee.

In Arlington lies a monument, hewn from granite and bronze, a reward to the cannon fodder of the Secret War. In their motherland lie many more monuments – millions – strewn in paddy and forest, rusted yet primed, awaiting the plough or the little hands of the inquisitive.

BENEATH THE DASHBOARD

Burma

I MEET HER IN DOWNTOWN Milwaukee, at a Moroccan restaurant, a favourite place of hers. Sitting on the terrace, she orders a hookah, I take out my notepad and we chat in the warm summer evening.[1] Brady Street bustles below, with buses and shoppers. She is a young woman of thirty-two, though she looks younger. She has a bright disposition, wears an expression both mirthful and mischievous, and has her hair arrayed in a shock of coffee-coloured curls. She sits with ease yet speaks with animation.

Mar Mar Lin recalls her escape from Burma. She can remember the churning waters and the cloying jungle along either bank, sitting in the canoe with her mother, Ni Ni, her cousin and the smuggler who, at the stern, operated a little outboard motor. She was thirteen, fleeing upriver. A military outpost loomed up ahead.

'Heave to,' boomed a megaphone. 'What is your business? Who are these?'

---

1   A hookah is an instrument for smoking flavoured, vaporised tobacco.

A machine gun swivelled, its muzzle sniffing them out.

'They are my wife and children, Sir,' said the smuggler. 'We are visiting relatives.'

'Is that so?' said the sergeant. 'Okay. First we will need to take your women ashore. For inspection.'

'No Sir, please. My wife is too sick. And my daughters are too young.'

'They don't look too young to me! We've *inspected* younger before!'

The other soldiers chuckled. Apart from the youngest, who went pale.

'Perhaps, Sir,' said the smuggler, 'perhaps we can offer you a gift?'

'An inspection would be a fine gift.'

'Look, please, take this,' said the smuggler, flashing notes like a fan.

The officer snatched the money and waved them on. A good chunk of Ni Ni's savings, hard earned, gone in a snatch. When, after an eternity, they rounded the next bend, the smuggler sighed and Ni Ni wiped away her niece's tears. This is not an adventure any more, thought Mar Mar.

The sinking sun threw whorling shadows before them. With darkness descending, a square shadow ghosted up, tethered mid-river: a bamboo hut on a pontoon. Here they rested for the night. The shrieks and cackles beyond stoked their fears, the gurgle below was their scant lullaby. Mar Mar lay awake listening and conjured images of the hideous monsters or the creeping, crawling terrors that might release such sounds. She worried about how hungry they might be.

They set off again at dawn and continued upriver until dusk. There were three days of this: swatting flies, telling old yarns or just gazing languidly. The jungle on either side crept ever closer until finally the stream was little more than a streak of mire. The smuggler dragged his vessel up the sticky bank and the women said their goodbyes, wishing him the best. He had risked much in denying the military their inspection.

Mar Mar gaped at the canopy far above, creepers dipping and soaring all about, swaying skylights shedding scraps of sun on the earth. Some hidden creature crooned. She was a long, long way from the streets of Mawlamyine.[2]

Pig heads would greet her downstairs every morning before school. Pigs and any number of other grimacing carcasses – along with vegetables, rices and spices. And her grandmother would be among it all, humming and chopping and stirring and mopping. It is a busy bustle, running a family and a restaurant. Mar Mar was a guinea pig at breakfast and she loved it: trying all the aromas, the textures, the flavours. Her fascination pleased her grandmother and she was soon promoted from guinea pig to chef's assistant – provided it did not encroach on her schoolwork.

In the early grades there were no books; chalk and boards had to suffice. With powdery scratches they would conduct their exercises, up to fifty children wedged into a classroom. Sexes were corralled to either side. The school was a cluster of huts with a single lavatory for its over two hundred students. And yet she enjoyed it, drinking in the Burmese, mathematics, English, science, geography and history almost as quickly as she did her domestic gastronomy.

School and cooking: these were her two duties as a child, and her grandmother would permit little else besides. She did not often allow Mar Mar or her younger sister to venture outside. Her

---

2   Mawlamyine, formerly Moulmein, is the capital of Mon State, southeastern Burma.

mother agreed and so did her grandfather, webbed in his ancient tattoos. But he had not coined her 'Little Rebel' for nothing: she was imbued with a sense of adventure from an early age, and as she grew she would wander farther and more frequently from this imposed realm of books and pots, fraternising with her two companions from down the street: a little girl and a little boy. They would spend hours together in the summers, when not at Buddhist school, teasing, giggling and devising their own entertainments under the glinting gold spires and colonial facades of the riverside city of Mawlamyine.

The boy's parents predicted that he and Mar Mar would be sweethearts one day. There were elaborate and exotic plans made for just such an eventuality, not entirely in jest.

'One day,' Mar Mar said, 'we will get married. I will be a school teacher and you will be an important general, with a fancy uniform and a great big cap!'

But the threads of this childhood reverie were soon to unravel.

There was perhaps a reason beyond childish romance for Mar Mar's whimsical thoughts of betrothal. There was a certain loneliness in her life. While her grandfather was ever-present, her father, Sein Htay Aung, had not lived among them for two years. Throughout this time her mother had to make do with the help of her parents while she raised the two daughters, trying to answer their artless questions as best she could. Her husband was a fugitive. His crime? The unutterable sin of democracy.

When revolution bubbled up in August 1988, Sein Htay quickly joined the cause.[3] For a tense but glorious few weeks in that autumnal heat anything seemed possible on the streets all across Burma. Farmers, students, clerks, monks, sailors, even a few defectors from the army, surged in defiance, crowding about

---

3   The uprising against the junta, the military dictatorship, was named the 8888 Uprising, after the date it began.

impromptu stages where upstarts sowed speeches daily. There were hopes for a foreign intervention or some other catalyst that might topple the authoritarian government. Finally, the military had had enough. Reinforcements were summoned from the borderlands, marched in and, with a withering volley, choked the would-be revolution in an eruption of smoke and blood. There followed a ruthless manhunt. Sein Htay, among thousands of others, vanished into the wild.

His family had no idea where he was, or how he was. Eventually, Mar Mar's mother heard a rumour of his whereabouts and ventured out to find him. After the rebellion was crushed by the military, he signed up with the Karen resistance and lived the uncertain and perilous life of a guerrilla, trekking from camp to camp, constantly manoeuvring, staying one step ahead of the government. Every day in the jungle was a struggle, even when not planning or escaping ambushes.

Eventually came the most dangerous mission of all: he was sent back to Mawlamyine to sabotage an electrical power plant, with several comrades and a pack of explosives. Shortly after they set off from the base, however, another group departed with a different mission: to liquidate the first group.

Somehow Sein Htay learned of the treachery and managed to escape. Apparently in-fighting and factionalism are not unheard of among the rebels, which is hardly surprising given the pressures and privations of the struggle, the unremitting brutality of the opponent, and sheer longevity: this is the longest-running conflict in the world. Caught between the rock of betrayal and the hard place of the junta, Sein Htay opted to lay low in a quiet Mon hamlet. There he entered the monkhood and retreated from the temporal. He lived a quiet life of prayer for many months. Until his wife found him.

The dust of 8888 had settled, she told him, and it was safe

to return to Mawlamyine. He agreed to return. There he was reunited with his daughters and parents-in-law. Very soon another child was on the way, a little boy. But the child did not live long.

Mar Mar lived through this grief and then suffered further as she watched her parents' relationship deteriorate and then crumble apart. Her mother left to search for her sister, who had not been heard from in several years, while her father went to Yangon, where he was born, and took Mar Mar and her sister with him. They moved in with his parents.

Mar Mar did not enjoy this new arrangement. She missed her grandmother, the kitchen and her two childhood companions. And, once again, she had to make do with a single parent. She settled into the routine of school and the rhythms of life in the one-time capital. All the while the military government continued its machinations: festering with corruption, crushing all dissent and waging a relentless butchery in the unruly peripheries.

One morning, in 1997, Mar Mar was washing dishes before school when her grandmother rushed in.

'Come with me, quickly!' she said.

'I can't, I have to finish my chores!'

'Never mind them. You must see this.'

'But I'll be late for class!'

'It doesn't matter. Come.'

When she entered the room her eyes lit up. She ran and hugged her mother.

'A May, a May, have you shrunk?'

'No,' her mother laughed. 'You have grown. It's been three years.'

They soon sat in the kitchen, poured tea, and Ni Ni told

Mar Mar her story, from the beginning. Ni Ni had embarked on the search for her sister knowing only this: she had crossed into Thailand some years earlier. There were no clues as to her whereabouts, or even if she was still alive. Neither this nor her lack of Thai had deterred Ni Ni; she just wanted her sister back. The borderlands are unforgiving, however. No sooner had she crossed over than her vulnerability was pounced upon; she was tricked and then enslaved in an industrial bakery. A whole year dragged by in servitude before she managed an escape. From there she got work in a factory, pickling bamboo shoots, which somewhat improved her situation and gave her more freedom to enquire about her sister. She was constantly asking questions, following up leads, hitting brick walls. There were no signs, no clues, so she set off again – this time for Bangkok.

The metropolis was a shock after the highlands along the border: dazzling skyscrapers vying with spectacular temples, thronged with masses of humanity from all over the globe, every shape and colour and class of person imaginable. Naturally she had to narrow her search, so she sought out the Burmese quarter, a dense district of fishermen and fishmongers, crammed up against the quays. She found employment in a metal workshop, scraping together enough to survive and continue her mission. There were questions, leads, more disappointments. Then, during a standard inquiry with a stranger, came some recognition and a phone number, just some inky digits on a scrap of paper. Dialling, she found herself put through to a phone in a refugee camp. And down the line, scratchy but unmistakable, came the voice of her long-lost sister.

'And that is how I found your aunt.'

'But where is she?'

'She is still there in the camp. I am going back to her.'

Panic welled up in Mar Mar.

'But,' her mother continued, 'I want to bring you with me. And your sister. That is why I am here.'

Here it was – what she had daydreamed about for so long, walking back from school or washing the dishes – an adventure. And besides, she was thirteen now, practically a grown-up.

Mar Mar's elation soon crashed against the concrete barrier of her father. Under no circumstances would he allow his daughters to go on such a foolish voyage, he declared. They were too young; they had school to attend and a household to maintain. His side of the family agreed. Ni Ni stayed for several days while it was argued back and forth. Finally, she convinced them to allow Mar Mar the choice. She chose to escape Burma. Her younger sister, however, really was too young, and no amount of arguing could change that. Mar Mar waved goodbye to her family, not knowing when she might see them again.

Mar Mar and her mother first went to Mawlamyine, where it all began, to visit her grandmother in the old restaurant for a few days. Mar Mar's cousin joined them here; she too would travel to Thailand.

After this bittersweet stay, the three of them took a ferry out of the city, upriver into a hinterland of paddies and scrub. As night fell they disembarked at a village and sought shelter. They had no plans whatsoever and even fewer contacts. A local woman took them into her home for the night and arranged a smuggler. They slept on her kitchen floor and set off in the canoe the following morning.

Now here she was, in the wilderness, a long, long way from Mawlamyine. They were among the Mon, however, the region where their ancestors came from, so despite the bewildering surroundings, there was a certain familiarity to be found in the manner and speech of the locals. Again, a village woman came to their aid, agreeing to guide them across the border.

Where Burma ended there was an outpost. Facing it, where Thailand began, stood another outpost. Barbed-wire fencing trailed to the distance on either side, and a dirt track ran through the middle, blocked by levered gates and soldiers. And yet, this helpless gaggle of women strolled right through, under the gaze of assault rifles and bayonets, stating simply that they were ambling across for an afternoon meal with relatives in the neighbouring settlement. That they spoke Mon themselves, that they had the hallmarks of their ancestry in their faces and that they had an experienced local by their side perhaps explains the surprising ease with which their transgression was achieved. They counted their blessings.

In the Thai village there was no time for sightseeing. They were immediately taken to a house and shuffled up into the attic, which had scarcely enough space for the three of them to curl up together. The people living downstairs were helping, but there were many in the village who would have been tempted to report suspicious interlopers. The mother, daughter and cousin settled down in this tight space; watched the afternoon wane through the gaps in the floorboards. Night cloaked them, the house below lulled into silence, and one by one the three refugees fell asleep in the pitch black.

Mar Mar sprang awake to a racket. The trap door scraped open and hurried whispers roused them. They had to leave, urgently. There was barely time to rub their eyes as they were clattered downstairs and out into the night. She could not see anything and had no bearings, but found herself crawling about among a confusion of strangers, all wide-eyed with fear, the fear of the hunted. They were scrabbling about in some sort of bottleneck. They had come to a fence.

'Mar Mar,' said her mother. 'If anything happens, just run. Don't stop. Don't worry about anyone. Run, do you hear?'

'Yes, a May.'

Before she knew it, the blundering crowd had ripped her away from her mother and cousin, and she found herself squeezed under the fence. While she tried to look back, she was ushered into a waiting pickup truck. They stuffed her beneath the dashboard on the passenger's side and sped off. A woman sat in the seat and a pillow was set on top of Mar Mar, packing her in further, into a tight ball. Then a baby went on top of this to complete the concealment. Not a peep of light penetrated this covert, there was just the growl of the engine and the screech of suspension at every bump. It reeked of oil and sweat.

Minutes passed, then hours. She lost track of time as her limbs went dead in the confinement. Every clatter hurt. Worst of all, she was thirteen and all alone in a strange land. Though in a vehicle full of people, she was confined within her own mind for that interminable night.

'Why?' she asked.

Then the wheels stopped, bobbed still, and the engine idled. The pillow was ripped away. Brilliant light blinded Mar Mar. Pins and needles broke out immediately. She stood, or stooped rather, in the middle of a street, rush hour buzzing all around her, a hive of scooters and tuk-tuks. She turned back to the pickup and saw a young man being helped out from the inconceivably narrow space between the passenger seat and the back wall of the cabin. He had spent that bouncing, bruising night centimetres away from her and had never so much as squeaked. Such is the life of a refugee.

A motorcycle swung over, stopping but still rattling.

'Hop on,' shouted the driver, a lady, through the din.

Mar Mar hesitated.

'Quick!'

'What about my mother?'

'You want to see your mother again? Then you'll have to just trust me. Besides, you haven't much choice.'

Mar Mar glanced about: at the battered pickup, at the strange city with its mysterious babble and its indecipherable street signs. She hopped on behind the lady.

They edged through the choking streets, the roiling fumes, then zipped past the outskirts into a fresh wind, green fields blurring past as they wound up towards serried hilltops. Finally, when they were well isolated, they came to a village.

Though they were in the heart of Thailand, the local people milling about seemed terribly familiar: their houses, their faces, their longyis. Then she heard them – they were speaking Burmese! Not only Burmese, but here and there a smattering of Mon, a sprinkling of Karen. This was a village populated entirely by exiles.

And there, in a nearby house, were her mother and her cousin. They hugged and cried and laughed.

On the restaurant terrace, with the hum of Milwaukee below, Mar Mar blows out a stream of hookah. She grins.

'That is how I left Burma,' she says.

'And your aunt?' I ask.

'We stayed in that village for a few days. We even got to celebrate the Full Moon there. Then we were shown how to get to the refugee camp. Where she had been living all those years.'

'How was it, living in the camp?'

'Boring,' she says, with a frown. 'Boring and … *bleak*. There is no opportunity there. You have to sit around all day. The Thai guards do not let you leave. Or do anything. They are very harsh, very corrupt.'

'I've read some stuff about that. Exploitation and extortion and the like. I've heard that some of the authorities there are dodgy divils. Work closely with traffickers. Or certainly throw a blind eye …'

'Yes, Thailand is not very kind to refugees. But they are a longtime ally of the US, so …'

'… no sanctions.'

'Exactly.'

We finish up with Mar Mar telling me about her more recent history. How herself and her mother managed to attain refugee status, how they made it to Milwaukee, their new home, and how Ni Ni opened up a shop specialising in Burmese produce. It has proven a boon for their family and also for the growing community of refugees who hail from Burma: Mon, Karen, Chin and, especially nowadays, the Rohingya, who are being butchered and dispossessed en masse as we speak – a fact generally ignored by the mainstream media.

She tells me of her marriage, to another refugee, an Iraqi, a Muslim – which would have been an impossibility in Burma – and of their young boy who has just had his fifth birthday. Her husband, Abdullah, owns a furniture depot and is well known in the Middle-Eastern community. Her younger sister eventually made it to Milwaukee too. Mar Mar made it back to Burma in recent years, in time to be reunited with her father after fourteen years' absence. He passed away shortly after.

She herself works for Hunger Task Force as a bilingual food share assistant and often finds herself working with and for newly arrived refugees. In their faces she can see her own past and her own struggles, but also their unwillingness to surrender to despair.

'One thing I learned,' she says, 'on that night in the pickup, in that tight little corner beneath the dashboard. Life is tough. Or, it can be tough. And so, you must live it to the fullest, you must have no regrets.'

A waiter jaunts past, a tray of delicacies balanced before him, wafting aromas. I fancy that Mar Mar has noted the food and is wondering what her grandmother would have thought of it, back in that busy old kitchen in Mawlamyine.

THE CAVALIER OF KUNDUZ

Afghanistan

WHEN I FIRST MET ZARHAWAR I was struck by an overwhelming impression of nobility. He had a chivalric bearing, evoking a bygone age. It seemed to emanate mostly from his eyes, a steady crystal blue, though he was also the possessor of a formidable black beard, which could have turned any respectable hipster green with envy. There was something in his countenance that brought to mind the farthest adventures of Alexander the Great or some character plucked from the pages of Rudyard Kipling. He was young, yet seemed very wise. The office – bleating phones and drudging suits – and the view out the window – a parking lot and the rusting corrugations of Milwaukee's factory district – was a poor backdrop for this man who I pictured instead perched among the epic mountain vistas of his native Afghanistan. Likely this was a ridiculous romanticisation on my part, but perhaps not wholly. I sensed I was not the only one in the Refugee Resettlement Department who was impressed.

He was standing patiently, good-humouredly even, while a group of us staff – resettlement caseworkers, for the most part –

deliberated over which pub to wander into after work. I was aware of the chasm between our schemes and his, and was somewhat relieved when the focus turned back to his case.

I sat in on a meeting between Zarhawar, his cousin and one of my colleagues, where they tried to ascertain his immigration situation. This involved seemingly endless phone calls and reams of charming on-hold music. Though he had been granted Special Immigrant Visa status, and had a green card on the way, he was eager to leave the US as soon as possible. My colleagues had been begging him to stay, but to no avail. His cousin, who wore a wide-peaked baseball cap and a baggy jersey, and who spoke with an American accent, could not budge him either. Apparently the whole extended family had engaged in this futile exercise.

'You are fortunate,' they told him. 'Getting into America is not easy. One shouldn't squander the opportunity.'

'No,' he said, in flawless, if accented, English. 'I understand what you are saying. But I must go back.'

Zarhawar had the steadfast assurance of a man with a supreme purpose. Perhaps this purpose is what leant him his air of nobility: he wished to tread the dangers of his homeland once more in order to reach his wife and help her to escape. Not only her, but the child she bore in her womb.

In Afghanistan, his life had been coming together satisfactorily. He was a professor of Dari literature and English, fluent also in Pashtun and Arabic, with the prospects of married life and a new home. But now it had, quite literally, gone up in smoke. Months earlier, in Kunduz, his marriage ceremony had been brutally interrupted by the gunfire and carnage of a sudden Taliban advance.[1] His two brothers disappeared in this chaos, one of whom has not been heard from since. Zarhawar spent his

---

1   Kunduz is a city in northern Afghanistan, the sixth largest in the country. It has often found itself on the front line of the war against the Taliban.

honeymoon on the run and all of his savings had to be mustered just to survive.

It was he, not his wife, who had been granted entry to the US; it was also he who was in greatest peril from the Taliban. Being a professor of English, or 'spreading the tongue of the infidel', was bad enough, but he had also offered help to the occupying forces as an interpreter. For this reason, he went alone to the US with all haste, knowing he could apply for a spouse to follow him over. He arrived in Milwaukee safe and sound, met his caseworkers, even had accommodation arranged. Everything was in order for him to begin the process of settling in. But as the days drifted by it became increasingly apparent that his wife would not be getting over any time soon.

She had become mired in the bog of bureaucracy that envelopes officialdom in Afghanistan. The legal system is quite different there: oftentimes, especially beyond Kabul, it remains heavily reliant on traditional practices that would appear somewhat exotic to the western eye. For starters, Zarhawar's wife's documents were all based in Kunduz, stored in an antiquated facility in the courthouse. They were mostly handwritten, unstandardised and in Dari. The US embassy insisted that everything be translated into English. This in itself was a mammoth task and required time and effort to find a translator. One document in particular proved to be a real spanner in the works; the courthouse kept refusing to release it because it was the only copy in existence, and they were afraid that it would be damaged or destroyed, and therefore lost forever. Finally they agreed to hand it over, but the authorities at the US embassy were unimpressed: it was a traditional document, written in scrawling calligraphy. Instead of official signatures, it was marked by the inky thumbprints of village elders.

In the meantime, Zarhawar's wife was heavily pregnant and

living with her father, who according to Zarhawar was unhelpful. 'Irresolute', as he put it. In the courthouse and among bureaucrats he would accept the answer 'no' far too readily where some insistence might have won the day. Zarhawar worried that the old man would get her killed somehow and that he was not up to the task of escorting Zarhawar's wife to Kabul. At any rate, it is inadvisable for a woman in Afghanistan to be with child while without a husband, or, in this case, without a *visible* husband. And, to top it all, the Taliban were slowly encircling Kunduz, gaining ground every day.

After another round of phone calls and further reams of on-hold music, Zarhawar received confirmation that he could leave the US and would be allowed to re-enter, so he borrowed money and booked his flights to Kabul.

I tagged along with his caseworker to visit him on the eve of his departure. We spoke of the very real dangers involved, but also of how we understood his motive. Most of all, the caseworker emphasised the perils of Kunduz; how he should confine himself to the relative safety of the capital and have his wife come to him there. We chatted about Afghani culture, languages and kahwah, a green tea infused with saffron and cinnamon, traditionally brewed in a samovar. Then came some Islamic theology. He spoke of the duties required of every Muslim. My colleague was very knowledgeable on the finer points. I acted as devil's advocate to an extent, gingerly dropping in questions now and again, which he was happy to answer. His explanations were lucid and enlightening. While I was hardly converted, I was deeply impressed by the spirituality, the philosophy and the variety available within Islamic thought – once it remains unfettered by certain extremes.

As we prepared to leave, we wished him the best of luck and shook his hand.

'Someday soon,' he said, 'after all of this is finished, we will drink tea together here in Milwaukee.'

'Inshallah,' I said. God willing.

After many hours of flying and several connections, Zarhawar landed in Kabul, and lost no time in getting to Kunduz. He made progress there in sorting out his wife's visa application, but it was too little too late – by the time the documents were in order she was too heavily pregnant to fly. They were essentially grounded until after the birth.

It was at this point that the Taliban launched a grand offensive and, after some vicious street-fighting, wrested the city from government forces. Zarhawar was behind enemy lines.

'For three days,' he said, 'I walked among the Taliban.'

The outcome, had he been identified, was in little doubt. Throughout their conquered territories, the Talibs establish checkpoints and roadblocks. At one, the rumours said, they had set up a biometric machine and were scanning people's fingerprints – the wrong match with their database and you would be dragged off somewhere, most likely a lonely ditch.

Somehow, and this I leave to your imagination as it is left to mine, Zarhawar managed to smuggle his pregnant wife out of the beleaguered city of Kunduz; through the war zones, across inhospitable wastelands and into the relative security of Kabul. Perhaps they stowed away in the cargo of some truck, or had enough local knowledge to hike some secret goat track, or perhaps it was simply a matter of enough money in the right palm. Zarhawar has not told us. His terse email to us merely said: 'It was a very scary time.'

Several weeks later, under the gaze of the snowcapped Hindu Kush, among the sprawling blocks and minarets of Kabul, a child was born: a little girl, healthy and safe. Her mother's documents were all in order. She and Zarhawar would have to attend an interview with their newborn and provide evidence that the baby was theirs before they flew – a tedious if fairly routine task.

In Milwaukee, we anxiously await the return of the man from Kunduz. Of course, nothing in life is guaranteed. But soon, God willing, we will sit together and pour some of that tea.

ARCHIPELAGO

South Africa

NOLWANDLE PULLS HER BLOUSE SLEEVE down over the bruise and sets two plastic cups on the dining table. The purple welt, angry with veins, peeps out as she pours the peach juice, but the children are too busy scrambling up into the chairs to notice. By the time they have drained their drinks, she has unclipped a schoolbag and spread some homework out on the table.

'More when you finish, okay?'

Fezeka, her eldest, nods and Nolwandle ruffles her hair as she opens her textbooks. Nolwandle flicks on the television for the youngest, her five-year-old, her baby boy: Bongani. Fezeka is nine, or, rather, nine and a half.

'We'll turn it low,' says Nolwandle, 'until Fezeka has finished.'

'Yes, Mummy.'

Bongani is sitting on the carpet in front of the screen, already immersed in his favourite programme, set in an animated hospital where his hero doctor sews up injured dolls and patches up teddy bears.

Nolwandle pauses before starting into the pots and pans. Just ten pages, she thinks, and smiles as she plucks a book from the crammed shelf – African history, spiritual self-help, Nelson Mandela – and sinks into her wicker armchair. She loves to read. Reading has brought her through a lot, let her escape just often enough to remain sane: growing up in poverty in a township on the outskirts of Port Elizabeth, with her father committed to an asylum and her mother struggling alone with four children; overcrowded and underfunded classrooms; corporal punishment; apartheid oppression; political violence in the streets. Her neighbours' entire house was once consumed by a petrol bomb, 'Impimpi' sprayed on the pavement: *Informers*. Their skulls were later uncovered in the cooling ash. Her first marriage, to an older man, had been arranged while she was still in school.

But she is not reflecting on past troubles now. There is only the inky magic pulsing before her eyes, transforming into scenes and scents and saviours. There is just the quiet scribbling of Fezeka's pencil and the faint bantering of neighbours, the dappled afternoon light dancing through the tree in the garden, and the mild July breeze. Cooking can wait: five minutes, or to the end of the chapter. Whichever. The end of the chapter.

The metal gate outside swings, clangs against the wire fencing; many footsteps trample down the path and the front door bursts open. Five strapping men surge in, yelling at her, at the kids, pushing her over to them, herding them all past the table and into a corner.

'Where is he?' they shout.

'I don't know! I don't know!'

The children cower, Bongani wailing.

'Stay there,' growls one, a silver chain hanging over his floral shirt, as he jabs a finger at Nolwandle's face, glowering at her through his eyebrows. 'Don't fucking move.'

The other four pillage the kitchen, toppling the wicker chair, the table, slamming open a cupboard and clattering brooms and boxes out onto the floor. They move with the confidence of youth and musculature; they have sharp haircuts and jewellery, branded jeans and jazzy shirts.

'Shut that brat up!' says Silver Chain.

One of the others kicks over a sack, maize meal pattering out like a sudden rainfall. They disappear into the bedrooms, beds scrape, clap against walls; there is a tinkle of glass, curtains whipping, cabinets crashing.

'He's not here.'

They tramp back in, panting, sweating. The cartoon is still chirping away on the television.

'He can't hide forever,' sneers Silver Chain.

They stream out. The front door slams, the metal gate swings.

Nolwandle spreads her arms around the children, mother hen, clasping their shuddering shoulders and tear-streaked faces into the frills of her blouse.

On the street corner, outside the gates of a standard single-storey house that her husband has converted into a mechanic's workshop, she cranks the handbrake. She climbs out of the car and weaves through the crowd of bystanders in the yard.

'What has this neighbourhood become?' an old lady sighs.

The others tut in agreement.

Inside, a shelf has collapsed, the floor is scattered with nuts and bolts and bottles of fluid. The assistant mechanic, built like a recently retired rugby player, is shepherding other locals outside. Nolwandle's husband, Pascal, is staring at the mess. He is tall and thin, has trimmed curls and a sharp chin. His shirt is ripped open. One nostril is streaming blood, his lip is cracked, an eye puffed.

'Nolwandle?'

'They came here too?'

'The neighbours saved us,' says the assistant. 'As soon as the scuffle began, they streamed in, thank God.'

'They'll come back,' says Pascal. 'Tomas, close up.'

Pascal grabs Nolwandle's arm, pulling her out into the yard and back into their car. He drives like a madman, hunched over the wheel, squinting through his puffed eye, overtaking, hammering the horn. They speed through the leafy neighbourhoods, out into empty lots, unshaded wasteland, a crowded slum, building sites, more leafy neighbourhoods. She glances over at him, at his bad ear, the lobe shot off in some long-ago skirmish.

'Who are these guys?' asks Nolwandle.

'You don't want to know.'

'Are they from your homeland?'

'Does it matter?'

'They had French accents.'

He sighs.

'Are they rebels? Former comrades?'

'Here we are.'

Pascal jogs up the steps into the police station. Nolwandle follows.

Inside, the officers laugh. And laugh and laugh.

'I love your stories,' says one. 'Hilarious.'

'You have too much time on your hands.'

'We're too busy to listen to this shit.'

'Don't humour him, fellas.'

'If it's too dangerous here, then go back to your own country.'

'Yeah,' says another. 'Back to the jungle. Where you belong.'

The couple slump back into the car.

'Who are they?' Nolwandle asks. 'Do you know? Why is this happening? Is it *them*? Are they after you again? I thought it was over?'

He growls, tears at his hair. He still refuses to reply while he drops the handbrake and revs off. He breathes heavily as he drives, eyes darting back and forth, cracking his neck repeatedly as he always does when thinking.

His mechanical training, basic as it had been, was perhaps the only blessing from his time at war in his homeland. It allowed him to find work as an assistant mechanic when he escaped to South Africa and, after a couple of years, to become head mechanic.

The extortion began soon after he set up his own workshop and over the years it has woven into a miscellany of debts, both finance and favours, that have become as much a part of his workshop as the wrenches.

He had always been somewhat uneasy about his time in the war. An orphan, wandering the roads after his village had been massacred, with not even a shirt on his back, he had been easy prey for militia recruiters. He has spoken very little about what happened thereafter. The local gang, the unspoken menace of this township, are comprised of Pascal's compatriots. His secrecy and evasiveness piqued their interest, almost as soon as he moved here. They knew he had a dark past, some unpaid-for sin, and had used it mercilessly to their advantage, trapping him in their unending game: tabby cats toying with a mouse.

They arrive back at their house. Pascal sends Nolwandle inside to the children while he punches a number into his mobile phone. A few minutes later he storms in.

'One suitcase,' he tells her. His voice is clipped, militaristic. 'Just the basics. Clothes for you and the children. Birth certificates, passports, all important paperwork.'

'Where are we –'

'Now!'

She pulls him into the bedroom, away from the children.

'I need to know what is happening. What are we doing? How am I supposed to –'

'The less you know the better. You must listen to me, follow my orders and you will be safe. I was a soldier once, don't forget; I know what I'm doing. There is no time for emotions. Obey. We need to leave right now.'

'Leave our house …'

'Leave South Africa. Now hurry and pack, woman. No more questions.'

An hour later an SUV is humming outside, engine idling. Red sunset glints off its sleek black body. The windows are tinted, it is perched high on its wheels and is spacious inside. The lone suitcase looks small in the boot. Nolwandle huddles in the back with the children: their eyelids raw, but their tears dried. They are wide-eyed, but silent.

'This is Mario,' says Pascal, sitting in the passenger seat. 'You listen to him, you hear?'

'Salaam,' says the driver.

He wears a neat shirt, neat beard, immaculate skullcap. The car is spotless, and a freshener dangling with prayer beads from the rear-view mirror wafts sandalwood.

They roll out from under the dappled shadow of their tree. Nolwandle catches a last glimpse of the wire fencing, the motley lawn, the low eaves of their little red bungalow. Not a villa, but not a slum-shack. Home.

They cruise through undulating townships and then alongside the city outskirts. Nolwandle peers out beyond the slums, the low dark jumble, the corrugated poverty, to where gleaming towers rise, adorning the waterfront; their glimmering is a border, a meeting of worlds. Below the bright lights are restaurants, bandstands, cocktail bars. Somewhere out there, past palms and sand, the traffic and music fade into the crashing waves, and foam swirls in the darkness, sliced by fins.

The SUV pulls in. Pascal turns around.

'I'm going now, Nolwandle.'

'How will we talk?'

'Do as Mario says, children. Be strong.'

He hops out, slips into an alleyway and they are rolling again, out of the labyrinth of shacks, the ruts and potholes, ascending up into a stream of headlights speeding along the smooth highway, into the night.

Goodbye, Port Elizabeth. Farewell, Algoa Bay.

The asphalt wends up into the hill country, lamp-lit scrub on the verges races past, sinewy trees, signs. Hours slip past, too, as the headlamps around them lessen. The children are collapsed in sleep, dominoed against her. But she is awake, staring at the stars. Her husband is gone. He is a hunted creature, scrambling down some unknown rabbit-hole. Nolwandle is alone.

They are rising now, up through the night, into the grasslands of the highveld, a lone spaceship surging through the starry vastness. And then, spread out before them, a twinkling carpet. Johannesburg.

Nolwandle wakes, rolls over in the crisp sheets, reaches out in a panic. Bongani is curled up beside her, little back rising and falling softly. Fezeka is below, splayed out on a mattress. Beside her is the open suitcase, a cracked clam. Morning sunlight, softened by gauze curtains, brightens the room: minimalist and modern, cream walls, dark wood wardrobes, a wall-length mirror. Some calligraphy on the wall.

She slips out, careful not to wake them, and drifts into the kitchen. The countertops are clean; there is a giant steel fridge, a shiny oven, an island with a fruit bowl. Compact, neat, stylish. There are potted cacti on the narrow windowsill. Four stories below, in an unknown street, leafy treetops ripple with the traffic passing beneath them. Opposite are more apartments, mirroring this one. Unprecedented luxury. She nods, allows herself a smile as she flicks on the coffee percolator. It sputters, then streams.

Her smile fades as she thinks back to her conversation with Mario yesterday morning. 'Use the kitchen whenever,' Mario said. 'Cook what you like. I will be back and forth. It will take a few days to arrange.'

'Arrange what? Where are we going?'

'You'll learn in good time.'

'Who *are* you?'

'I'm a businessman. Now, I have to go.'

'How do you –'

'I'll be back later.'

The door clicked.

She drinks her coffee, explores the cabinets. She drags out a sack. It feels good, sinking her fingers deep down into the maize. Normality. She scoops some into a pot, boils it.

Soon the umphokoqo, a sort of porridge of maize and milk, fills three bowls on the island. Then three spoons are scraping.

'Can we eat breakfast in the sitting room?' asks Fezeka.

'No, finish it here.'

'Where's Daddy?' asks Bongani.

'He will be with us soon.'

'Why did he not come?'

'He is angry with us,' whispers Fezeka.

'No, girl, he is not.'

'He's always angry,' mutters Bongani.

'He is stressed. He will join us soon. Don't worry,' Nolwandle says.

'Why do we have to go?' asks Fezeka.

'There are some bad men, who –'

'Bad men?'

'We're going on a holiday, Fezeka, okay? Just for a little while.'

'I miss my friends,' says Bongani.

'Me too,' says Fezeka.

'You have each other now,' says Nolwandle. 'You'll always have each other, okay?'

They nod.

Nolwandle washes their bowls, while around the corner, in the living room, cartoons blare from the wide, flat screen. She gazes out past the cacti, to the outer world. Somewhere out there, though in what direction she has no idea, is Pascal. When will I see him again? She tries to read auguries in the soap bubbles, to figure the future barrelling towards her. They swell and burst: volatile, violable, so very very vulnerable. What will come after this apartment, this interior design limbo? Is this how trafficking begins?

No. I must trust the men. Obey.

It is day four after leaving the little red bungalow and Nolwandle is soaring, Johannesburg shrinking beneath them as they spear through the dawn-drenched clouds. The children are belted in beside her, with Mario somewhere behind. They arc high over the great grasslands and lakes and rivers of the continent, the spuming falls and cloaked forests, then sweep down over the northern deserts.

In Abu Dhabi, she huddles the children around her as passengers surge out the plane door and up the tunnel. They eventually reach the concourse, still in tight formation, where she spots Mario gazing at her. He turns away and melts into the crowds. No goodbyes. As discussed.

All she has are the children and the instructions: get on the night flight to Dublin. Or she could turn around. Back to Port Elizabeth. Go home? But with what? The suitcase is already out there somewhere, being trolleyed into the belly of another beast. What would they return home to, anyway? Waking in the night to the front door slamming open? To gunshots? Or a petrol bomb? To become a skull peering out of the ash?

Again they soar, above the moonlit gulf, above the dunes. The children are restless, moaning in and out of sleep, little eardrums throbbing. She too feels a pressure in her skull, a deep ache behind the bridge of her nose. She is not asleep, though not awake; she is in a trance, dreams flittering across reality in the dim cabin light, apparitions lurking behind the hostesses, vapour shimmering at the wingtip.

A memory returns to her. Every morning, as well as the uniform and schoolbag, Nolwandle had put on the ring. Outside, out of her mother's watch, she removed it again. She wanted to be a normal fifteen-year-old, like her friends.

Her husband was older, a well-heeled businessman from Equatorial Guinea in need of a long-term visa to keep him in South Africa. Her mother was in need of support, some sort of financial alliance that would keep them treading water above the abyss of poverty. There had been no stable income for years, ever since her husband had been committed. Apartheid asylums were not beacons of healing, especially not for blacks. Despite his youth and physical health, Nolwandle's father became a broken man.

The businessman was a decent fellow; he supported her family and her studies in the city. It might even have worked out, had she been older, had it not been arranged. In the end, he left on a business trip and never returned. He left Nolwandle with a baby boy, Anselmo, and a suburban house she could not afford.

She kept the landlord at arm's length for months, promising her husband's imminent return with the rent. When it failed to materialise, she moved out, downtown, to a bedsit. Her mother moved in too, along with her youngest brother, who was still in school. She provided for them and Anselmo and paid the rent, just about, with her job at the local library. She was promoted, but soon her sister moved in too, bringing them immediately back to the brink. One step forward, one step back. They were tough years, years of patching clothes and gluing shoes, but eventually her sister found work and her mother moved back to live with the eldest brother.

Then Nolwandle met Pascal. They moved into a new place.

Anselmo never took to his stepfather. The feeling was quite mutual. After getting caught up in a xenophobic riot, which tore apart Pascal's first mechanic's workshop while he was in it, Anselmo decided that enough was enough. He is in Equatorial Guinea now, a young man, working with his father.

Turbulence shudders Nolwandle from her doze. She has the thin blanket tucked up to her chin, but her arms lie out across it, over the seatbelt. The bruise is still there, the purple welt, angry with veins, though it has faded somewhat. They eventually do, mostly.

Yesterday, in Mario's tiled bathroom, she had stood, dripping, in the act of reaching for a towel, with her image caught in the tall mirror. They were all below the neck; tactical strikes. There was a dendrochronology in them, a reading of dates possible in their rings, some glaring, howling, some months old, faint discolourations, some invisible tendernesses, others mere memories, prehistoric, mythic.

She pulls her sleeve over the bruise. She rubs it. There is no bump, no lump, just smooth skin. She has felt his lumps, though: under the skin, hard and cold, the tautness shifting over them. Pascal has grown around them, and yet they remain unchanged, same as the moment they suddenly lodged inside him, ricochets spent. There they have sat since, sympathetic to coming rains, while their target healed around them, returned to the front, entered puberty, charged bunkers perhaps, or scrambled in trenches, or riddled tree lines, or ambushed convoys, witnessed yet-unspoken horrors, soaked in red clay, shivered at night, deserted the unit, defected to government troops, betrayed the camp, watched former comrades butchered, trekked over borders, settled in a new country, entered manhood, tried to forget his past, married a woman, Zimbabwean, who soon became pregnant. She brought a baby girl into the world, but did not live long enough to name her, dying from complications. Pascal was alone in a new country with a baby to raise and a mechanic's workshop to run. It was a neighbour who saw Fezeka's first steps, heard her first words, while he toiled and wrenched away in the greasy darkness of the repair pit. Some months later he met a volunteer working with displaced communities. Nolwandle.

Soon after they married, she witnessed the nightmares, the cold sweat, the hyperventilating, the terror on waking, sinking to confusion, then to sullenness. He often stood in darkness for hours, peeking out the bedroom curtains, or disappeared for the day, returning with bruises or his clothes in tatters. He made and remade and unmade plans to move house, city, even country. He never answered questions, never told her anything but the barest of details about his childhood, his village, his soldiering. He refused to have his bullets X-rayed, to even humour the idea of extraction. Questions led to anger, then, if persistent, to beatings.

'Therapy is for white people,' he told her.

'Look at my face. Is this white? Therapy worked for me, I was able to forgive my mother, to move on from the bitterness.'

Nolwandle had come to realise that her mother had troubles of her own: she too had been forced to marry young; she too had been raised by a lone mother. She had endured abuse from the neighbours, in her village in the Cape Province, for being mixed or 'coloured'. Her mother had been a domestic servant in a white-owned estate.

'I thought like you before it,' Nolwandle continued, 'but it worked. Please try, Pascal. I will pay. It will be worth it, I promise.'

'No.'

'Please,' she was beginning to beg, a whimper entering her voice. 'Please. For the children.'

'What did I say?'

'There is a woman, she has an office downtown. She is good, I can ring right now –'

And then the fists would clench. And swing.

But he worked hard for them. He suffered for them. He never meant it, with the outbursts. Not really. A short temper. A flaw. We all have flaws. Her dendrochronology, the children's dendrochronologies, are offshoots, accidental outgrowths. They can heal. He can grow. He will grow. He will shake off his dogged past and stand tall, a new man. What they all need is a fresh start.

Ireland.

'Where now?'

The taxi driver turns in his seat, his mass creaking and squeaking the leather, his pink meaty face frowning. They are outside the Office of the Refugee Applications Commissioner in Dublin. Nolwandle is quivering. She stutters.

'It is closed?'

'Yeah, so it says. Sure it's a Sunday, isn't it?'

'Oh.'

'So where now? A hotel? A hostel?'

'I can't afford …' The meter has ballooned since the airport, her cents trickling away. A horn beeps behind. 'What about the police?'

The taxi drops her, the two children and their single bulging suitcase out on the footpath below an old sandstone building. In the waiting room, behind a window, sits an officer: gelled fringe, blue shirt, navy tie.

'We can't help you, I'm afraid.'

The brass tie clip winks out at her.

'But I have nowhere. It's just for one night, Sir, please.'

'We're not the Hilton. Nothing I can do. Now, if you have a crime to report – or to confess – that'd be another matter.'

Outside, she hails another taxi.

'Where to?'

'Is there a mosque?'

'A few of them,' grumbles the driver. 'Which one?'

'The nearest.'

It is the middle of Ramadan, so many of the faithful are gathering at the Islamic centre, waiting for sundown to eat. One middle-aged woman in a hijab, Middle-Eastern, is friendly to Nolwandle, brings her and the children food and tea, finds them a place to sleep, mats and blankets. She also hands her some money for the taxi in the morning. Nolwandle forgets to ask her name. This is the kind stranger she needed. She is thankful now for her Islamic learning, even if it began with simple evening classes, which was a way for her mother to keep her out of the troubled streets after school.

They rise early, blue morning already warming, and taxi past the red-brick townhouses, the bushy parks with their black iron fencing, spear-like, blurring by. There are no monkeys tomfooling in there, no flamingos or springboks. Only pigeons and seagulls. Early birds.

They are some of the first at the refugee office. They pass under the metal detectors as the suitcase is scanned. Forms are filled. They sit. They wait.

The November mornings are lonely after the school buses have rumbled off from the security gates, down the country lane towards the main road. Nolwandle drifts back among the rows of chalets, as the salt-soaked wind alternates between making a shelter of their walls, then a funnel. The trees bunching up against the perimeter of the complex shed their leaves weeks ago: they branch up into the grey: black veins, crow-clotted.

Her chalet is attached to six others, a row close to the security gate. She pushes through her front door into the kitchen, which is divided from the living room by a countertop. There is an old chunky bench along one wall, its pockmarked wood topped with upholstery. There is a dining table and three chairs. A kettle, an iron, a sink, a fridge, no freezer, a stove, a microwave. No washing machine; instead, they have two days allocated in the laundrette. The television is a tiny box with a fuzzy screen. There are a couple of non-descript paintings drilled into the walls: 'You may not remove them,' she was told when moving in. 'You must ask permission to attach additions of your own to the walls.' Searches can occur at any time, for any reason, she was also informed, whether you are ready or not: 'You have signed the house rules.' Besides, the staff have a master key.

Nolwandle partakes in a few hours of activities each week. She attends lectures, organises a creative youth group and volunteers as an English tutor with some of the Syrian refugees in the complex. But, for much of the week, there is little to do.

Initially, Nolwandle had been happy to have the mornings to herself, time to read, to study, to hew tools useful for her future. But the weeks have worn her down. Now she dreads the silence of the house. Her only escape is the pots and pans, and she spends hours cooking even the simplest of meals: isolating each step, over-elaborating, clinging to the details. Forgotten is the rush of Port Elizabeth, when she was a mother and an assistant manager at the local library, when cooking was a stumbling block in the hectic schedule, a bemoaned chore.

She is grateful for the shop in the complex. According to some of the longtime residents, it was once a canteen with set menus: implacable blandness, unending genericity. Still, it stocks no Boerewors sausage or Nyal meal or cassava leaves; she cannot whisk up brief ghosts of home. But without it, the stretch of the mornings would engulf her. She has been interviewed twice by the IPO since her arrival, but there has been no further word.

Nolwandle bakes through the November dusk, flicks on the light switch with her elbow, hands sticky with dough. The children will return from school any minute now, a brightness in the oncoming night. She rubs her arm softly. There is no bruise, only memory. He arrives tomorrow.

Pascal found a chunk of wood at the periphery of the complex, where some contractors have been spewing sawdust into the winter sky as they fell old ash trees overhanging the staff car park. He has been sitting in the armchair since morning, flicking chips off the chunk with a penknife. There is a pile on the worn carpet. He breaks now and then, gazing out the frosty window, clicking his neck. Then the chipping continues. Nolwandle pads about the kitchen, winces at the slightest creak of a cabinet or clink of a dish. She has apologised twice this morning; she knows that a third apology will invite fresh welts.

Pascal took care of their affairs in South Africa somehow, then slipped over the border, laying low in Zambia. He refuses to discuss their accounts, the breakdown of their joint finances. Such things are for the man. Everything Nolwandle has ever owned, all her earnings, are in his wallet now. Now they are reunified. For better or worse.

He stands up suddenly, blows on the wood, grunting in satisfaction. He holds it up in the wan light. A long thick spoon.

It is not, she soon learns, for cooking.

'Lay still,' he growls.

Pascal is hunched over Bongani, who lies with his belly on the floor in full school uniform.

'One.'

Pascal raises the thick spoon and whacks it down on the boy's rear end.

'Two.'

Another whack.

'Three.'

The boy yelps.

'Quiet! Four.'

The boy twitches.

'Five. And another – six – for moving.'

Pascal points the spoon at Nolwandle, who is advancing, begging.

'Don't even think about it, woman.'

'Pascal, please, he's five!'

'You shut your mouth. Don't undermine me. Obey.'

Bongani scrambles silently over to his mother and Nolwandle scoops him up and into the bedroom. His little cheeks are glistening. Fezeka is sitting silently at the dinner table, not daring to look up. Pascal stands over her.

'You think these books make you smart, do you? You gonna fill your head up with shit, like your bitch of a mother, that it? Ideas about this and that? It's all shit.' He sweeps the pencil cases and copybooks away, scattering them across the room. 'I don't like this attitude you have now. Well, things are going to change around here. Father is home. Respect your father, do what you're told. Follow your orders. You obey *me*.' He thumps his chest, leans down, into her face. 'Understand?'

Fezeka sniffles.

'Now shut up and do your homework. I want to hear the news.'

Pascal slouches in the armchair, pulls it in even closer to the television, so that it blocks the screen, the dome of his skull silhouetted in a flashing halo. Nolwandle eases the bedroom door shut. The neighbours must have heard everything; she certainly hears their every bump and chuckle.

Within days of his arrival, the old regime has reintroduced itself, sweeping aside the little routines and traditions and creature comforts that had held them steady, sometimes even made them smile. By now the conquest is complete; the regime reigns supreme over every inch of its domestic dominion, every corner and cupboard, with fresh dendrochronologies of the flesh to prove it.

A deep voice booms and mutters throughout the house now: decrees, edicts, commands. Pascal has forbidden his wife to continue her activities: no more teaching English to the Syrians, no more organising the creative group for the young people, no more attending lectures on international development. It is his old totalitarianism: at home he had forced her to quit her career, despite the ziggurat of promotions she had carved out for herself and polished with sweat, blood and tears.

The hopes that she had for a new beginning with Pascal are stillborn. Deep down, Nolwandle has always known it would be so. But, oftentimes, delusion is all that sustains.

The mug of coffee explodes against the wall.

'I'll fucking kill you, you bitch.'

Nolwandle flings the chair over, tripping him, and dashes out the front door, slamming it behind her, but he kicks it out and charges after her. The February cold slams her uncoated body as she darts around the corner, out onto the road leading to the security gate.

'Come back here, you whore,' he screams. 'You hussy.'

Security emerge, frowning in confusion as she staggers among them, panting. The short distance is fortunate.

'Please. He's crazy.'

One stands beside her, crackling a report into his walkie-talkie, as the other advances towards Pascal.

'*Putain!*' shrieks Pascal. '*Garce!*'

'Stop there, Sir.'

Pascal streams abuse at her, past the guard, darting his head left and right as he is shepherded backwards.

'Come on, come on, Sir! Have we to call the police?'

It is a long time before he finally disappears around the corner of the chalets.

She expected a reaction, but not like this. She has just informed him that she has had enough and that she has made a report of her injuries, first to the doctor, then to the women's refuge in town. This came just after the teachers' prying phone calls about Fezeka.

The child's head is shorn smooth, save for the odd tuft here or there, or scab. She had sobbed as he snipped away in a frenzy, braids tumbling to the threadbare floor, where they lay, for hours, until Nolwandle, herself crying, swept them up.

'I'm cutting off your attitude,' Pascal had told Fezeka. 'Maybe you'll learn some manners now.'

She looks skeletal. Onlookers gasp: out among the chalets, in the classroom, on the school bus. She never smiles any more, she stays indoors during break time. The other pupils do not taunt her; she is now beyond even the cruelty of children. Tears wet her pillow each night, with the shame.

'I need to be transferred,' Nolwandle tells security. 'It is not safe for me there any more. And the children too.'

'There's nothing we can do until the morning.'

'But you saw what he is like!'

'We don't have the authority. You'll have to put it to management tomorrow.'

She stays on a neighbour's couch that night, wondering how she is to rescue the children. Security have promised to keep a close eye on her chalet, but she lies awake, listening. She jolts up in the witching hour, hearing a screech, but it is only an owl. She lies back down.

Lines run through her mind, from *Long Walk to Freedom*:

I had no epiphany, no singular revelation, no moment of truth, but a steady accumulation of a thousand slights, a thousand indignities and a thousand unremembered moments produced in me an anger, a rebelliousness, a desire to fight ...

Next morning an Irish woman in a trouser suit, the manager, speaks with her, arranges a new place on the far side of the camp, a ground-floor apartment in a two-storey terrace. But only Bongani can accompany her. Fezeka is not her biological daughter. She has always looked at the girl as hers, has always been glad that she never knew what it is to be born into a category, to be baptised into a caste, to have genetics decide destiny. Except that now Fezeka's genes *have* trapped her.

'I'm sorry,' says the manager. 'Our hands are tied.'

Nolwandle stares at the pill bottle on the kitchen counter, wonders how many are in it. The silence of the new house is rearing above her, surging overhead, about to plunge. She grabs her anorak and dashes outside. There is a low stirabout sky, clawed by the twining treetops, as she passes through the rows of chalets.

She meets no one out here, as is usual. A ghost town. The empty footpaths and roads do not often betray hints of the hundreds of inhabitants, the beings between the walls, breathing and waiting. A signpost whistles in the wind, she tucks her chin down into the collar of her anorak.

The new house in the complex is decent, the neighbours upstairs are quiet, but every day, whether walking to the shop or to the school bus, she must pass by her old house. More often than not, he spots her, bursts outside in a torrent of abuse. He follows close behind, shouting, slandering. Passers-by swerve away, curtains part, gathering gossip. 'Bitch! Whore! Putain!' She stares down at her marching feet, wills her ears to shut, reddens. Afterwards, on her own in the kitchen, kettle boiling, she cries.

The years of volunteering back home, working with refugees and asylum seekers and trafficking victims, could never have prepared her for this life. Role reversal had been simply unthinkable.

Her weight fell away sharply in the first weeks after Pascal's return and she went gaunt over Christmas, but now it has swung back and beyond. When not cooking, and sampling, she lays in bed or on the couch, watches the day darken about her. But she always has the lights on for Bongani; flicks on a smile too – just as mechanically.

It is lonely without Fezeka. Her girl. Her female companion. Worrying too, to imagine her alone with the brunt of her father, flinching under his wooden spoon and vicious tongue. Looming over all this, a sinister cloud bank, is the slip of paper that is lost somewhere in the fog of the bureaucrats, which, at any moment, or not for years, will be stamped. Yea or Nay. Acceptance or deportation.

Nolwandle stands on the ridge by the perimeter fencing and gazes out over the windswept gorse and marram grass to where the brown lip of the sea is churning the sands.

How many rocks in how many pockets would it take?

An oystercatcher glides over her, red beak arrowing through the salty clarity as it floats high above the hedgerows and the lichen-speckled roofs of the chalets, row after row of them, grids of stasis, an archipelago of inner worlds.

Red-brick facade on a bright spring street: her new home, amid the bustle of the city. Another transfer. In the mornings, she walks Bongani along the sunny footpath to the school around the corner. And then the chattering and innocent inquiries are over and the vastness of the day stretches before her while she trudges back on the shaded footpath, weeping, to her room.

I should be glad. Happy with the transfer. We are among the population, not shacked up on a lonely coastline. We are safer now. No wooden spoons here. No ambushes of abuse. The bruises have faded. The echoes have died.

And yet she finds herself crying all day, flooding tears at the slightest provocation, in her room, in the corridors, outside.

Somewhere, in the back halls of her awareness, she knows people stare. This turns her in on herself even more, into an ever-darkening interior, circling down into the vortex. In her self-imposed isolation she feels her five languages merging together. English, Xhosa, Tswana, Sotho, Zulu become a new language, or unlanguage: silence. In the worst moments she almost misses the smattering of Afrikaans.

How many rocks in how many pockets would the canal demand?

Bongani, cling to Bongani. Bongani the beacon, Bongani the purpose. Nolwandle is always early at the school gate.

Bit by bit, day by day, she crawls up out of despair. Pills, she decides, are not helping any more; she enrols in some therapy instead. She helps Bongani with homework, brings him down to the courtyard, where a playground sticks out of some tired grass, while men in hoodies lounge on the benches, sipping coffee and smoking cigarettes.

She gazes around, up at the red brick all about her, the granite lintels and pointed arches. It had once been a place of education. It had been communal, dynamic, full of life and prospects. Back then the arches may have felt supportive, the red brick might have had a fiery warmth. Now it is dull red, brown almost. The arches have a Gothic drear to them; a penal authority in their points. They are arched eyebrows, eyeing in judgement.

Nolwandle seeks activity, life outside the suffocating brick-work, a place in the sun.

When she is invited to an outing in Blackrock, she agrees, despite her nerves, knowing it is an opportunity to meet new faces, see new places. A chance to get out in the open, if only for a few hours.

She takes the DART in the morning, zooms along between back gardens: ivy-wreathed walls and timber fencing, allotments of tranquillity, strongholds of stable respectability, unattainable Shangri-Las. Then they burst out along the waterfront to the sight of two distant chimneys, skinny legs in stripy socks; a purple headland on the horizon; a ferry creeping landward; a flock of tiny sails flittering out from the mouth of a great pier, butterfly wings on the waves. Sunlight and shadow patch the ruffled bay, like a cowhide shield. She drinks in the scenery, lets it fill her. Before the therapy, she would have choked on it, coughed it back out.

She smiles, snaps a photo of it for Bongani. They will come here for ice cream some weekend.

Her phone rings in the station.

'Nolwandle?'

'Yes?'

'This is Maria here, from management.'

'Is everything okay? Is it Bongani? What has happened?'

The phone crackles. Nolwandle checks the reception, hurries through the turnstile, out into the car park, holds it back to her ear.

'Hello?'

'Hello? Yeah, Bongani is fine, he's in school. A man called for you.'

'A man?'

'He said he's your husband, that he wants to see his son.'

'My husband.'

'He said his name is Pascal.'

She stares at him, aloft in the witness stand. Collar buttoned, clean-shaven. She has just exhibited a stack of photos to the judge: bruises, cuts, bandages on legs, ribs, shoulder blades, on the arms that met the swing, on her, on the children. A picture of the shorn and scabby scalp. Another of the wooden spoon. One picture, flash-bright, shows the side of a child's face. There are four long welts along the cheek. Angled like spokes. His fingers.

Nolwandle has spoken of the abuse, verbal, physical, digital: he often logged into her social media. Financial: he had sold all their possessions in Port Elizabeth, told her nothing, gave her nothing. Psychological: the depression, the self-loathing, which lingered long after the dendrochronologies had faded from her flesh.

She recalls the day she returned from the outing in Blackrock. He had left behind an envelope. 'For support.' Two hundred euro. She is puzzled by this exchange rate. A euro per insult? Per bruise? Per half-bruise, per tenth-of-a-bruise? How do you even measure a bruise? How wide is the standard? How long? How enduring? Or was it in fact a glimmer of regret? Some decency welling up? There had been charm once, at the start, when she found him. Charm and fragility. She had held him after the nightmares, sobbing.

The judge asks Pascal to speak.

'These are not bruises, your Honour.' He avoids Nolwandle's stare. 'She is lying. She has a blood condition, you see; it causes these markings to flare up from time to time. It has nothing to do with me. I helped her, if anything, nursed her, whenever they appeared.' He shakes his head sadly, sympathetically. 'She is hysterical. We need to get her some professional help.'

What horror darkened your heart, Pascal? What canopy closed over your skies? What seam swallowed your wonder? Whose nightmares did you partake in, Pascal, feet loose in big boots, shoulders stooped under the weight of your bullet belts, eyes lost under the impossibly wide rim of a man's helmet?

He shrinks in the stand, is a boy again, trembling in the downpour, peering out over a parapet into no man's land.

She has not seen him since that day in the courthouse. It is well over a year since they shared a roof. The judge issued the safety order, photographs of Pascal were given to security at the centre. His local garda station has him on file. A new chapter, it seems, is beginning.

Though Bongani is safer now, Fezeka is still trapped with the spoon carver. Nolwandle is working to liberate her too, to attain guardianship. She has sent reports on the abuse to Tusla, the Child and Family Agency. And to the guards. But the response has been sluggish. She has given them permission to interview Bongani, but months have passed. How accurate can a seven-year-old's memory remain? She will keep trying. As Mandela once said: 'After climbing a great hill, one only finds that there are many more hills to climb.' Nolwandle is at the foot of a daunting hill, but does not need to reach its summit to know another awaits her, and another.

Still, she is glad she is not climbing this particular hill back in Eastern Cape, where the police would likely as not tell her that domestic abuse is just that: domestic, none of their business, and so to be dealt with within the home. Or be bribed by the abuser. Back home a woman accepts her beatings, learns to cope somehow, to compartmentalise and forget as much as possible, and to pray the next assault is not fatal.

Nolwandle still lives in the red-brick building. She walks her son to the school around the corner every morning, collects him every evening. Bongani loves school. Nolwandle is happy that he does not have to attend the bottom tier of a three-tier educational system, is not lost among forty or fifty other pupils, does not have to leave class to march for freedom, or arrive in the morning to a pile of ashes. She is glad her son gets to use equipment that is not absent due to poverty or theft, does not get beaten with rods, or force-fed an oppressive language. But mostly, Nolwandle is determined to allow Bongani to finish school, enter college, to soar into whatever dream might beckon him.

Nolwandle fills the days with work, cleaning houses, clients lining up as word spreads. The old ban on asylum seekers working, as well as the prohibitive payment for the work permit, was abolished at the start of the year, deemed unconstitutional by the Supreme Court.[1] It is progress, but many challenges remain. Driving licences are as yet unobtainable, which puts a lot of jobs beyond reach, especially for those in rural areas. Bank accounts are difficult to open. The right to work is just one hill at the foot of a lofty peak: the access to work.

When she has a chance, she drinks coffee with friends, meets solidarity groups, strolls in the greens and museums of the city, or along the reedy canal. Sometimes she sits on the bench, gazes into the ripples at the reflections strolling to and fro, unshackled, unmired, free. The feeling flits over her that she will remain in direct provision until doomsday; that she is watching the incense stick of her life smoke slowly along, leaving only a whisper of ash.

A scruffy writer listens to her story in the local cafe, scribbling frantically on a notepad as she delves deep down into the dark well of the past, hauling memory after memory to the surface, holding them up to the sunlight. It is a relief.

A daylight relief. At night, she prays, tosses, sweats. Still there is no answer from the Department of Justice and Equality. No yea or nay. Two years have passed. Still she is waiting. She is displaced, marooned in an archipelago.

---

1   In May 2017 the Supreme Court ruled that the ban on asylum seekers working was unconstitutional. The ban was formally struck down in February 2018.

ILLUMINATION

Burma

I

A GUARD WAS HUMMING OUTSIDE. Azhar blinked as dawn flooded into the cell – sun split between bamboo bars, spilling in stripes across the earthen floor. A fetid stench hung about, that of hard-worked, unwashed bodies. He mouthed a prayer through cracked lips. So began day twelve at the plantation.

A latch rattled and the door swung open.

'Right, you swine, to your feet.'

Azhar stared at the black boots: tight laces, tucked trousers – baggy and olive.

'Come on, *kala*, get busy,' said the voice.[1]

He gazed up the olive legs: firm belt, new holster, baton gripped by a vein-bulging hand, ammo pouches, and shirt pockets stuffed with cigarettes – to the sneering face under the cap. The soldier had the red badge of the Tatmadaw, the Burmese military, on his shoulder, and an alcoholic fume wafted down off him as Azhar creaked upright: head going light, belly rumbling.

---

1 'Kala' translates as 'dirty foreigner'.

Outside, a cluster of guards sucked on smokes, spitting tobacco flakes and taunts towards the stream of prisoners filing out of the huts. One had an assault rifle cocked on his hip, another held an Alsatian: poised, licking its chops. The prisoners were counted and parcelled out into teams in the yard, sunlit barracks to one side, the edge of a grove on the other: ranks of cashew trees throwing their shadows westward as the sun shimmered aloft from behind the distant hills.

They trudged into the foliage. Among the low canopy the workforce shuffled, plucking and placing into baskets the precious fruit of their labours. Sweat gathered on brows and soaked armpits, flies buzzed in the dead heat and soldiers lolled about, rifles slung. Azhar and his cousin were working side by side – they had been abducted together. Azhar glanced around, leaned across.

'If we stay here, Tuahid, we'll die,' he whispered.

Tuahid did not reply, just kept picking.

'We get weaker by the day,' Azhar continued. 'If we don't do something soon, it'll be too late. We'll be like … *them*.'

He nodded towards a pair of wretches – sharp cheeks, blank eyes – harvesting robotically nearby. His cousin dropped his arms, slouched.

'We must be brave,' said Azhar. 'We must escape tonight.'

Tuahid snatched a cashew apple, seemed about to crush it, then placed it into the basket. He sighed.

'You are right,' he said. 'What is your plan?'

II

Azhar explained his simple plan in a moment and in another moment his cousin agreed. They had all day to ponder it, its details, its time frame, its chance of success. There were risks, vagaries and consequences to conjure. Azhar tried to focus on the cashews, tried to put only his next foot forward.

His mind drifted to his childhood. He had come shrieking into the world, thirty years earlier, among a cluster of cabins on the outskirts of the township of Maungdaw, in Rakhine State, western Burma. A tree stretched above the gable of his family home. As a little boy he had longed to climb it. There were many futile efforts and scratches. One sunny day, however, he succeeded. From its upper branches – slightly but disturbingly bouncy – he had gazed about at the huddled roofs of nipa palm and the surrounding patchwork of paddies, orchards and fields, laced with glistening streams and tracks to neighbouring villages, the larger brick buildings of the town visible in the distance. To the east the blue sky was green-silled by a serried spine of hills; to the west was the estuary, its waters churning brown and turquoise where the River Naf met the Bay of Bengal. Seagulls flocked over the distant fishing villages and tiny boats bobbed on the swell. He could close his eyes at a breeze and smell the salt. Beyond those flecked waves lay other lands, of which he knew nothing. He peered up through the leaves at the wisps in the azure, at the black-tipped gulls wheeling. Staring into those fathomless heights, illuminated by the sun, it was hard to imagine that a heavy blanket smothered him and his village, smothered all his people.

They were Rohingya, Muslims, which made them a species of vermin in the eyes of the Buddhist fundamentalists in power. The Rohingya are non-persons, a vulnerable minority on the western periphery: stateless, friendless, hopeless. The branch groaned, so Azhar descended hurriedly to his place, a creature of the earth.

At school, he swiftly received his education. Here he was told that he was different, was cordoned down the back of the classroom where the other students would turn at their desks and laugh at his clothes, his accent, his mannerisms.

'Shut up, Bengali,' they would hiss. 'Bow to your mat!'[2]

At times they would spit, or even shove. Their laughter echoed at night in his head. Even among the teachers he could find no ally; they would turn blind eyes or make cruel quips. His errors were magnified and broadcast, his victories skimmed over, ignored. And yet, somehow, he thrived. He learned to become invisible, to camouflage himself against the crumbling plaster of the back wall like some studious chameleon, noting everything, imbibing sums and conjugations and dates along with the taunts of his fellow pupils.

'You must be patient, Azhar,' his father told him. 'You must work hard. Be kind. Forgive – even he who strikes you. This is the way of our ancestors.'

Azhar was the firstborn. As he grew up he gained siblings as frequently as he advanced in school grades: in the end there were nine of them living in that little bamboo cabin. He was the firstborn and also the first hope of the farming family. His parents struggled to make sure he got as much support in his studies as they could manage. This meant only the most rudimentary supplies, for which they saved, scrounged and haggled. His father once went hungry for a set of pencils. Azhar spent the early mornings squinting at notes before the rag wick of an oil lamp. It had a personality of its own, and a cantankerous one at that: shuddering and spluttering and spewing horrid fumes. Candles – bright, steady, smokeless – were a preposterous luxury. All this was more than most Rohingya could manage. Poverty and discrimination are attritional forces. And cumulative: the few schoolmates he had who were not Rakhine Buddhist were whittled down steadily until only a handful remained – not in his school, but in the *entire* township

---

2   Though Rohingya have lived in Rakhine State for centuries, they are still classified as illegal immigrants by the government. This derogatory term insinuates that they belong in Bengal, not Burma.

of Maungdaw. The so-called superior caste – Rakhine or Bamar Buddhist – who often ended up in the military or the police, civil service or education, took this as a sure sign of their superiority.

'Stupid smelly kalas,' they would say. 'You see? They are lazy, it is in their blood.'

In 1994, along with several hundred other students in the township, Azhar graduated from high school. The vast majority of his peers were Rakhine, with all the advantages that accrued. Few Rohingya had survived to the final year, let alone graduated. Azhar did, though. He came second. Out of the whole township.

He applied for university courses, in engineering and medicine, but somewhere in the swirling labyrinth of bureaucracy and without any satisfactory explanation, he was denied the place that his score should have granted. The Rohingya are characters in a vast Kafkaesque nightmare. Discrimination in Burma often manifests itself in a sneering face or a kick from a jackboot, but other times it is faceless and nameless, an impalpable machine that cannot be reasoned with. On a document, an Arabic name tolls like a leper's bell. In it, the administrator hears echoing minarets, wailing dunes and clashing scimitars.

'Our nation shall not be swallowed by quicksand, but by outsiders,' as the Burmese proverb goes. It is inscribed and venerated on walls throughout officialdom.

Azhar reapplied, this time for agricultural science at Yezin Agricultural University. To his surprise, he was accepted. Accepted in the merest sense. For a Rohingya to leave even their own township, he or she must apply to the local office for a travel permit, a 'Form No. 4', which takes time and, more importantly, money. Although it was officially free, in reality it required hefty bribes in order to grease the gears of the bureaucratic machine. After he applied at the township level, he had to apply at the district and then state levels. Each required a generous greasing.

This was no small endeavour for the family. Every drop of sweat and toil in the fields, every ounce of their collective savings was squeezed – had been squeezed for years – to prepare their young hero for his adventure. Their dreams rested on him.

The application process took so long that Azhar missed most of his first semester. At the dreary office in Maungdaw, an aging administrator, slouching behind his desk, stamped the permit: 'There you go,' he droned. 'You have forty-five days to report back to me and get your form stamped. Understand? Report back before the expiry or become a fugitive of the law.'

He was permitted a month and a half, including days spent travelling, and yet he paid, like his fellow students, for four and a half months of tuition.

Azhar had never been away from home before; his world had been bound by hills on one side and an estuary on the other. Now he had to journey beyond. It began in a pickup truck, which he had to charter – just a local who had scraped together enough for the vehicle and was eking out a living with his little service.

They headed east. Soon they came to a checkpoint, what they call Three Mile Post, where they were pulled over and ordered out. The soldiers searched the vehicle and the two men. A small sum was paid and they continued on. They crossed those hills that had framed Azhar's childhood. It took them hours, though a crow might have flown it in minutes. The roads were slender, sinuous, crumbling, the driving cautious and bumpy. Descending into the plain beyond, they arrived at Ten Mile Post. Again they were manhandled, searched and extorted.

'Okay, drive on,' the soldiers droned, bored now.

They soon arrived at the town of Buthidaung. Azhar was dropped off beside the river. At the jetty, he had his documents and baggage scrutinised again. Another bribe was slipped into another soldier's hand. An officer strutted over, his bright beret like a cockerel's crest, his braid glimmering like plumage.

'Stop there,' he said to Azhar. 'What is this, Private?'

The soldier jerked from slouch to statue in an instant.

'Just checking the Form Four papers, Sir.'

'Hmmm' – the officer eyed both Azhar and the soldier – 'Rohingya?'

'Yes, Sir. This one's from Maungdaw Township. Speaks Burmese.'

'I see. Where are you going, boy?'

'Yezin, Sir,' mumbled Azhar.

'What? Speak up!'

'Yezin, Sir,' he said louder.

'Yezin? Whyever would you go there?'

'To study, Sir. Agriculture.'

The officer did a double take, looked from Azhar to the soldier and burst out laughing, holding his sides, howling, until the private joined in, until Azhar released an uneasy chuckle and all the other troops nearby, in their green helmets and red neckerchiefs, were grinning too. Passengers ambled past, some giving curious glances. The officer stopped suddenly, spoke in a monotone:

'Forget about it, boy. Just go home. Go back to your hovel. You will not survive in academia – your brains are not evolved for that stuff. What would you do? No one will hire you. Go home, if you know what is good for you.'

'I would like … to try … Sir.'

Azhar picked up his suitcase. The officer stiffened, seemed about to strike him.

'"I would like to try",' he stuttered instead, then guffawed. 'Very well, you will provide entertainment.'

The soldiers sniggered after him, all the way aboard.

'See you next week, kala,' one chirped.

The ferry followed the River Mayu downstream towards the coast. There were police circulating aboard, who questioned him more than once, and, after a day's sailing, another checkpoint. In Sittwe, the capital of Rakhine, Azhar sought out the Immigration Office where he filed an application to leave the state. This took several bribes and days, during which he had to stay in a hotel. Eventually, and with no small amount of relief, he was granted permission and boarded a plane.

An hour's flight brought him to the bustling metropolis, the nation's capital: Yangon. After the airport the going was much easier. He was in now, though he still required his sheaf of documentation when he booked his train ticket. Twelve hours up the tracks, into the heart of Burma, and he pulled up, finally, to the station at Pyinmana. A bus waited.

On the cusp of arrival, and very much fatigued, Azhar spotted some surveyors hammering stakes in a vast grassland. He discovered later that planning had begun for a sprawling new capital, constructed entirely from scratch. It would abound in towering monuments, broad boulevards, administrative complexes, military bases, parade grounds, gigantic statues and a great golden pagoda. No dense populations would environ this haunting city, nor throng its streets. They had learned from the events of 1988.[3] It was to be called Naypyidaw – *Abode of Kings*. Surrounding this future splendour were swathes of paddies, tilled by stooping peasants with tools that would not have astonished Ashoka.

The bus turned off the road and into a campus. He gazed up at the crest as they passed under the gate. *Uplift the Nation through Agriculture*, it said.

---

3   A nationwide uprising that blossomed in August 1988, only to be crushed weeks later. Aung Sang Suu Kyi gained her international renown in the aftermath.

There was no time for orientation: work began the moment he dropped his bags on the floor of his room. There was lost ground to regain, as well as new material to grasp. By day, it was the lecture hall, by night, he pored over books and scribbled notes. Luckily for his eyes, he did not have to contend with the spluttering and spewing of an oil lamp. Instead, he could flick a switch and fill his room to its very corners with unwavering illumination. Now the preposterous luxury was sleep. There was not much time for mingling with the other students, even if there had not been those odd looks and abrupt responses. Lectures ended, there was a frenzy of study for a few weeks, exams blurred past and suddenly he was stirring awake as the pickup truck rattled to a halt. Last stop: Maungdaw. He met his family, who gave him a hug, and he met the slouching administrator, who gave him a stamp.

'Well done,' said the administrator sardonically.

Several semesters passed in this way, back and forth.

In the student hostel, he had a roommate. He had never before met a civilian Bamar, and was shocked to discover he held no animosity and was unversed in terms like 'smelly kala' or 'lazy Bengali'. He was a studious fellow and, like Azhar, a picky eater. Neither would partake in the hostel's food. Azhar wished to avoid pork and his roommate wished to avoid all meats, at least in his relatively pious phases. They became firm friends. This proved instrumental to Azhar: he honed his spoken Burmese, but more importantly, he learned that Buddhist babies were not born with hatred in their hearts.

In 1997, halfway through his degree, the university shut down. A lecturer turned up one day and told them to go home. There had been no ripple of discontent, no student gatherings in cafes, heated discussions or whispered conveyor belt of plans and rumours. It was only afterwards that they heard about

Yangon, where democratic protests had been bubbling up in the campuses, poised to unleash a wave of demonstrations in the streets until, at the last moment, the military had swept in and arrested the troublemakers, locking the lecture halls and laboratories indefinitely. Despite the oblivious serenity at Yezin, it too was closed.

Azhar went home. Already, however, his studies were bearing fruit. The hunger, the taunts and the spluttering lamp were redeemed somewhat when he got a job in Maungdaw that year. Much of his boyhood studying had revolved around English. He had also gained a wealth of experience in the few months between school and university when he had worked for the UN, as a World Food Program supervisor, where he improved his English and interacted with westerners for the first time. When Azhar arrived home from Yezin, CARE Australia was implementing a number of humanitarian projects among the Rohingya: agriculture, forestry and plotting gardens for impoverished families. He was offered a job as a translator and soon became a junior project manager, involved in launching new initiatives in the township. The UNHCR was there too and in dire need of interpreters; they also hired him. This work was meaningful to Azhar and it paid relatively well. Most of all, it allowed him to be near his family and friends. He might have even been content, if he had been considered a person by those who held sway over his life.

In 1999, the university reopened. Azhar continued working for another year until, strongly encouraged by his colleagues in the UNHCR, he returned to the campus in Yezin.

Graduation was bittersweet. He was aware of the pride of his family, but he was also very much aware of the plains and peaks stretching between them. They had not been granted travel permits. He sat by himself in his ceremonial robes while all around him students and their families laughed, hugged, took photographs.

'You must be patient, Azhar,' he heard his father say.

III

His degree gathered dust. No one would hire Azhar. Government institutions and respectable companies always insist on all the formalities: résumé, identity documents and, of course, another bureaucratic odyssey. They always insist on proceeding by the book and the book in Burma is a racist tome. The officer at the jetty was still howling with laughter.

Instead of uplifting the nation through agriculture, Azhar ventured to the teeming streets of Yangon, where he was hired by a construction company. It was run by a Rohingya man, a rare enterprise indeed. Perhaps this canny businessman, this compatriot, would recognise Azhar's talent. Perhaps he would not have to return home empty-handed after all. But, after barely a year in the big city, he left. It was too risky working there without the necessary permits. Besides, his grandfather was ailing and he wished to see him. This was September 2005.

On arrival, he dropped his suitcase in his parents' cabin and strode next door. There was a curtain hung across the entrance to the back room. He peered into the shadowy chamber.

'Look at this big city scoundrel!' said his grandfather, from his cot. 'How are you, my lad?'

Azhar told him about the journey home. He told Azhar of recent goings-on. And, when that was done, he began to reminisce.

'I was thinking only yesterday,' said the old man, 'of the time we choose your name. You know the meaning of your name, Nati?'

Azhar smiled, he knew he would be told regardless.

'You are a ray of light, a bright lamp, an illumination. The village is proud.'

The old man turned to his daughter, Azhar's aunt, who was feeding him a bowl of soup.

'He's a bright boy, is he not, Hazerah?'

'He is, Au Ney,' she said, her eyes glimmering in the dark.

IV

Some weeks later, Azhar was in his grandparents' house. He was chattering with his grandmother and several of his aunts, sitting around on the rug, drinking tea and chewing betel.[4] Grandfather was sleeping fitfully in the back room. Cousin Tuahid was there too: out of work, like himself. The men were away in the fields; outside the children pranced about, playing.

Without warning a motor roared up outside, there was a squeal and the door burst open, soldiers stampeding in, pointing weapons and fingers, bellowing questions.

'Where is he? We know he is here. Where are you hiding?'

Azhar – the only Burmese speaker – stepped forward, wanting to reason with them, but his grandmother grabbed him. The soldiers began tossing over furniture, tearing down sheets.

'Stop!' screamed his aunt, Hazerah. 'You are mistaken. He is not here.'

In Burma, the Rohingya are stopped and harassed, even if they stray only as far as the neighbouring village, and are met with the greatest suspicion at checkpoints further afield. They are interrogated, humiliated, sometimes beaten or worse. They are restricted in every movement. Every movement, that is, except

---

4　A vine native to south and southeast Asia. The leaves are chewed as a stimulant, much like khat or coca.

one – emigration. The authorities are happy to see them leave, happy to see that swallowing quicksand recede.

An uncle of Azhar's had consoled them in their anxiety many years previously, when he set out beyond the waves of the brown and turquoise estuary. His wanderings had brought him to Saudi Arabia, where he had carved out a life for himself making furniture. But now his father was sick and duty called him back. He had only recently returned, in a shroud of secrecy. This day, he was in another village, staying with distant, less obvious, relatives.

'Keep your hands up,' a corporal shouted.

'Please,' Hazerah said, approaching. 'We don't –'

A soldier whipped around and slapped her. When she fell, he yanked her across the room by the hair.

'You want to say something? Tell us where he is.'

A child cried. Azhar and his cousin rushed over, begging, beseeching, but the troopers turned on them like a pack of wolves, raining rifle butts and punches, then dragging the pair outside where the beating continued while villagers stared from doorways or cowered away with ears blocked. A kick shucked the wind out of Azhar and dust filled his mouth. He was dragged by the collar, drooling blood and spit, and flung into the back of the truck. Tuahid tumbled in on top of him. The doors slammed shut and the truck revved off.

So began day one at the plantation.

Day twelve was fading. The sun set and the ladies sat on the laps of soldiers in the yard. A radio lilted pop music out over the cashew grove while the women, in bright lipstick and leather skirts, sold rum or smokes or led their next client into the belly of the barracks. Azhar licked his lips. The air smelt of roasting pork. He had been fed his meal earlier: a handful of gritty rice.

He was serving his captors: filling jugs or stacking firewood by the crackling brazier. Tuahid too stood at their beck and call, even after the backbreaking toil of the day. The moon rose and drew a certain lunacy from the garrison, who grew drunker and more revelrous, howling war songs at the sky to accompany the bedspring crescendo inside.

Azhar nodded at Tuahid. He placed the jug on a table and bowed to the nearest soldier, who was tickling a woman under the chin. She wore his cap and giggled. Azhar coughed.

'Sir,' he said. 'May I use the –'

'What?' – the guard turned with a frown – 'Yes, yes, be quick.'

Azhar tramped to the edge of the brazier's halo, where the bushes they used for latrines crested darkly. Moths flittered past. He moved, calmly on the surface but quivering within, then winced as Tuahid shuffled over towards him.

'One at a time!' he imagined the troopers shouting. But they were preoccupied.

He and his cousin looked at each other and back at the yard. Then they were sprinting, vaulting a drainage ditch, and tearing through the rows of cashew trees. Shouts rose up and the pop music was choked. A gunshot cracked, followed by a whole salvo: bullets buzzed by, chunking into branches or wailing into the night.

The fence loomed up, old and rotten, and Azhar charged into it, bursting through in a shower of bamboo, feeling his shirt catch on something, then rip free. He heard Tuahid clamber over and then there was scratching and swishing through the thicket. Azhar was in a milky moonlit clearing – a giant striding in the open – then, suddenly, beneath canopy and creepers. There was only the static of cicadas beyond his hammering heart. He slowed to a jog.

'I think,' he panted, 'we should …'

But his cousin was not there.

'Tuahid?'

He peered back in a panic: shadowy phantoms wavering, un-wavering, sinister. Trunks? Or foliage? Or, my God, he thought. They got him.

Vomit welled, but then a dog barked and a machine gun erupted, scattering bullets his way. Azhar fled into the depths of the forest.

'But you can't go,' said his mother, a tear streaming. 'You've only just come back to us.'

The oil lamp – calm now, an old friend – lit their faces: the whole family was gathered in the front room. Some were hastily dressed, dishevelled, or still clasping blankets about themselves. Azhar had eventually emerged from the forest into the fields outside his village and slunk across them. A dark, twining figure had met him outside his cabin: the old tree by the gable, clutching the moon with its twigs. Azhar remembered the view from its branches: the hills in the east and the waves in the west, beyond which he knew nothing. The cabin had been deathly silent when he ghosted in the doorway.

'I can't stay,' said Azhar.

'They already got Tuahid,' said his father. 'They will come for Azhar too. He cannot stay.'

He opened a tattered tin box and handed Azhar a bundle of notes, neatly bound.

'Here. For the journey.'

It was 50,000 kyat: over thirty dollars. Azhar looked up from the money at his father, but his father closed his fingers around it.

'You will need it. I wish we had more.'

The family huddled. They cursed and wept and hugged.

Such is the life of a refugee.

V

At dawn the trucks arrived and soldiers spilled out, surrounding the village, bursting over thresholds, but the fugitive was nowhere to be found.

He was bobbing on the estuary. The oarlock clinked and the oars strained and slopped, strained and slopped, the skiff soaring up summits and surging down troughs. Sky, water, sky, water: greys warming slowly into lavender and saffron. Azhar, green in the gills, gulped repeatedly.

'Not far now,' said the ferryman with a knowing chuckle, his arms still rowing somehow. Was he a saviour or a psychopomp? Azhar had stuffed 10,000 kyat into his hand at the embarkation, trying to smile affably, or, at least, normally. That was a fifth spent already, but it had staved off any awkward questions. The other passengers, a chain-smoking merchant and three fishwives, chattered among themselves. The fugitive kept quiet.

At the height of the next wave the mist ahead parted and Bangladesh fuzzed into existence.

Past the mud and the rocks there were groups of people buzzing about: fishermen loading boats and traders selling from stalls. There was a smell of warm seaweed or slime, and seagulls flittered, pecking at this and that, cackling. Azhar inquired about the refugee camp. A young lad piped up, told him he knew how to get there. The lad walked him inland, up a dusty road shaded by trees and lined by fencing and thickets and huts of brightly painted corrugated steel. After a long walk, they came to a cluster of cabins at a junction. A colourful bus was idling, crowned with trunks, baskets of fish and cages of chickens. The lad shouted up at the driver, above the rattling engine, where to drop the foreigner.

Three hours later, he stepped down and watched the bus trundle away into silence. He was surrounded by fields, shimmering in the noon. A track led off the main thoroughfare, snaking away into scrubland, behind which rose forested mountains. A group of young men approached along the road, carrying sacks on their shoulders, wearing longyis. One had a straggly beard; another wore a white kufi skullcap. Then Azhar heard their voices.

'Are you Rohingya?' he asked.

'Yes, brother,' they said. 'As-salamu alaykum.'

'And upon you, peace. Do you know the refugee camp?'

'We do. We're going there now, we live there.'

'Can you take me? I'm visiting friends.'

'What are their names?'

He told them.

'Ah ha, I know the old man well! Of course, come along. Do you have papers?'

'I don't.'

'They'll turn you away at the front gate.'

'They?'

'The guards. No matter, we know a quiet way in.'

'What is it like?' Azhar asked the nearest.

He replied by bulging his eyes and spitting out a brown stream of betel.

They walked an hour down the track, then parted from it before it brought them to the camp, hiking cross-country through dense scrub in order to avoid the main gate. Azhar's legs ached. His stomach grumbled. Finally they emerged from the bushes at a quiet, unguarded stretch of the perimeter fence and squeezed through a gap in the wire, into a crevice between two shacks. On the far side they shuffled out into a narrow earthen street, a chicken scurrying past them into a low, dark doorway. The huts were all connected, their walls a curious mixture of bamboo trellis, daubed mud and plastic sheeting. The roofs were a patchwork of tents and various materials, strewn with palm fronds. Children ambled by, some naked, all filthy, and were scolded by a flock of women in floral hijabs, hauling buckets of water. Mire oozed down the middle of the dusty thoroughfare, flies swarmed throughout.

He was led deeper into this warren, across a reeking trench, past a crowded pump and a goat being bled out, kicking faintly, then finally he stooped in under a doorway, low and dark like all the others.

His family friends, a husband and wife, poured him water and gave him crackers. They sat together on a mat. The interior was tiny, more cubicle than cabin. There were clothes hung on a line, some pots, two stools, a broom and a Quranic verse painted on a plank. He took out some money to pay for the food.

'No, brother,' said the husband. 'It is custom. Besides, I know your father.'

'I owe you, brother,' said Azhar.

The wife's eyes crinkled in a sympathetic way.

'Tell us your story,' she said.

After a pause he began. They listened silently from beginning to end.

'Brother,' said the husband, 'it is truly terrible what has happened. We will do what we can for you. But I must tell you, you cannot stay with us, not for long. We have children. If you are caught here, we might be thrown out.'

'I understand,' said Azhar. He rubbed his forehead. 'I was thinking, perhaps, of going to Malaysia. I have a friend there, an old neighbour.'

'That is a wise plan,' said the wife.

'We would go ourselves,' said the husband, 'if the little ones weren't so young, so frail.'

Azhar nodded and ruffled the hair of the little boy standing beside him. His ribs protruded over his baggy shorts, his eyes were large. And yet he smiled. The husband continued:

'Of course, you can stay here for a little while, until you have made your arrangements.'

'Thank you, brother,' said Azhar. 'Thank you, sister. God protect you.'

'God protect all of us,' said the wife. 'The people who fortune forgot.'

The open ocean. That turbulent estuary at home seemed like a mere cattle trough now. Azhar clung to the ship's gunwale and vomited into the Bay of Bengal. There was water all around: choppy, heaving, cresting water, diminishing out to the curve of the earth. The deck behind was empty, save for a couple of the crew smoking by the deckhouse.

'Hey, hurry up,' barked a sailor: bare-chested, wiry and missing half an ear. 'Get below.'

Down the ladder was a multitude. The ancient wooden fishing boat – paint peeling, bolts rusting, chimney belching – was stuffed with refugees: one hundred Rohingya rolling the dice of destiny. They had been herded below deck at the first moment and were kept there, allowed up only to relieve themselves off the stern, one at a time.

On the fourth day an old woman died and was cast into the churning foam of the wake. On the sixth day, an infant. Azhar's crackers ran out on the ninth. The fellow beside him split his last slice of betel nut, sharing it with Azhar. By the evening of the tenth nobody had any food left. Except for the crew, but that was for them. People were seasick, others drank seawater and contracted diarrhoea. Not everyone could quickly clamber up the ladder. By the eleventh day the floor was a slimy mess, streaming fore or aft with each undulation.

They were among each other, like a netful of shrimp. So

tightly packed were they between bulkheads that a mouse would have struggled in vain to squeeze through them. Skin, damp in the humidity, slipped against skin, elbows and knees dug into backs.

By day they sweated, by night they shivered. Azhar lay twisted awkwardly between two snoring bundles. He could not sleep, only stare at the formless black ceiling and imagine how the stars and galaxies might be twinkling outside. The sleeping bundle on his left rolled over, the sleeping bundle on his right snorted, a toddler was grumbling, an elder was bawling, the engine hummed and the propeller chopped, the keel creaked and the bow-wave shushed – all the bodies in that hold quivered, coughed and breathed in increasing synchronicity until they melded together into a perfect rhythm, a unified dirge, a giant body laid out in a coffin drifting across the deep.

There were twelve such nights. On the thirteenth morning a beach and jungle lay before them. Thailand.

Rowing boats relayed them ashore: gaunt, faint, trembling. They reeked but no longer cared. Azhar looked back at the haze, but the coffin ship was gone. Silent men with clubs and batons marched them an hour through the forest to more boats, which ferried them across to the mainland: another beach and jungle far from any civilisation or sanction.

They were packed into trucks and then had their skeletons jolted for several hours before tumbling out again, this time at a holding station run by the smugglers. It was less campsite than menagerie. Cages stood all about, dappled by the bleak grey light falling through the canopy. They were bamboo lattices, reminding Azhar of giant fish traps, as if some hoary sea god had ripped them from the surf and hurled them inland. He recalled the traps in the estuary, poking out of the stinking mire at low tide, scraps of seaweed clinging on or bunched inside. Now, in the jungle, people clung or bunched in the traps: emaciated, moaning, dreadful to behold. Faeces lay here and there. Apart from the swarms of mosquitoes, Azhar saw neither beast nor fowl in that forest. Perhaps they knew better than to come to such a place. There were huts for the guards, who lurked with batons. Few had guns: the quarry was weak. And they remained so, fed just enough dirty rice and watery sauce to pump hearts, piston lungs.

Night fell over the cages. Azhar lay twisted awkwardly between two snoring bundles. He could not sleep, only stare at the formless black canopy and imagine how the stars and galaxies might be twinkling above. How many such nights would there be?

'Two escaped last week,' said a man, lying next to Azhar. 'A fellow called Abdul Razaq and his friend. From Sittwe, I think.'

He had wispy hair and his missing teeth gave him a piano grimace as he wheezed after each sentence. He was younger than Azhar.

'They caught them, before long,' he continued. 'Dragged them back into the camp, right over there, where that barrel is. We could all see. The dogs had already had their go, but then the screws started. There must have been ten of them, with clubs, a few with iron bars. They just laid into them, again and again. They curled up, tried to fend them off. That sound: bar against bone. I'll never forget it.' He coughed, spat. 'The screaming stopped, eventually. One of the guards pulled Abdul Razaq's head back by the hair and slit his throat. The other, they shoved into the river.' The man let out an extra-long wheeze, closing his eyes. 'That was a message for us. "There is no escape."'

He rolled away, facing the bamboo ribs of the cage.

Azhar had known the journey would be tough, possibly even fatal, but he never imagined he would encounter such evil. But, as with the fly in the web, it was already too late.

'Who are they?' asked Azhar. 'Thai?'

'Most. Some are Rohingya.'

Azhar stared at him.

Next morning two guards dragged him out of the cage, prodding him to a trestle table that was set up outside one of the huts. A tarpaulin hung overhead, shading the agent who sat there. He had a thin moustache and wore sunglasses perched on top of his slicked hair. His eyes were reptilian.

'You have a pal in Malaysia?' he asked.

'Yes, Sir.'

'Good. It's good to have friends. We like to hear that.'

Azhar regarded the earth. He felt dizzy.

'You have a number for him?' the agent asked.

He set a clunky cellphone on the table.

'No, Sir,' said Azhar. 'But I can get one.'

'That's good.'

He nudged the phone across the table and lit a cigarette, staring at his client. Azhar dialled in the number of the only phone he had ever rung. In a cabin, in a village in Rakhine State, northwestern Burma, a teenage girl stopped stirring her pot and answered. She gave her greetings and took Azhar's message and the number. She told her younger brother, who ran out to the roadway. A farmer, leading an ox and cart full of firewood, was passing and noted the details. In the next village a woman bought a bundle of sticks from him, then jogged into her neighbours – Azhar's parents. They sought out the family of Azhar's pal, who were glad to hand over the Malaysian number. Azhar's father hopped on a bicycle and pedalled back to the first village, where the teenage girl was by now scrubbing the pot. She dialled and handed him the phone. Azhar was fetched from the cage again. The voice was crackly but unmistakable.

'Azhar, futu, are you okay?'

'I am, Baba. I'm somewhere in Thailand, I think. It is good to hear you. How are –'

The agent slapped the table. 'Quickly,' he said. 'This is not a tea party.'

Azhar scribbled down the Malaysian number.

'Okay, Baba, I have to go. Tell them all that I am well.'

'Wait,' said his father.

There was a staticky pause. The agent gestured to hurry, Azhar strained his ear.

'Baba?'

'Your grandfather. He is gone to Allah.'

Azhar wept as he was shunted back into the enclosure.

Later that afternoon he was summoned again. To ring Malaysia. His friend agreed to help without hesitation, taking the bank account details and arranging the deposit of 1,800 ringgits as soon as he hung up.[5] In a lavish apartment in Bangkok, a man with a crisp shirt and a pot belly logged on to his razor-thin laptop and, confirming the transaction, punched out a text message. In the jungle, on the trestle table beneath the tarpaulin, the cellphone chirped. The agent with sunglasses grinned at Azhar.

'A good pal,' he said. 'You are lucky. Now, where will we send you?'

'Penang,' said Azhar.

VI

Azhar and a handful of others were mustered the following day and led out of the camp under escort. Dozens of eyes followed them from the shadows. An inexplicable guilt followed too.

---

5   About 400 dollars.

They trekked all morning through the undergrowth, down winding but well-worn tracks, to a creek full of unseen croaking creatures where the branches embraced overhead or dipped timidly into the coffee-coloured water. A raft took them across the border and a brief march took them into a safe house on the edge of a town.

After a few hours, Azhar was collected by a driver in a shiny car. Its seats were soft, its interior pleasantly cool. The radio burbled folk music, lulling Azhar into a drowse. A ribbon of glossy tarmac bisected forests and truncated outcrops, spiriting them to the outskirts of the city in a matter of hours. Horns honked, drills rattled and cafes buzzed as the buildings spurted up ever taller. A cry echoed forth from a minaret: haunting but also assured, rooted. Was it all a dream? The cages and the coffin ship and the plantation? The gaunt faces and the blank stares?

VII

Azhar sat gazing out of the shack as a shiny convertible rolled in the entrance off the busy street. He wore not a longyi but a white shirt and tie, tan trousers and cap: the uniform of a parking attendant. He had been one for several months now.

His old neighbour, Mustafa, a single man also in his thirties, had met him when he arrived in the car from the jungle. He took him into his home, a neat little apartment on the outskirts of Penang. The second bedroom was cleared out and some spare clothes found. Azhar spent several days mesmerised by the food in the fridge, the shower, the clean bedsheets. After some weeks, he began to grow uneasy in the apartment. And yet, it was risky to be out and about, especially when everything was so new and so strange in that neat, modern, rushing city. Malaysia does not recognise the term 'refugee' and so those who flee misery or carnage are categorised as illegal immigrants. This makes them vulnerable: they have no authority to appeal to. Azhar was still a non-person. However, cabin fever eventually set in, so he ventured out into the world.

He first found work in construction. The work was brutal: his scholarly frame, weakened by recent privations, creaked under the heavy hods of brick. He lasted three days. Next, he applied to a nearby cafe – they accepted him and so he spent the next six months out in the back among steam and soap and stack upon stack of dishes. When not scrubbing, he explored the neighbourhood, connected with local Rohingya and steadily built his vocabulary of Malay – a construction project to which he was much more suited. In his bedroom, while his pal listened to music in the front room, Azhar would read books in his latest language, trusty notebook by his side. His speaking improved and he was hired as a parking attendant.

Policemen, now and again, would stop him in the street and barrage him with questions. They would prod and paw their prey with a feline cruelty until an offering was made. Usually a few cigarettes or a wad of ringgits would do the trick. It was relatively harmless: petty schoolyard extortion. Local gangs were more of a worry; they could act with impunity on non-persons. But what kept Azhar constantly poised, ever ready for flight, as he strolled to work or met up with friends, what made him jolt awake at night dripping in cold sweat, were the immigration police. They did not stroll the beat, like standard officers. They were not so predictable or avoidable. More often they inhabited rumours and tales and dreams, becoming a sort of boogieman in the Rohingya imagination. No amount of cigarettes or weeping or gnashing of teeth could steer them to clemency.

Azhar was gazing out the shack window, thinking of unwrapping his lunch, when, at the corner of his eye, two tall figures, clad darkly, loomed in the doorway. He did not need to turn, he already knew. He tried to explain, then to plead, then fell into a profound silence as they led him into the van, hands cuffed.

He spent three months in prison and then was driven to the Thai border. When the blindfold was removed an old acquaintance was standing before him. He had a thin moustache, slick hair and reptilian eyes. Twisting branches and noose-like creepers squeezed out the sky. Three hundred ringgits is what they had sold him for. In America or Europe this might afford you a three-course meal. He was back at the fish-trap menagerie again, could smell the filth and despair.

'Ho, ho,' said the agent. 'This one is plump.'

He sat under the tarpaulin again, at the trestle table. Azhar wanted to straighten up, to look him in the eye, and ask him: 'Do you not recognise me? Was I just cattle? Am I not a man?' Instead, he regarded the earth.

'So,' said the agent, rolling himself a cigarette. 'Where would you like to go? We can take you anywhere you want, as long as you have the money. Don't worry, we are in charge, the police do what we want, we can get you anywhere. You want to go to the US? We'll take you. Or how about Germany? In Australia they hunt kangaroos, would you try there? I would go there.'

'What if I don't have the money?'

'They would be hard to hit, though,' mused the agent. 'With all that hopping.'

'I'm not a rich man! Do you think I can afford such –'

The agent smirked, leaned forward and blew a steady stream of smoke into Azhar's face.

'Walk away,' said the agent. 'Just stand up and walk out of this place. Or run, if you prefer. See what happens.'

This time, Azhar's boss bailed him out. Eighteen hundred ringgits. A sum of sweat and toil that would take many, many months to repay. Like before, the money was deposited and the agent was informed. They ferried him up the creek, across the border, and drove him back to Penang. He knew he was fortunate. He had learned much about the trafficking camps after his first stint, about what happens in that strangling jungle, that heart of darkness. Those who cannot get their ransom and who do not die in the cages are eventually sold off. The women get sucked into the mire of the sex industry in the big cities and the men are sold to the slave fleets, to haul fish day and night, far from land, month after month, until they can go on no longer and become food for their erstwhile quarries. Few escape or survive long enough to earn their freedom.

Back in the city, Azhar became a recluse, terrified of the outer world. He goaded himself to return to work, especially after the help his boss had given him. But it was no use. For months he remained in Mustafa's apartment. Sometimes he would stand by the window and gaze up, over the rooftops, hoping to see a seagull or, at night, a star: something unique, some celestial companion. In Malaysia thousands of Rohingya live in shadow, in the undergrowth or in dark crannies, ready to scurry away the moment a torch beams upon them. Every so often, authority will stamp on one, crushing mercilessly. Such is the life of a refugee.

Eventually, however, Azhar ventured out. He was hired, again as a parking attendant. He settled into routine. Two years drifted by. One day, while gazing out the shack window, two tall figures, clad darkly, loomed again in the doorway. Again, he knew. This time he did not try to explain. He was bundled into a van and driven away.

It was a long building, sparse, a hall with high horizontal slits for windows and a pitched roof. It was designed for about three hundred, but spread across its floor, snoozing or chattering or just staring – in a mosaic of fabric, flesh and hair – were twelve hundred detainees baking as the sun seared the tin overhead. Fleets of flies circulated, landing just often enough to prevent sleep. Azhar batted one away. How many have I swatted here? he asked himself. Thousands? Millions?

Thanks to a deal brokered between the Malaysian government and the United Nations, the illegal immigrants were no longer being sold back to traffickers. Instead, they were being quarantined in detention centres to await an interview with UNHCR representatives. They would decide who were the genuine refugees. They held the thread of fate.

Azhar had festered here for months, watching others turn slowly insane and wondering how far down the slope he was himself – if he was not there already. To drink tea, to sing songs, to sit on a rug with friends and discuss funny things, happy things: all seemed preposterous wishes now. How long will I remain in this place? he wondered. The guards did not care, the warden did not care, the police on the outside certainly did not care. But the UN, if they were to come, to hear his story, he might have a chance.

Twice a day they would stretch out in a line, like a colony of ants, and jerk forward to get their portion: dry bread in the morning, watery curry in the evening. The toilets were appalling – portals into a feculent underworld – and there were no baths. The guards were not sadists, generally, but they were nevertheless attached to their employment. Each had his reasons. Beatings did happen, when necessary. At night one could not sleep: every toss or turn rippled through the packed ranks and amplified. Mosquitoes feasted throughout, uninterrupted by any sort of netting. Convicts – murderers, rapists, paedophiles – received better treatment, even in Malaysian prisons: small, neat, underpopulated cells with clean toilets and solid meals. A dream life.

The high horizontal slits poured in amber light, turned fiery and darkened. Azhar lay twisted awkwardly between two snoring bundles. He could not sleep, only stare at the formless black ceiling and imagine how the stars and galaxies might be twinkling outside. How many such nights would there be?

A guard was humming. Azhar blinked and dawn flooded in – concrete walls and bamboo floor, creams and tans and split sun between window frames. A fetid stench hung about, that of underfed, unwashed bodies. He mouthed a prayer as footsteps clunked towards him.

'Right, wake up, to your feet.'

Azhar stared at the black boots: tight laces, tucked trousers – baggy and olive.

'Come on, get busy,' said the voice. 'The UN are here to see you.'

VIII

I am alone in a snow globe. Through crisp carpet I trudge, lit by streetlamps, my prints filling immediately with fresh flakes. On my back is a satchel; within, a notebook thirsty for ink. Over the two-storey rooftops of cafes and bars and hair salons, the towers of downtown Milwaukee pulse through the flurries. I jog across the roadway and down a side street.

From a row of picket fences and porches I choose one and ascend, rapping on the door. It opens.

'As-salamu alaykum,' says Azhar, smiling.

'And upon you, peace,' I reply.

We shake hands.

'Come in,' he says. 'Come in from this blizzard.'

We take a seat in his front room, on a pair of couches. I open my notebook. It is warm here, there are rugs spread all over the floor, shoes arranged by the door. Azhar has made a home for himself. He works long hours as an interpreter with local hospitals, dipping in and out of his English, Burmese, Rakhine, Malay, Urdu and, of course, Rohingya.

When the UN found him in that fetid detention centre, they were impressed that he had not required any translation. They believed his story and granted him refugee status. They also hired him as an interpreter and that is how he supported himself while he waited in Malaysia to be resettled. It took five years. In June 2015 he flew here. He did not fly alone.

A little girl runs in, hugging a fuzzy giraffe and smiling out shyly from behind it. In the corner of the room, by a small desk, sits another girl, five years old, poring over a chunky book full of pictures and short sentences. A lamp cranes over her, putting a steady shine on her black bob of hair. It does not splutter or spew.

'Hello,' she says. 'How are you?'

She giggles and goes back to her reading.

A woman enters, resplendent in a scarlet longyi, its many folds and creases glittering with golden flora, her dark hair in a bun, shining like her daughter's. Najma lights up the room.

'Thanks very much,' I say, as she sets down tea cups.

'You're welcome,' she replies, with an infectious grin.

She excuses herself and hurries out to the gurgling of a baby in the next room.

'We met at a laundromat,' says Azhar, his eyes creasing at the recollection. 'I went there to clean my clothes and I left with a date. We would meet at cafes and restaurants in the evenings, stroll along the avenues. Then we got married. It was a love marriage.'

After the stories about the plantations and the camps and the coffin ships, I cannot help but chuckle.

'Of course,' Azhar continues, 'we rang home to ask permission. Out of respect. They said: "Good luck. We bless your decision. We trust you. If you are happy, we are happy."'

He tells me how the ceremony was a subdued affair, in a neighbour's house, with just an imam and a dozen or so close friends. Like his graduation, it was bittersweet. At home the wedding would have been a lavish affair, with the village throwing a huge feast, slaughtering calves and hanging bunting. Hundreds of guests would have trekked across the countryside to be there.

'Of course, those weddings do not happen so much any more.' The sparkle in Azhar's eyes dulled, then doused. 'I have told you about Rakhine in my time. Everything I described to you has gotten worse. Education is more difficult, healthcare is less accessible, movement is more restricted. The military and police have marched thousands of troops in, set up many more barracks, checkpoints. They sweep through villages, beating men, raping girls and shooting anyone who resists. Helicopters circle the sky, hunting for fugitives. The Buddhist population has been incited by the nationalists: monkhood, government, media. They are full of fear, full of anger. They hate us. The settlers are the worst of course. They are poor, hungry, desperate. They do what they are told and hate who they are told. They are given land confiscated from Rohingya. The government has learned a lot from the Israeli settlement program. They have good teachers.'

'Where do they bring them from, these settlers?'

Azhar laughs dejectedly, runs a hand over his face.

'From Bengal.'

I shake my head and can scarcely whisper it: 'Hypocrites.'

'When a riot happens, they burn our villages, attack people like wild animals. They rape and kill. I've heard that they often beat their victim until they cannot get up, then pour petrol over them. The soldiers and policemen watch.'

'Jesus.'

'Naturally, many more people flee. Today, the camps are even more crowded, the trafficking ships more numerous, the agents fatter. That cage in the jungle in Thailand … if that was not hell, then there is no hell.' Azhar takes a sip of tea. 'But they say it has become worse. I ring my family there and they are afraid. If the US government would allow it, if it was easy, I would bring them all here, all of them, so they could be safe and …'

Azhar stops, embarrassed. His eyes have brimmed. I stare down into the patterns of a rug. He has told me of the nightmares, of Tuahid's face being swallowed in a quicksand of cashew nuts.

'When I reached Malaysia, I began to hope again. I felt I might survive. Then I met Najma. She is from Maungdaw too: she saw the same things, the same struggles. In Milwaukee our hopes have grown stronger. We dreamed of a life for our children. I have no wishes for myself. I want my children to have a place they can call home, to have a place where they can get an education. I don't want my kids to go through life as I did: people looking down on you, spitting on you, hitting you, shifting you, selling you, using derogatory words, degrading, racist, discriminatory, xenophobic words. Even here, though, the struggle continues. There are some who do not want us, some who see us as bad people. But becoming a refugee is not a choice. Who in the world would choose that?'

I shake Azhar's hand at the threshold.

'We will talk soon, brother,' he says.

'We will indeed,' I reply. 'And thanks again for the tea.'

We both grin.

I stroll down a side street, cross the main road and hop on a bus into snowbound downtown, where I enter a bar and jostle through the crowd – young, affluent, free – a privileged caste. My friends hail me with shouts and slander through the blaring tunes, and the night descends, pulsing, into a frothy swirl of pints.

My mind drifts back again and again, however, to a bamboo cabin in the twilight, where a little boy is scratching notes earnestly in the flickering of an old oil lamp. The world slumbers. He chews his pencil and gazes out the door as a brilliant beam cracks open the eastern hills, illuminating a thousand paddy fields.

REEDSONG

Afghanistan

'Since I was severed from the bed of reeds,
in my cry men and women have lamented.'
- *Song of the Reed*, Rumi

A Modern Wedding

BREATHLESS, THE BOY SLAPS MONEY down onto the
shop counter, grabs the batteries and darts out again into the
moonlit streets of Herat.[1] His bony feet patter on the cobbles and
his overlarge tunic billows behind him. He pauses briefly among
a cluster of tradesmen gathered below a pole. A loudspeaker is
perched on top: crackling voices are refuting rumours of disquiet
in the government, passing quickly on to rapprochement with
Pakistan and budding ties with Egypt and Saudi Arabia. Far
far overhead, a pair of winged metallic monsters drift across the
cosmos, warily eyeing each other – Skylab and Salyut.

The boy runs on, emerging from a warren of tenements,
passing between walled fields and orchards, to the wrought

---

1   Capital of Herat Province, Afghanistan.

gates of the Grand Hotel. Overflowing flowerbeds perfume the courtyard: tulip, nargis, jasmine. Fronds high above slide over the stars; a colonnade of tall trees encircles a fountain, which burbles orange in the swathes of light that slant down from tall windows, where silhouettes mingle. A cacophony babbles from within; a large, jubilant crowd.

The boy wriggles into the jammed foyer, through a gaggle of old women in their finest hijabs, around some grey-bearded elders in turbans, past children his own age – moptops, silky shirts and bell-bottom trousers – past suited men, clean-shaven, moustachioed, and women in skirts and blouses, lipsticked and rouged, glamorous, covered in no more than loose neckerchiefs. He is aware of his own threadbare tunic, its rustic simplicity.

He arrives at the stage panting, and a woman with a tambourine drops the instrument and snatches the batteries from him. A debate erupts with her four bandmates as she tries to jam the batteries into the speaker.

'Quick,' says the tabla drummer, 'we're thirty minutes behind!'

'You think I don't know that?' snaps the tambourinist.

'Didn't bring batteries,' mutters the harmonium player.

'Oh, leave her alone. She thought they'd be provided,' says the cymbalist, as she settles on her cushion. 'We all did. This is our first modern marriage. Our first time playing to men, as well as women. Let's show them what we can do.'

A clap rings out and the hall hushes. The guests part, opening a route across the dance floor, into the foyer and out the yawning front doors, where moths flitter in the scented night. At the front gates, cars pull in and chauffeurs emerge, opening back doors.

A stocky young man steps out of one, in an immaculate black suit, with a bright patterned tie, bushy brushed hair and a neat moustache. Then in resplendent white emerges the bride, her cascade of dark curls uncovered but for a white veil clinging to

her chignon. She too is young, and stunning, like a Bollywood
princess. A buzz passes immediately through the guests; many
have never been to a mixed wedding before, with both genders
present, let alone seen anything but the traditional green hijab,
the tunic and waistcoat. Immediate family members form a
procession behind the couple as the speakers crackle into life
and the band lifts into a slow solemn march to accompany the
stately parade indoors, through the ranks of fixated faces and up
to the dais where the wedding thrones await. As the couple sit,
the march ruptures into rapturous melody, filling the dance floor
immediately. Those not swirling and stepping or clapping along
fill the surrounding tables. Platters arrive: silver teapots, sugar
bowls, bulbous glass cups.

Soon wellwishers are queuing up to sit either side of the
couple: say their few words, offer their blessings, then let the
next person sit in their place. Cologne and perfume embrace
thickly.

'Salaam, brother,' says a man.

He is four years older than the groom, but of similar features.

'Salaam,' says the groom. 'A long journey from Kabul?'

'Oh it was nothing.'

'All the same, Emmaduddin, thanks for making it.'

They embrace again. They have seen little of each other in
recent years, ever since the older brother moved to the capital as
a teacher.

'This is great,' says Emmaduddin. 'I've never been to one of
these new weddings before. At least not in Herat.' He points at
the men and the women together throughout the hall. 'What
atmosphere, hey?'

'Modernity.'

'And no mullah?'

'Baba will read for us.'

'Of course,' says Emmaduddin. 'None better.'

It is the first modern wedding in the Saljuqi family, perhaps one of the first in all Herat. There are men and women together in a single venue which is not a family member's home.

'It's quite welcome, as far as I'm concerned.'

'I'm glad,' says the groom.

'I can't believe it's come to this. Little Nasruddin, a man now!'

The groom chuckles.

'It seems only last week you were in trouble over the cannon. Do you remember that? Quite the ... *explosion*, one might say!'

They both laugh, though Nasruddin can still feel it, the sting of this story, in the soles of his feet. Even now as they lay ensconced in their silken socks and polished brogues. He shifts in his chair involuntarily, wriggles his toes.

His wearing of such westernisms, and their accompaniments – slacks, shirt, tie, blazer – had begun as a young boy. He remembers loitering after breakfast at the front door, in their grand old hallway, with its polished tiles and hanging tapestries.

'Why do I have to wear these stupid shoes, Mama?'

'Because, the school says so.'

'Why?'

'Because the Shah says we are a modern nation now.'[2]

'Why?'

'Nasruddin.'

'But Mama, the street boys will laugh at me! And the vendors too.'

'This is the 1960s, my boy, not the 1860s. And baba agrees. Now, run along, or you will be late.'

The street boys did laugh, and taunt, so he devised a method

---

2 The Shah was the monarch of Afghanistan at the time, in this case Mohammad Zahir Shah, of the Mohammadzai dynasty.

to please both street urchin and schoolmaster. Next morning, he slipped out the front door in his traditional tunic and baggy trousers, skullcap and sandals. Behind the school wall, Nasruddin plucked the bizarre western garments out of his satchel, one by one, until dressed. Then he stuffed his traditional clothes deep inside, under the books.

Somewhat ruffled, he joined his class in the courtyard. A couple of hundred boys were arranged along lines painted on the concrete, streaking up to the facade of a single-storey brick building, a shaded arcade in front and, to their sides, wings full of sash windows; an almost Victorian-style building – a remnant, perhaps, of the farthest grasps of the British Raj, an architectural daguerreotype of the Great Game, of pith helmets and elephant-towed artillery.

Each class stood stiffly to attention while the principal scanned them up and down, tapping here at a loose tie or pointing there at a grubby hem – a colonel inspecting his recruits. They recited the poem of allegiance, as every other pupil in the country was doing at precisely the same moment, finishing with a smart salute towards Kabul, where, across hundreds of kilometres of valleys and mountains and deserts, the Shah was no doubt gratefully acknowledging their efforts as he set about another day of kingship.

Then followed guidance, encouragement, news of upcoming events, which were all uttered in Pashto, Nasruddin's second language. At home he spoke Farsi, even though his clan, the Saljuqis, were Turkmen, descendants, some say, of the Seljuk horse archers who skewered the Byzantine cataphracts at the Battle of Manzikert in 1071.

It was here, at morning assembly, that punishments were meted out, lashings of humiliation before your classmates: shoes untied, socks plucked off, feet held up – soles to the sun – for the metre-long willow rod, for its swing and smack.

At noon, on a hill overlooking Herat, an ancient cannon would boom, the herald of lunchtime to the clockless citizens below. Magnificent trumpet. The boys would down pens and devour their meal: a loaf of bread and a small tin of condensed milk. The condensed milk was nothing compared to the fresh local produce, but that was too expensive for daily consumption. Each day a different child would be given a sack of flour, to be brought home, baked into loaves, and distributed to classmates next day, alongside the milk. UNICEF supplied these vittles.[3] As for everything else, education in Afghanistan was state-funded, including pencils, crayons, inkwells and paper.

The teachers ran a tight ship: in class there was a shorter rod for poor spellers, the tardy and daydreamers. It was disciplined, it was routine and it was, at times or even oftentimes, monotonous, but it was otherwise fine with Nasruddin. He did not get in much trouble. In fact, he thrived in school. It was elsewhere that little Nasruddin learned the sting of willow.

When the final bell rang each afternoon, they would trot down the street and around the corner to the mosque. They were not free after school to explore and play, but instead had to attend religious lessons, taught by the mullah, the clergyman.

What was worse, summer brought no liberation, but rather a more complete capitulation to the mullah: instead of geography, mathematics, science, it was Quranic catechism reeled off in the musty prayer room. It smelled of youthful sweat and ancient books. Nasruddin would daydream through the drone of doctrine, gazing at clouds in the high window, musing on the things one could see and do on the outside.

He longed to kick a football, toss a marble, or climb a mulberry tree and forage until his smile went purple. Maybe afterwards

---

3   The United Nations International Children's Emergency Fund.

play cards in a cool porch or volleyball in the park. He might even fabricate a kite: hack bamboo into rods and bend it into heart-shapes, carve a spindle out of softwood and then, for the fighting kites, crush glass into fine powder. Mixed in glue, this powder was then applied to string to strengthen it for the aerial clashes.

But most of all Nasruddin yearned to see the cannon in action. As did his friends. The problem was that they were always in the clutches of the mullah during daytime. The one brief glimpse of freedom in these humid summer doldrums was the few minutes of break time at noon. But because it was of course the cannon that released them, they were always inside when it thundered. It was insufferable to Nasruddin that something he heard every single day of his life should be off limits. But he was not discouraged.

One day, at about mid-morning, Nasruddin's hand rose.

'There are forces,' droned the mullah, 'forces at large in our country, boys, new ideas, dangerous ideas, sinful ideas, you must be the generation to rise above – yes, Saljuqi, what is it?'

'Mullah, may I use the facilities please.'

The old man nodded, waved him away.

'Now, where was I, boys? Ah yes, these new ideas, you must rise above them. Even the Shah, it seems, is not immune to these outlandish follies …'

In the arcade he met the other four: each boy had raised his hand, asked permission, exited and waited. Now that the last of them was out, the next phase could begin. They stole out of the madrasa and into blazing morning sun. Safely around the corner, they laughed and wrestled, free. They galloped through the city bustle, rickshaws and donkeys, the packed teahouses and the hookah dens, jostled through the bazaar, past saddlemakers and shoemakers, coppersmiths and locksmiths, out along cypress-lined boulevards to the outskirts.

Nasruddin beaded with sweat as he reached the brow of the

hill. There it was. Slanting forward on its throne, snout poised over the city, the chronological keeper itself: lord of their days. The gunners stood beside it, in their threadbare uniforms. One snapped shut a pocket watch and nodded at his colleague, who dipped a smoking match.

The great beast bucked on its chassis. Nasruddin's skull was ringing; he coughed out the acrid cloud and cheered as thunder reverberated. All across Herat, from the red-brick citadel to the stadium, among the elegant townhouses and the tenements, noon had arrived. Nasruddin yelped and capered with his classmates in the drifting smoke, the gunners smiling at their antics.

He winced when the willow smacked his sole, three days later. His gunpowder plot was short-lived: as the last echoes had rolled out over the hillside, he had realised the enormity of what they had done. He did not return after the lunch break, but instead slunk home. The next day, he lay in bed, 'sick'. The day after that, Emmaduddin castigated him.

'Please don't make me,' whined Nasruddin.

'You have to! You can't stay in bed for the summer!'

'Won't you tell the mullah I'm sorry?'

'Okay, I'll convey your deepest, most sincerest apologies, your highness.'

'Let me know what he says ... perhaps I will return tomorrow ...'

Surprisingly, the mullah accepted, asking only that his esteemed pupil should return to class. Nasruddin did and realised the trap he had strolled into on seeing the mullah's crinkled old face. The redness in it was released in the lash, like the pressure valve of a steam-shuddering boiler. Nasruddin hobbled for days afterwards.

But he had witnessed the cannon of Herat.

✦ ✦ ✦

'Nasruddin,' hisses a voice. 'Nas! Rudd! In!'

His mother, Aamena, marches through a cluster of wedding guests and moves in behind his chair, forcing him to turn.

'What is it, Mama jo?'

'Are you mad?'

Emmaduddin turns also.

'How could I have let you organise this on your own? And to think you would manage!'

'What is it, Mama?'

'You have, what, two hundred and fifty guests out there, yes?'

'Yes, Mama.'

She sweeps her hand at the crowded conference room. Many guests have finished their tea and have begun to swell around a tall door. The rest, still chatting at their tables, will soon follow.

'You have hardly enough food for fifty. At best!' Her eyes are wide with anger. 'Catastrophe! One little shaft with a table squeezed in, it is preposterous.'

Nasruddin grins, causing her to puff.

'This is no laughing matter, sonny! You can't have people travel – Saljuqis, no less – some on the road all day, hungry, into this magnificent hotel, expecting a feast, expecting comfort, luxury –'

'It's okay, Mama,' says Nasruddin. 'That is only one room. There are four more dining rooms; all have the same amount of food.' Her expression softens. 'We told the waiters to keep each door closed until the room filled, then to open the next room. The crowd will spill into each room as the previous one fills.'

'Like a fountain,' interjects Emmaduddin.

Aamena nods. Then she coughs, straightens up and slips away, to find something else to take care of.

Nasruddin shakes his head with a smile. He has been frantically busy for some weeks now, making sure that his mother's fears are not realised. He was up early this morning, overseeing the food deliveries and making sure that everything was clear with the hotel chef and his staff. Nasruddin had even bought the food; they simply had to cook it.

Nasruddin has explored every nook and cranny of the markets with a fine toothcomb. He has seen the lambs bleating in their enclosure – ten of them – slapped the burlap sacks of rice – fifteen of them – and sniffed at the spice samples – dozens of them – in browns, reds, ochres, greens, and enough white crystal to form a dwarf-sized pillar of salt. He has selected nets of onions and pyramids of tomatoes, forests of lettuce and barrels of oil. In the tea and coffee houses he has haggled fervently. He has bought basket-loads of sweets: split geodes gleaming with a rainbow of gemstones.

On the kitchen counters, at dawn, he stared at the miniature meadows of mint and fields of lemons, the piles of spinach, carrots, raisins, almonds, nougat and caramel. He felt nervous, explosive, the feeling on opening an exam paper when the questions leap out all at once, each jostling for attention, each a stumbling block or a time-sucking swamp. How, in a matter of hours, could it possibly be ready?

Somehow, it is. By now the conference hall is emptying and Nasruddin is ushered out of his seat, along with the bride and the immediate family. They will eat separately from the five crowded banquet halls, in their own private chamber. It is richly adorned in tapestries and cushions. As they sit around the dining mat, Nasruddin looks about at the cheerful faces, ruddy under the electric chandelier. Rice, spice and lamb fat fill his nostrils. There is little talking, much chewing.

His younger sister, Zaheda, pours him a glass of water. He stares deep into the churning sparkle, recalls the old cistern of his childhood.

As a boy, he was sent every day to the cistern to collect the household's water for the day. There was no plumbing in Herat, only communal fountains, pumps, cisterns, or even the River Hari that wended its way through the valley, giving it a level of fertility that has been world-renowned since antiquity. The Greeks lauded its vineyards and, even as a boy, Nasruddin knew that Herati raisins were considered to be the best in the world. On hot days, he would linger underground, in the shadows of the vault, sucking in the cool damp air, splashing the water with his jug, watching the ripples roll out. Then he would load up and trudge back home.

Home was a high wall along the road, in the middle of which were tall gates. Inside, a yard led to the facade of the old post office, part of a regional network established generations earlier. It had been a ruin, for a while, before Nasruddin's family moved in. The old sorting racks, towering to the ceiling, cobwebbed, had still been standing, inhabited by spiders and by the ghosts of a million letters. The first act had been to dismantle the ramshackle furniture, then the clearing, cleaning, plastering could begin.

To either side of the yard was an orchard and behind each of these, in the corners of the compound, was a stable, where the post horses had once been fed and shoed, readied for epic races to faraway lands, to fairytale realms. The local children, Nasruddin's friends, loved to hear such yarns, and loved even more to climb the trees, run around the garden, or splash about in the irrigation ditch that ran along the back wall. Only, of course, when not confined in the school or the madrasa.

A camel could have fit through the threshold, so tall were its thick wooden doors. The ceiling inside was very high, owing to its official origins. The rooms were spacious, airy.

One day, around the time Nasruddin might expect his friends

to call around, there was a rap at the door. It was, he noted, heavier than usual and prompter. He reached up for the wrought-iron handle and dragged it open. A large shadow loomed over him, blocking out the sun. The man was in a brown uniform, buttoned tight up to the chin, where his red jowls rested. A peaked cap was tucked under his arm. He wriggled his grey drooping moustache.

'Good evening, young fellow. May I speak with your father?'

'He is still at work, Sahib.'

'Your mother?'

'Nasruddin,' said Aamena, 'who do you have there, is it –'

She stopped when she saw the old man.

'Peace be upon you,' he said, fist over heart, bowing curtly.

After a pause she greeted him and showed him in to the living room. He was brought tea and food. Who was this old man? Later, Nasruddin heard his father, Mohammad Omer, greeting him in the room and soon the voices were rising, racing, debating something important. The old man, Nasruddin learned later, was a retired army officer, from a town many miles away. He had been stationed in Herat during his service and had somehow found himself in possession of the post office. He, like many of his old colleagues, liked to remain in uniform long after retirement: it turned heads in the street, caused people to smile wider, bow lower. It said: 'I am part of a brotherhood, my dear fellow, and it would behove you to remember that.'

The Saljuqis had been renting from him for years, but now he wanted to end the arrangement. They had made their home there, were raising young children. The old officer, however, wanted to sell them the house; it was too far away and he needed the money.

'Won't you take it?' he said. 'It's a bargain.'

'No,' said Mohammad Omer. 'I'm afraid I can't.'

'There are others clamouring for it, they will be only too happy to step in.'

'That is well, Colonel. May Allah grant them a joyous life here.'

'Come on, why not? Your kids love it here, you need a nice big place to raise them.'

'My family have some properties already, we don't need to buy a house.'

'Surely not as nice as this? With the orchards and the river?'

'The ditch? No, I'm afraid I cannot. My decision is made, Sir.'

'I see.'

The old officer ruffled his moustache, jowls glowing.

'Of course,' said Mohammad Omer, 'you can stay with us for as long as you need to. Or until you make a sale.'

Three months later, he was still living with the family. As he was entitled to, by the law of hospitality. It had taken several more days to finally convince the old trouser that the answer was indeed final. Since then, he had been searching for a buyer among other locals. When he found one, the Saljuqi family were ready to move.

Many miles from the city of Herat, up the winding valley, lived Grandfather Saljuqi. His little estate, on the outskirts of the village, was a close-knit community: several cabins clustered about the manor and stables. He had grown even closer with his farmers since his wife passed away; it was their wives who fed and looked after him in his old age. But the loneliness crept into his very bones. He spent hours fawning over family photos.

When his son, Mohammad Omer, arrived one day, to collect some paperwork, he greeted him heartily. They sat in the porch, sipping green tea, overlooking the fertile sunlit terraces.

'And how are my grandchildren?' asked the old man. 'How is Nasruddin? What is he, eight?'

'Growing fast, Baba.'

The old man nodded, eyes crinkled at the corners.

'You should bring them here,' he said suddenly.

'What?'

'Yes, why not? Aamena too of course. It will be good for them. They can eat healthy country food, get out of that city dust for a while.'

'But what about school, Baba? My children will be educated children.'

'There is a school in the village!'

'Ah, Baba, I don't know …'

'What?'

'Those village schools …'

'It will do no harm for a few months. Besides, what can some city school teach them about life that their grandfather cannot? Ey?'

Mohammad Omer grinned through his frown.

The family arrived the following week. The children ate well every day, the fat of the land: melons, rice, tomatoes, aubergines, cucumbers. The country air filled them with confidence and they grew rosy-cheeked and strong-limbed, chattering like the brook at the bottom of the wheat field. But, as the months passed, Aamena began to miss the bustle of the streets, the children grew tired of the hour walk to school and most of all they missed their father, who had to stay in the city because of work, only making the trip to the village at the weekends. They saw out the school year but then returned to the city dust.

Grandfather Saljuqi missed the children's laughter. He missed the talk of poetry with his son and daughter-in-law. Rumi, Jami, Ferdowsi, Saadi of Shiraz, among many, many others. He missed listening to Aamena's sparkling voice reciting entire poems over the cricket song of sunset.

So, after a few months of silence, he packed his suitcase and took a donkey as far as the village. In the village square, at the foot of the old shrine with its crumbling plasterwork, he nodded goodbye to the farm boy and the donkey and hauled himself aboard a bus: exposed engine, curvaceous mudguards and riotous paint patterns. It left each dawn, trailed by a truck crammed with produce for the bazaars of the city. Each dusk they returned – such was the village's communication with the wider world.

The bus rattled into life and, with a cough and splutter, pulled out of the square. The old man had left exhaustive instructions with his trusted tenants for the running of the farm; made sure they could repeat them back to him. He had done all he could do, now it was in God's hands.

The bus trundled down the valley. The sun rose behind it and sparkled on dewdrops across the croplands: verdure hugging the river and spreading out to where distant conifers climbed the lower reaches of bare brown ridges. It passed villages and then walled houses and orchards, which gave way to dense townhouses and traffic and minarets. The towers of the Great Mosque sprouted into the sky like tulips, their lapis lazuli tiles glinting in a lapis lazuli sky, a jewel among mud bricks and crumbling plaster.

After this, mighty ramparts loomed overhead, perched along an outcrop, a series of squat round towers, angry arrow slits staring down, scanning for foes as they have done throughout the ages since Alexander built them. It was in the shadow of this citadel, where the bazaars bunch together and the spices mingle in the air, that the bus pulled to a halt. The old man took his suitcase and strolled into a nearby alley.

Miserly windows, set high in the spartan facades with which Herati townhouses meet the outer world, frowned down upon him. But within these walls were courtyards and salons, troves of tapestries, silverware and heirlooms, crossed jezails and scimitars, flowers, fountains, poetry, music, tea, conversation.

He entered a gate into a small yard surrounded on three sides by the walls of a two-storey house. There were overflowing flowerbeds and, in the middle, a well.

'Babayi!'

Nasruddin ran out and hugged him.

'Nasruddin,' said his grandfather, 'have they taught you about your ancestors?'

It was the fourth morning of the old man's visit. They lay on cushions, drinking tea. Bulbuls chirped at the windowsill.

'Yes, Babayi, I think so.'

'You know about the mosque around the corner? You know why there are so many of our kin living here around the citadel?'

The boy shrugged his shoulders.

'Your great-grandfather, my baba, was a great mullah. People far and wide knew him for his great wisdom and his kindness. He built the mosque around the corner, the Saljuqi mosque, as locals call it, so that he could share his knowledge with the people of Herat. It was small, but famous. It became almost a university of theology, where thousands learned, who passed it on to further thousands, so that today thousands upon thousands of people carry his wisdom in their hearts.'

'Babayi, they never told me in such a way! Thousands upon thousands?'

The old man nodded.

'Now, Nasruddin, *you* must tell *me* something.'

The boy nodded.

'Where is it you go each evening?'

'To listen.'

'Listen? Listen to what?'

'To the voices.'

'The voices?'

'Baba,' said Mohammad Omer, entering. 'It is the radio. There is a loudspeaker in each neighbourhood.'

Mohammad Omer pulled on his blazer, ready for another day behind the headmaster's desk. Grandfather Saljuqi nodded, munching on a fig. After a pause, he asked:

'How much are they?'

'The loudspeakers?'

'No, no. The machines, these *radios*.'

'Baba, they are too much.'

'How much? Tell me.'

'Two thousand Afghanis.'

'I will buy one.'

Nasruddin looked from his grandfather to his father and back, eyebrows shot up, barely able to stay calm.

'Baba?' Mohammad Omer was frowning.

'Yes, yes,' scoffed Grandfather. 'It will be a gift.'

He winked at Nasruddin.

They sent for Abdul Razaq, the local expert, and paid him as a consultant to accompany them into the city centre and peruse the radio shop. He helped compare models, choose the best and negotiate a fair price. Back in the house, he helped install it and gave the gathered family a painstaking tutorial. The room filled with static, then little whines and shrieks while Razaq fiddled and suddenly the strumming of a rubab and the tapping beat of a tabla surrounded them.

Nasruddin's jaw hung open. Grandfather ruffled his hair, then, chuckling quietly, eased on to a cushion, closed his eyes, and drank in the music.

'Worth every penny,' he sighed.

Nasruddin was besotted immediately. The radio sat on its throne on a cabinet in the centre of the living room. When the others were not around he would kneel before it and admire the shiny speakers, the dials and buttons. Such witchcraft: to twist a knob and hear a voice on the other side of the world crackle in your home!

Three years later, his grandfather passed away. Though he was strong as an ox, still tall and square-shouldered, with wits and appetite as strong as ever, his appendix burst out on the farm and no doctor lived near enough to save him. He was ninety-two. Nasruddin was eleven.

'*Mister Saljuqi!*' An English voice greets Nasruddin. The bride and groom are again seated on the dais, the band plays and the guests banter over tea or jive about on the dance floor.

'Ah, Professor Bailey, good evening!' Nasruddin switches immediately from Farsi to English. 'Sit.' He pats the chair. 'Are you enjoying yourself? Did you get enough to eat?'

'I got plenty,' smiles the professor, patting his stomach. 'The lamb was exquisite, I must say.'

'And the musicians?'

'Fascinating. I'm trying to bloody well relax and enjoy the evening but I can't very well help myself. I keep taking notes all the time!'

'I am sure the ladies will speak with you at some point. Their husbands also are musicians. They will all be interested, no doubt, in your studies.'

The professor is an ethnomusicologist. He has travelled to conduct an extensive study of the traditional music of the region. His assistant is Nasruddin's sister's husband. He is a firm friend of the family now, hence his invitation tonight. The professor and his wife are two of the very few guests who are not in some way related to the bride or groom. In a few weeks, he will return to London, to Goldsmiths University. But he will be back. They have all promised to stay in touch.

Though the English couple are the only foreigners in the room tonight, they are far from unique in the city itself. Herat is in the midst of an unprecedented tourism boom and has become an unmissable waypoint on the Hippie Trail. Westerners journey, like the pilgrims or caravans of old, through cities such as Istanbul, Tehran and Mashhad before arriving in Afghanistan. They come – with their long hair, flowers and striped kaftans, sexes barely distinguishable – in Volkswagen vans, hired cars, bicycles and on foot. Some even on horseback. They stay for days or weeks, enjoy the music and the cuisine, the hookahs and hashish, sleep in hotel rooms or sleeping bags, in parks or on rooftops, sleep with each other, and then drift onwards to the Bamiyan Buddhas, Kabul and beyond the Khyber Pass towards the white beaches of Goa or the snowy summits of Kathmandu. Restaurants, cafes and hotels are sprouting like mushrooms all across the city. Bazaar hawkers have learned a strange new lexicon: mark, frank, lira, pound, dollar.

These outlanders are welcomed by most because of their wealth and because of the ancient duty of hospitality, and by some, mostly students, because of their stories and swagger. Others, however, eye them from a distance, reproachful and bitter.

They come to view the Great Mosque and stay to chat with the many local scholars who use its colonnades for study, swapping idealisms and idioms. It was around the time that Nasruddin began secondary school that the trickle of tourists first began to swell into a great flood. During study breaks he mingled with travellers from the farthest reaches of the globe. Even, once, a group of Irish, who told him of their little green island, and how peculiar it felt to be in a landlocked country, with no waves and little rain.

A pair of bell-bottoms billowed along the pavement, step after step, almost covering the shiny toecaps beneath. They passed multitudes: baggy calf-length trousers, tattered sandals, ground-sweeping skirts, bare feet, boots, hooves, paws, poultry claws, and, every so often, groups of high-heels and tights, click-clacking. Nasruddin wore a turtleneck and a blazer with the bell-bottoms and he ran a comb through his moptop as he sauntered down the street.

He was no longer ashamed of modern garb on the walk to school. In fact, as he saw it, he had progressed beyond straight slacks and bland blazer, the square style advocated by the Shah. A smooth face was a must, a burgeoning beard an early indicator of backwardness. Nasruddin was a man of the future, a man of sophistication. Or he would be, just as soon as he graduated from secondary school.

Someone clapped his shoulder, he spun around.

'Come on, man,' said a teenager, in similar attire, 'you're going to be late.'

'Late? We've at least ten minutes before class starts.'

'No class today, Saljuqi!' The teenager chuckled. 'Haven't you heard?'

A horde of boys coalesced around a bulky building of rough stonework. It had high windows and a vast roof. The old ware-house had been converted into a school, years earlier. Inside, classrooms had been fashioned out of thin partitions, hugging the original, load-bearing wall. This left a spacious central hall onto which every classroom door opened, a lofty nave that reverbera-ted with the crush of the crowd gathering below. Despite the

feeble protestations of teachers, their pupils crammed into the
place, roaring, and surging forward towards one end, where five
of the oldest ones balanced on some sort of makeshift podium.
To Nasruddin they seemed to be sailing on a sea of scruffy
heads. One of them, after several attempts, managed to calm the
audience. He had a sharp chin, like a shovel, curly hair.

'So, classmates, you've had enough?'

The crowd erupted in cheers.

'Enough of stuffy curriculums?'

They cheered again.

'Enough of conservative professors?'

And again.

'Enough of the Shah?'

This was the loudest cheer of all.

'Well then, comrades. Join us. We too have had enough!'

Chaos engulfed the building, which itself seemed in imminent danger of collapse. The hall had completely filled by now:
boys perched on each other's shoulders, swung from piping,
clambered up bookcases to cheer on the leaders. The speaker conducted this cacophony with gestures. Not without difficulty, he
won a hush.

'Today, comrades, we take the revolution to the streets. We
march on the city! We must be bold. We must be brave. The Shah
will send his henchmen to crush us, but we will sweep them
away, like a wave on the sand. We will send them fleeing. We
will awaken the people.' He paused while the roars echoed down.
'Now, comrades, listen, this is crucial: when the coppers close
ranks before us, wait for my order. We will withdraw ten steps.
Then, before the police know what has happened, we will charge
into them and break their ranks. The only question that remains:
are you ready?'

The boys went wild.

'Are you willing?'

Wilder still.

'Then let's march!'

Nasruddin had always been a diligent student, ears open to his teachers and mouth mostly shut. But he suddenly found that even his fist was raised in the air, tightly clenched, and even his throat was unleashing some hitherto pent-up frustration.

In secondary school Nasruddin studied algebra, physics, geology, theology, geography, history, literature and Mao Zedong Thought.[4] The Maoism was not strictly curricular, but it may as well have been: nearly all his classmates were budding Maoists, as were many of the students in Herat. It would be their job, they believed, to drag Afghanistan into the future, to build a socialist republic on the ruins of tribalism, feudalism, traditionalism. There were others too wooing the heart and mind of the student body all over Afghanistan, all raging against the Shah. For the Maoists, the Marxists and the Republicans progress was too slow; for the Islamists too fast.

The tide of students flowed through the streets and into the square, where a line of police stood shoulder to shoulder, an impenetrable grey dam. Nasruddin gulped. Their caps were pulled low, hiding all but their grimaces. Their knuckles were white, fingers tight around the batons. Behind the thin grey line, officers barked orders, directing reinforcements into place.

'No more Barakzai corruption!' shouted the protesters, raising fists in the air, or shaking them at the uniforms.

'End feudalism!'

'Serve the people!'

---

4   Mao Zedong Thought or Maoism was the ideology of Chinese communist leader Mao Zedong. It differed from Soviet Thought in that it emphasised the rural peasant over the urban industrial worker as the harbinger and safeguard of the revolution, leading to something of a split, bitter and often bloody, in communism across the globe.

'Long live Chairman Mao!'

In unison, the grey dam took one step forward, batons wagging. The tide ebbed suddenly as the students stepped back, a no man's land yawning open, a beach, slogans and taunts dying down. The square was almost silent, but buzzing. Tension shimmered off the cobbles.

Though far from the front line, Nasruddin wished he were back in the school, studying English with Ms Bib, the young American who glided to lessons on her bicycle, books jammed into the front basket, always friendly, always elegant. She was with the Peace Corps, who had established English departments in many schools. It was Nasruddin's favourite subject. He was one of the most gifted students, and, as such, he had been offered a place in their advanced evening classes.

His urbane English teacher was the tip of an ideological iceberg, however; a race by the superpowers for the good graces of the Shah and his subjects. Afghanistan was a no man's land in the Cold War, a void between the entrenched power blocs. Perhaps it was even, some theorised, the key to final victory. The Soviets modernised the army, the US provided NATO advisors; the Soviets financed a hospital, the US built an airport; and on and on. Educators spread Cyrillic and Latin alphabets, spoke of sickles and stars and stripes. Rubles and dollars poured into the country.

'NOW!'

The students charged, crashing into a threshing machine of truncheons, ramming shoulders into stomachs, wriggling past strong, uniformed arms, punching in under cap peaks. The grey dam collapsed and the square became a bellowing maelstrom. There were wet thwacks as polished wood struck skull. Police reinforcements baton-charged from a side street and the students fell into full retreat, galloping, jostling, tumbling. Many of those who fell were kicked and clubbed into unconsciousness, others were lucky to crawl away. The heavy black boots thundered after the routed schoolboys, shepherding the frightened flock down the road, into the schoolyard and up the front steps. Like trapped rats, the students turned about and fought, grabbing chairs, using them as shields or tridents or missiles. But the police hemmed them in and began to fell them in droves, batons blurring. Nasruddin could see the classmates in front of him struggle and collapse in turn, could see the glaring eyes of the lawmen, their buttons glinting, their spittle flying, their truncheons bleeding.

Then a police officer collapsed. And another. Thunk. A brick shattered on the concrete. Some boys had broken into the construction site next door. The police were now cowering, holding their arms up, glancing from sky to students to sky as they retreated. A bombardment of red bricks hailed down and it was their turn to flee. Nasruddin, pale, watched the shoulder blades and heels pumping away down the road.

The students jeered. Some teenagers staggered around, clutching their crowns, blood streaming down their faces; others lay out cold. A urine tang hung in the air. Despite the casualties, the number of protesters had grown: fathers, uncles, older brothers, concerned citizens, fellow rebels, many had witnessed the brutal baton charge and were now mustering rapidly. Even a handful of teachers rallied to the cause.

The fury of the newcomers propelled the schoolboys into a counter-attack, sweeping back down the street in hot pursuit of the police, fanning out across the square, staving in the doors of the police headquarters. The police had evaporated, leaving only their grey uniforms, tossed about, discarded. Within minutes flames were licking window frames, the crowd cheering and chanting out in the square. Vehicles too were lit, or anything else with police insignia.

By noon, the streets were silent. The police cars were charred husks and the barracks a blackened shell. Everyone had gone home.

The burning of the police barracks was the climax of the student protest. After followed a strike and a closure of all schools in Herat. Nasruddin and a handful of his best friends, worried their education would wilt, arranged to enrol in a school in Badghis, a poor province along the Turkmenistan border. It was so impoverished that they brought along everything they could think of, including food and furniture. Famine was ravaging several provinces, further stirring discontent.

After hauling their luggage north, finding their accommodation, and moving in, the boys visited the local school, where they entered the headmaster's office.

'Good day, Principal Sahib,' said Nasruddin, extending a hand.

The headmaster did not shake it.

'We are here to enrol, Sir, in your, eh, fine institution.'

'Absolutely not,' thundered the headmaster, his face reddening.

There was a portrait of the Shah behind his desk.

'Pardon me, Sir, but why?'

'Why? Why? Do you think I am stupid? You think you city louts can just swagger in here and trick the simple rustic? You are rabble-rousers; you are atheists! I heard all about your antics in Herat!'

'But, Principal Sahib, we just want to study.'

'Study how best to drag the town into chaos? You want to spread your propaganda, poison my pupils' minds – well, guess what? Not on my shift. Now please leave.'

There was no arguing and so they sold their possessions

and returned to their families, mere days after departing, with nothing.

Luckily, an agreement was soon reached between the students, teachers and government, and classes resumed in Herat. In the end, Nasruddin missed only a month and graduated with high marks. His enthusiasm for Mao Zedong Thought waned, leading him to dabble with the Islamist student groups briefly before turning his back on politics altogether, not an easy task in a highly polarised period.

In the meantime, the Shah was finally deposed. By his cousin, of all people: former Prime Minister Daoud Khan. July 1973. A bloodless coup, more or less. Daoud quickly abolished the monarchy, proclaiming a Republic of Afghanistan, with himself as president. For his momentous move, he had forged a broad front of accomplices in the political shadows, including a minor party by the name of the People's Democratic Party of Afghanistan (PDPA).

Nasruddin was hired by the Ministry of Telecommunications. He was trained in as an administrative clerk at the Herat telephone exchange. It was a magnificent, modern building on the eastern edge of the city, like something from a film: two stories of polished plate glass, German-designed, funded by Siemens. Inside, serviced by a spaghetti of wiring, was row upon row of whirring machinery, with clusters of blinking lights, gathering ten thousand voices and dispersing them again, a billion blips of energy, a conclave of the entire country. It was a building unlike any other.

Three hard but satisfying years passed here. Until, one bright summer's day, a letter landed innocuously on his cluttered desk.

From the Ministry of Defence of the Republic of Afghanistan.

The following week, at dawn, a dozen buses lined up in the stretching shadow of Herat stadium. Nasruddin struggled in the rush to push his trunk up onto the roof of the bus. Tied tightly to it was a rolled-up mattress and a rug. Inside were his clothes, sheets, cushion and some food, tea, toffees. He was surrounded by young men: some of them former classmates, many of them strangers. All had been summoned here to this convoy by the same little letter.

They packed into the bus and it revved up and rumbled off.

'Hard to believe, hey?' Nasruddin said to the fellow sitting beside him, a brawny labourer.

'What's that?'

'That we're leaving Herat.'

'At least you only got a year. I've no bloody education – that's *two* years for yours truly! In Kandahar of all places.'

'That's how this conscription business works. Better to get it over with now and be done with it.'

The bus jumped. A pothole. Outside, craggy ridges and sparse vegetation skimmed by. Nasruddin missed the orchards, parks and leafy boulevards of home already, the pistachio groves and the sounds of shepherds fluting swaying down from the hills.

'Cheer up, lads,' said a bespectacled youth across the aisle, grinning. 'It's our duty to the republic. It's an adventure!'

The labourer muttered and pressed his forehead against the glass.

Some weeks later, Nasruddin sent home a letter.

Baba & Mama,

I trust all is well at home. As for me, I am healthy and fitter than ever. Do not worry. Though the weather here is unmercifully hot and the training intense, I am luckier than most of my peers. They have singled me out because of my schooling, and made me clerk of our company. (You were right about studies paying off!) This means I am often stuck in the office (little more than a shack), inundated with paperwork. Still, it is better than inundation with sweat, out in the desert, hauling mortars and machine guns, or going for interminable callisthenics!

The base is enormous, there are 15,000 of us here. Within the wide walls are ranks of barracks, Medical huts, parade grounds, officers' quarters, latrines, leafy parks for exercise, tanks, trucks, cannons. Much like the base at Herat. Some of the fellows call it 'the Prison'. We are only allowed out for three reasons. One: for gunnery practice in the desert. Two: on our weekly free day (they let us wear our own clothes and stroll into Kandahar city for a few hours). Three: I hope does not occur. There is no sign of unrest in Kabul or in Herat, is there? Things are quiet here, at any rate.

The first day was dreadful; hours of waiting around while officers parcelled us out into our proper regiment, battalion and, finally, platoon. Then they lined us up for our inoculations. A sergeant strides out with a great glass cylinder in his hands and says: 'Right, who knows how to inject?' To us he said it, the beginners, fresh off the bus! We hadn't even received our uniform yet. One of the boys put up his hand, and the sergeant hands him the cylinder. It was full of liquid; an enormous syringe! One needle for fifty of us. Funny, no?

Then they shaved our heads. Less funny.

Anyways, I am quite settled now, though, needless to say, I am counting the days. The bulbuls sing much the same here; yet their song fills me with home-longing.

Every few weeks, our platoon gets mess duty. We spend the day from dawn til dusk in the kitchen hut. Then at breakfast, lunch and dinner, the other lads in our regiment line up and we ladle the grub into their canteens. They carry it outside to eat. It is hard work, but then again we get the choicest cuts. Last time we managed to whip up some kebabs for ourselves, much to everybody's delight.

The uniform is a simple affair, dull brown like the wilderness beyond the base. There is a soft field cap, sturdy boots and a belt with a golden eagle on the buckle. It is actually quite airy, though it sill does not stop this poor Herati from melting, from yearning after our famous breezes.

Kandahar itself is quite charming. Nestled under undulating mountains, it has some nice bazaars and teahouses, though not nearly as good as ours. They have much wool here and the pomegranates are delicious. I have seen the mausoleum of Ahmad Shah Durrani, a magnificent edifice with a beautiful blue dome, as befits the father of the nation.

Well, that is all I have for now. I trust my recollection of the banality of military life will put your hearts at ease. Give my best wishes to Emmaduddin and Zaheda. And tell Abdul Azim to stick to his studies; he will need to, if he really does wish to go on to Medicine after school!

Your son,
Nasruddin

'Saljuqi! Private Saljuqi! Where is he? Ah, Saljuqi, the captain says you are to report to the exercise yard immediately.'

Nasruddin was cramped in his desk behind towers of files, hammering away at the typewriter. A fan was wobbling frenetically but barely stirred the lazy heat beaded on his forehead.

'What can I do, Corporal? As you can see, I'm swamped!'

'It doesn't matter, come on.'

'But, Sir, I –'

'The pen pushing can wait, Saljuqi. You've missed too much training already. This is the army, not the library!'

The march was exhausting, swimming through the blurry air, over baking rubble. Now Nasruddin was in deep desert. Yellow wasteland stretched to the horizon and pure fathomless blue vaulted above. An aircraft was circling overhead, sputtering.

Behind him stood the entire platoon, staring at him. As was the captain, with his halo-broad cap and glinting braid. In front of him was a tripod, its thick solid legs meeting at about chest height. On it, slanting up towards the sky, sat a heavy machine gun, a monster of a weapon, Soviet-built, with a great bulbous snout and twin crescent-shaped butts to snuggle each shoulder into. There were two rings perched on top, wire sights side-by-side: one for target direction, the other for range and velocity.

The captain gestured to proceed with a flick of the hand, then grinned at the troops as if to say: 'Watch this.'

Nasruddin wiped his brow. He grabbed the grip, snuggled each shoulder into each crescent-butt, and ever so faintly contacted the trigger. The aircraft skimmed past. Beneath it, a white blossom opened out against the blue, a parachute, with a cylindrical grey weight under it, swinging like a pendulum.

'FIRE,' cried the captain, and Nasruddin's bones were jolting, teeth clenching, eyes squinting. Shells rattled on the rubble and lightning poured forth from the muzzle. He held the trigger, feeling the monster bucking and barking, following the declining parachute as it sank lower, lower, missing, missing, and – POOF – the grey weight, a sack of dust, exploded, leaving a burst in the sky sifting earthward.

The platoon roared and cheered; Saljuqi turned, grinning. The captain, astonished, strode up and shook his hand.

'Good grief, Saljuqi, I never took you for such a marksman – especially after all the training you've missed!'

'Thank you, sir.'

None was more shocked than he.

A sheet hovers over the heads of the bride and groom, held at each corner by a relative. Nasruddin gazes out at the crowded hotel hall, then down into a mirror and meets the big brown eyes of the woman he is to spend his life with. Azizeh. They exchange golden bands, drink from each other's goblets, while guests dip their fingers in bowls of henna ink, drawing circles on their palms. They swap fleeting niceties from the corners of their mouths, aware of their centrality to proceedings and the five hundred eyes glued to them. Nasruddin's father, deeply versed in theology, reads from the Quran. Nasruddin closes his eyes as the ancient words echo.

She was there when Nasruddin returned to his job after military service, a phone operator at the Ministry for Telecommunications, jamming plugs into jacks, rattling questions down her microphone, listening to her earphones intensively. She was one of dozens, lined up at their switchboards, all women, wearing skirts and high heels and lipstick. But Nasruddin knew she was the one for him.

There was one slight problem. He did not know her and neither did his family. No one he knew had ever chosen their own wife before; that was always left to the diplomacy and machinations of elders. But this was a republic, a new modern Afghanistan. And Nasruddin was a modern man.

Azizeh was the daughter of migrants, rural Pashtuns from the Helmand Province to the southeast. Her father, suffering from a respiratory illness, was advised to seek out a softer clime. And so he settled his family in Herat, where Azizeh was born. She was the second youngest; there were six girls and three boys in the Bris family. This was not their surname, they had no notion of such a strange concept, but they were the only members of the Bris tribe living in Herat and so went by its name.

Months slipped by, of furtive glances across the exchange, of racing thoughts and plans when he should have been focused on paperwork. A year passed. Finally Nasruddin plucked himself up and made his move. He turned for help to his father, who made inquiries at the mosque and learned that the Bris family were wealthy and pious, the father being a much sought-after accountant among the merchants of downtown. This was a good start. Next, a delegation was sent to visit the young woman's family: Nasruddin's mother, aunt and sister spent an hour as guests there, introducing themselves to the women of the household, eating pastries, drinking coffee. It was deemed a success, so, some days later, a delegation of men was sent in – father, uncle, brother – while Nasruddin twiddled his thumbs at home and drank seven cups of tea, reorganising the bookshelves.

He could picture the scene, see his folks arguing in his corner, painting a flattering portrait, speaking of career prospects and family standing, wealth and health.

'He has all his teeth,' they would say. 'He is in his early twenties, young and handsome, only a year older than your Azizeh. An excellent match: how many young maidens do we see these days being snared by wrinkly old fossils? Such a pity, ey, when that happens?'

They would produce a photograph of him, for the girl to ponder over. In truth, he had very little money, though he had been working steadily in the telephone exchange since returning from conscription. His father, however, would sell a parcel of the ancestral lands, out on Nasruddin's grandfather's estate – a fairly common solution.

Nasruddin prayed Azizeh would read his heart somehow, through all the haggling, and see into its deep well of love.

He heard the front gate clink, footsteps and chatter, and he dashed out to the courtyard.

'Well, what did she say?'

✦ ✦ ✦

Like the summits of the Hindu Kush towering above the plain, the white cake ascends from the table: a five-tiered ziggurat of icing reaching a dizzying altitude of over forty inches. The bride and groom sit behind it, some young women at their sides, bare-armed, hair tumbling over their shoulders, and an older woman in a hijab. Children swarm behind, in colourful shirts and blouses, posing, play-acting – someone snaps a camera and captures the moment forever.

It is four weeks since Azizeh said, 'Yes.'

The couple hold a knife together and plunge it into the pristine icing. There is a cheer, the slices are distributed, washed down with yet more tea, and the music explodes again, filling the dance floor with a revolving circle. Onlookers yip and clap as the dancers swirl and step, swirl and step, on and on, well past midnight.

Flight

Lucio Barnetta
Herat Caravan Hotel
Herat
Afghanistan
7.9.78

Marie,

Greetings! I hope things are well back in dull old Zurich! (The photo is a snap of the tomb of Queen Goharshad, I figured you'd dig her.) Erni, Jaki and I arrived on Monday on our trusty bikes – well worn, I can assure you. It was rather a tough leg, across the border and up the valley, but we're here now and it's groovy. Nice to see some city life, haven't had much of that since we left Tehran.

We've holed up, for now, at this charming little hotel, The Herat Caravan, right in the city centre, in among all the action. We've eaten a lot of our meals here, delectable food, and have spent the evenings in the saloon, where they have the best of local music each night. They've got a stage at one end and everyone sits against the wall on cushions or rugs. They have these little mini tables, low, so you can sip your tea or drag on the hookah. Lots of other Europeans come here too, not just the hotel guests. I even saw a couple of Russians, but they seemed pretty square and serious, didn't mingle much. I guess they work here. 'Advisors' probably.

The part-owner, Herr Nasruddin Saljuqi, is a pretty cool cat, a young fellow, our age. He's up most nights hanging out with us guests. I don't quite know how he does it: he goes into work each morning to the ministry of telecommunications. His wife must never see him. He needs to kick back and chill; all that hard work is going to give him a heart attack!

At night we unroll our sleeping bags on the roof and crash out under the stars. It's far out, Marie, and especially with this prime Herati hashish they've got here, which, like the hotel, costs a pittance. An absolute pittance. Best grass in the world, man. I may never leave!

In the morning, we'll wander in the bazaars or rent a horse to trek about in the hills. Maybe fly one of their kites. Or else just lay out in the park with a doobie — all depends on how we're feeling. Because tonight we've got something special planned.

A kid in the street got us some 'midnight oil'. Grade A stuff. Said it goes down well with candy, so we got some of that too. Local stuff, very sparkly. You know how I've always joked about dope; well now is the time to try it I reckon. Some yankees here have recommended it too, say it's the trippiest high going. I'll let you know in the next card! Now must go, squeezed enough on here.

With love, Lucio.

Jakob Schneider

Room 106

Hotel Inter-Continental Kabul

Afghanistan

23.9.78

Dearest Marie,

I'm so very sorry to have to write this letter to you. They'll have told you by now of Lucio. We have been living our own hell here, for over two weeks. I think I need to write this. I hope it does some good for both you and I, if that is at all possible.

The three of us were found vomiting and writhing in the hotel room and were immediately taken to hospital. Our stomachs were pumped. We told them about the opium. I was too sick to be embarrassed, but I am now. How can I forgive myself? How could we have thought it was a good idea? We – Ernst and I, that is – are truly idiots. I don't know how I will face his mother. I don't know why we two survived, but somehow we did. And Lucio did not. The police came around and tried to blame it on Mr Saljuqi, the hotel owner; roughed him up a bit. We pleaded with them to leave him be. It was he who had looked after us here, gave us such hospitality, so far from home. A decent man. He knew nothing of our stupid scheme.

It is small consolation, of course, but I want you to know that we are safe. We are staying here at the hotel in Kabul until our flight back to Switzerland. Never thought we would return like this. I am so very sorry, Marie. I must stop now. I'll visit you in Zurich as soon as possible. Please be strong. 'It's not always going to be this grey.'

Sincerely, sorrowfully,

Jakob

It is only mid-morning, but Nasruddin cannot work. He needs to get out of his office, to get home to his family. Early this morning, rumours began streaming in; that something was afoot in the city, a vague tension was growing, people were nervous. Now, mobs are swarming in the streets.

The republic was toppled almost a year ago, last April; a coup triggered when President Daoud took steps to hamstring all opposition. He was too slow to arrest the leaders of the PDPA, who struck before they could be snuffed out. He had viewed them as a mere tool in his own coup, when in reality they were riding piggyback, waiting for their moment. Their leader, Nur Muhammad Taraki, became president of the newborn Democratic Republic of Afghanistan and immediately allied himself with the Soviet Union.

The new government lost no time in launching their social programmes, most notably sweeping land reforms, ostensibly to end the exploitation of the peasants. It was conducted in an over-hasty, ham-fisted manner, a one-size-fits-all implementation by urban intellectuals after little consultation with their rural comrades. They banned usury, the primitive system of loans in use throughout the countryside, but replaced it with nothing, grinding the rural economy to a halt. Instead of bringing more equality, this resulted in chaos and chronic food shortages, infuriating practically everybody.

The flag was changed, dropping the colour green, which had long been a reassurance of the roughly Islamic sympathies of previous regimes, however vague. It is red now, with a yellow cog-wheel and ear of wheat in the top corner. This was the first of many slaps in the face of fundamentalism. But what really infuriated the religious conservatives was the declaration of full equality of the sexes. Women were actively encouraged to participate in education, business, politics, healthcare and every aspect of Afghan life.

Ideas were one thing, but the sudden severity with which the PDPA enforced them was unprecedented. Even Moscow was alarmed.

Little had changed at Nasruddin's office, however: phone lines still needed maintaining, whether the calls were made by subjects or citizens or comrades. Until earlier this week, when the staff at the telecommunications office were advised to horde supplies in case of a collapse of services. Nasruddin didn't take the threat too seriously; his family were self-sufficient, with the crops from his grandfather's farm. He did, however, purchase ten tins of Klim, powdered milk, for his newborn son, Elyas.

Now he wonders should he have taken the advice more seriously. There is something in the air that reminds him of the student protests. But it is more serious this time, somehow. The mobs are fuelled by conservative, anti-government, anti-modern, fervour. And here he is, sitting in a government building, in his modern suit.

I must get home, he thinks. He grabs his jacket and keys, signs out, and quickly passes the receptionist in the lobby. He hops on his bicycle, wheels around the corner and down a quiet alleyway.

A voice hisses out of a window.

'Hey, you!'

Nasruddin looks up.

'Saljuqi? It is Saljuqi, isn't it?'

'Yeah … yes.'

'You work in the Ministry of Telecommunications?'

Nasruddin tries to peer up but can not recognise the shaded face between the shutters.

'Who is that?' he asks

'Do you value your life?' growls the voice. 'Are you crazy? Turn around, get back to the office. They'll string you up, or worse.

You work for the government; you're an infidel as far as they're concerned. Go now, don't delay.'

A screech of jets rattles overhead as he returns to the lobby. The staff are gathering at the top of the stairs, peering out the mezzanine windows towards downtown Herat. Nasruddin joins them. Again the screech approaches and two stubby straight-winged bombers zip past. There is a flash among rooftops – the eruption sounds a split second later, clouds boiling into the sky.

There are several gasps. More jets screech, more bombs explode. The whole staff are panicking now, running hands through their hair, stroking their smooth cheeks, or gesticulating wildly.

'Quiet! Quiet.'

The director general strides in among them, immediately silencing the pandemonium. He is totting a Kalashnikov. Soldiers stream in behind him, crusty boots on the spotless carpet.

'Do not worry,' he says. 'We will all be safe here. We are well protected. The army is on the way, from Kandahar and Kabul. They will crush these reactionaries, these terrorists, under their tank treads. The air force, as we can see, is already taking care of them.'

He is a loyal party man, a firm believer.

'What about our families?' says a secretary.

'Yes,' says a janitor, 'they need us.'

'What can we do here?' says a clerk.

'We are useless here,' says a typist. 'Our folks need us.'

Nasruddin and several others gather around the director. He is listening, nodding.

'Look,' he says. 'I think you should stay here, it's safer. This thing will blow over soon.'

'But, Sir,' says Nasruddin, 'my wife is at home. It's just her and the baby and my elderly parents. They need me there.'

The director rubs his chin, thinking.

'Okay. I can't say I recommend it, but I can't stop you. Family is family. Those who insist may leave, but I will send an escort with you part of the way. There are savages in the streets.'

Most stay, but Nasruddin and five others go. Two soldiers unbolt the foyer doors, peering out into the deserted street. They nod and the little group, five staff and three soldiers, slink out and down an alley. The soldiers march behind the staff, assault rifles pointed at their backs. They have been ordered by the director to treat them as prisoners, so they won't be suspected of working for the government. The five have bicycles though, so only one hand can be held in the air in surrender, while the other guides the handlebars.

Smoke soon fills their nostrils. They see carts upturned, bazaar stalls torn apart, windows smashed. And gutters streaming with gore. Bodies lay on the pavement, blood spattered on the walls above them. Some lie in improbable contortions, like dropped puppets. Many wear suits or uniforms, are clean-shaven or are, in some other superficial way, modern-looking. One is pale, blonde, a soviet technician, perhaps. Red flags are torn down, ad hoc green flutters in their place. Rumours spread that an entire army division has mutinied. Gunshots rattle in the distance, grenades burst, jet screeches diminish, skimming away low across the hilltops, returning to base for a frantic reload.

Miraculously, Nasruddin makes it back to his townhouse without encountering a mob. He slips in the gate, bolts it tight and goes inside to hug his wife and baby.

'They tried to break into the hotel,' says Azizeh.

'What?'

Nasruddin lowers the baby into the cot.

'Yes,' she says. 'But the staff locked the doors, stayed quiet, and the mob moved on. They were lucky. Other places have been attacked, they say. There have been killings.'

'But our hotel? Whatever for?'

'All the tourists there. They think all foreigners are Russian. Or godless. Or something, who knows.'

'Most of them are simple country folk,' sighs Nasruddin. 'They are starving, miserable. They are angry.'

Over at the Great Mosque, in the shaded porticos where Nasruddin once debated with hippies, officers bark orders at frightened conscripts. Army loyalists, those who have not mutinied, along with government officials, party members, and Soviet advisors flood into the sanctuary. Loudspeakers bellow to remain calm, that order will soon be restored in the streets. Tanks back up against the mosque's arches, machine guns bristle from its parapets and snipers roost in its minarets; all pointing outwards at a city in revolt.

It is March 1979. The Herat Uprising has begun.

An airliner speeds down the runway. It slices through the heat mirages, past Soviet fighter-bombers, helicopter gunships, armoured cars, tanks and Red Army paratroopers marching in squadrons from the belly of an enormous cargo plane. The airliner lifts off, skirts the rugged hilltops and banks high above Kabul. Nasruddin gazes down at the city, at its gleaming domes and Babur Gardens, at the old jumbled districts and the recent grids, all nestling between ridges that lay out like shrouds, rising in undulations towards the northeastern horizon, where lordly peaks jut from cloud.

Nasruddin is not flying into the Hindu Kush, however; he is headed west, back to Herat. He ponders all that has happened since the revolt last March.

In the days after he left work, he remained at home in the townhouse as the explosions crescendoed and lulled, holding his wife and baby. An armoured column appeared on the outskirts, unnerving the rebels, until the crewmembers opened their hatches, unfurling green banners and chanting 'Allahu Akbar'. Crowds of protesters rejoiced, gathering around the tankers, praising them for their mutiny.

When the tail of the column finally arrived and took up positions, they dropped the green, closed their hatches and began blazing all about. Thousands fell. So much for mutiny. These loyalist reinforcements quickly linked up with the loyal garrison at the Great Mosque and soon much of the city was wrested back into the government embrace. The insurgents melted back into the countryside. But, as soon as they had regrouped, they began launching forays into the city and ambushing government forces that ventured out. Herat became a city under siege. Rebels would enter a neighbourhood, engage the soldiers and disappear again by the time the jets screeched overhead. The bombs rarely caught the Mujahideen guerrillas.[5] Instead, it was civilians who were atomised or crushed under collapsing masonry.

Azizeh's family home, on the other side of the citadel, was obliterated. Thankfully, nobody was in the house at the time. Their shops too were destroyed, as was much of the street. Ruin fell on them from the bomb bay doors, but from the Saljuqi front doors came welcome. They moved in with their daughter and in-laws.

The battle for Herat became increasingly bitter, with less and less room for neutrals. The government was fully capable, it seemed, of liquidating opposition – Maoists, Islamists, even the moderate faction within their own party, the Parchamis – perhaps even down to those who had dabbled in student politics, Nasruddin thought. Another reason to leave.

Nasruddin applied for a transfer and sold his half of the

---

5   The anti-government, often Islamic fundamentalist opposition forces soon became known worldwide as 'the Strugglers', the Mujahideen.

Herat Caravan Hotel. Luckily, he was able to arrange for an internal transfer to the Ministry of Telecommunications office in the capital.

For weeks he has been living with Emmaduddin, who has been teaching in Kabul for ten years. Nasruddin is flying home to arrange the transfer of his furniture and to collect his family. There is no question of travelling by bus: the roads have become death traps, with wide swathes of the countryside out of government control. Government employees are fair game for the Mujahideen who stalk the mountain passes, waiting with snipers, rocket launchers and even boulders. Nasruddin has heard that in the canyons it is impossible to place the gunshots; the echoes engulf all.

Himself, Azizeh and the baby will travel by airliner while their furniture will take its chances below them, in a hired truck.

The Herat Uprising was only the beginning of a succession of revolts that tore across Afghanistan. For each city revolt that was crushed, a whole swathe of countryside would rise up. Soon no-go areas were spreading like wildfire. Rebellion sparked repression which sparked rebellion as the violence snowballed exponentially. The government begged the Kremlin for intervention, the Soviets declined, wary of stumbling into their own version of Vietnam. Again Kabul begged, again Moscow declined.

In September, after a subtle internal tussle, Taraki was ousted and, later, smothered in his bed with a pillow. The new leader, Hafizullah Amin, however, failed to halt the growing instability, despite his ruthless determination. He had also angered the Soviet leader Brezhnev, who had sworn to protect Taraki.

On Christmas Eve 1979, Soviet airborne forces landed in Kabul and on 27 December, the presidential palace was stormed by elite Spetsnaz operatives. Amin was killed, either executed or in the crossfire. Babrak Karmal, from the moderate faction, was appointed president.

Meanwhile, Soviet troops poured across the border. It had begun. The Rescue. The Invasion.

Nasruddin blinks awake from his snooze and sees the wide green valley far below, beneath cloud wisps. For a moment he forgets everything and marvels at this bird's-eye view; the serpentine river, the patchwork of croplands, the wrinkled hilltops on either side, like crumpled foil. Perhaps he is passing, right now, directly above his grandfather's estate, where he had spent that bright fresh year of his childhood.

He had once been sent back to the farm, just before he began secondary school, to request a load of firewood be delivered to the townhouse. When he had delivered the message, the tenants made him dinner and, afterwards, prepared him a bed. He asked one of the farmers to wake him in time for the dawn bus. He was woken, but far too early; the stars were still twinkling. Before he set off, the farmer gave him a loaf of bread for his breakfast. Nasruddin arrived in the village, after an hour's trek, and was immediately surrounded by a pack of feral dogs. They began circling him, licking their lips, growling. At that moment, he remembered the bread, threw it to the hounds, and fled to the mosque, to sanctuary, to await sunrise.

Though it was not funny at the time, he has always loved telling this story. He chuckles. Then he remembers that it is a battlefield he is gazing down on, and perhaps, right now, he is directly above an ambush or reprisal.

Herat is his bed of reeds, his home, has always been and will always be, and yet Nasruddin must wrench his heart out and transplant it, for the sake of his baby. His parents will have the townhouse to themselves for the first time. He has already made arrangements to move out of his brother's house when he returns to Kabul. With wife and child, he will move into a house in Khair Khana, a suburb in the northwest of the capital. There he will share the ground floor with his sister, her husband and their three children. The landlord lives upstairs. With any luck, the furniture will make it to Kabul without any little souvenirs of potshots from distant cliffs.

Nasruddin will continue his work in the Ministry of Tele-communications, a quiet position, a harmless post, where perhaps he can focus on paperwork while the countryside tears itself apart.

Nasruddin places the Kalashnikov against the parapet and blows hot air against his cold-crippled fingers. It is the winter of 1981, only a few months since he moved to Kabul.

Below him stretches the city, streets of slush, white rooftops, and beyond, the snowcapped mountains. His hands warm but it only makes the rest of him shiver; the drab grey military tunic and soft cap are scant protection against the bitter gusts sweeping down from the Hindu Kush. He longs for a heavy winter overcoat, or a toasty ushanka, like the Soviet troops sport as they stand guard at the presidential palace or rumble past in their trucks. But Afghan conscripts are the scrapings of the barrel, woefully under-trained, under-equipped, under-motivated. Some, albeit decreasingly, are true believers. Others are spies or saboteurs. Most are simply doing time, at best stooges, at worst cannon fodder; they shirk through their tours, clinging to cigarette breaks or dinners, counting the days until completion or waiting for their chance to escape and perhaps make some money by selling their weapon to the Mujahideen. Some even join them.

Nasruddin can do nothing of the sort. He has a pregnant wife and a toddler to look after. He had considered himself immune to conscription, having served his year in Kandahar, during the rule of Daoud. The rules had been altered, however,

as the Karmal government desperately needed to fill the ranks in
the national army, with casualties and desertion mounting every
month. All under the age of forty are now eligible, regardless of
previous service.

The Soviets too have had their losses, and have been forced to
commit ever more numbers of men and machinery to the fight.
The Mujahideen show no signs of collapse, though thousands
have fallen. They are becoming increasingly tactically astute and
carry increasingly sophisticated weaponry to the field. In the
beginning, many a helicopter pilot joked about the lead musket
balls clinking like hail off their flanks, laughed at the puffs of
smoke from antiquated jezails no different to what had sniped at
redcoats a century earlier. Now, though, helicopters are erupting
in flames, whirling to earth, penetrated by Redeyes, the latest
in ground-to-air missile technology. It is quite clear that these
have not been raided from government stocks or fashioned by
gunsmiths in hilltop villages.

Nasruddin is luckier than most. He has been posted to the
military hospital in Kabul, rather than some outpost in the
wilderness, and so he can still return home after each shift.
Azizeh's sister is married to a high-ranking military doctor, who
managed to claim Nasruddin as a clerk in his office. He still wears
the uniform and occasionally performs sentry duty, but mostly he
is inside, filing documents or distributing newspapers through
the wards.

It is on these rounds that he witnesses the horror of war. He
learns how a bullet, no bigger than a bee, can rip a man's intestines
to shreds in a split second, or shatter a leg. He sees how limbs
can be burned to the bone or faces melted into unrecognisable
seas of scar tissue. He sees grown men weeping for their mothers
and mere children, with hardly a wisp on their chins, quivering
like geriatrics. Others lay there and stare through you, trapped,

unblinking, in some irreversible split second, in the atomising of a comrade or the following of an order or the unravelling of some atrocity.

In the night, the screams are always the same, whether in Russian or Dari, in Hazaragi or Pashtun.

Every morning, there are empty beds, cold and neat, wailing women and children, trembling old folks. The carpenters in the basement have never been so busy; their output is stacked in rows in the car park, filled, slid into trucks, lowered into pits. In the dumpsters, reels upon reels of reeking bandages are tossed. The sewers beneath the building run red.

Nasruddin peels his cuff back from his watch. Lunchtime. In Kabul, as in Herat, there had once been a cannon, a thunderous timekeeper, but at some point, which Nasruddin cannot pinpoint, it ceased. These days, the city bristles with many thousands of cannon, in every calibre imaginable. And a noon boom no longer has an innocent ring to it. People would duck now, rather than dine.

Inside, down in the cafeteria, he grabs a tray and sits. But he cannot eat. Through the steam, the bland rice aroma, the Silo Factory bread, there is still the smell of disinfectant, and behind that, perhaps merely by association, is the sickly ripe stench of decay.

An officer marches in.

'You, soldier, are you on sentry?'

'Finished, Sir,' said Nasruddin. 'For today.'

'Okay, come with me. You too, and you.'

He summons any grey uniforms he finds among the white lab coats, the hawks among the dove flock, and leads them downstairs and outside. They mount a truck and when it is full it revs up and rumbles out into the street. They are less hawks than bewildered cygnets.

The tailgate drops open and the soldiers drop out. They are in a windswept field, hidden from the city by a rise. The officer points to some shovels and picks.

'Dig,' he barks.

When the virgin snow has been scarred, and the yawning pit sunk, the trucks return and unload the coffins. Through the snowstorm the distant peaks are barely distinguishable against the swirling sky. Grey ghosts, hunched and shivering, scrabble dark soil out onto snow. The coffin trucks return, again and again, the picks continue to swing.

When more diggers arrive, Nasruddin slips away and hurries home.

1986. Nasruddin stares out the airplane porthole with wide-open eyes. A white peak soars up out of the surrounding purplish earth, tapering like a held tablecloth. Passing over it, peering into the caldera, he thinks it resembles an anthill. It is not Mount Fuji that shocks him, though it is impressive, even for an Afghan, but rather the sprawling cosmopolis creeping over the horizon, utterly alien, utterly bewildering, bristling with towers, pulsing with bullet trains, glinting like a chandelier. Tokyo.

In the taxi from the airport he watches the city slip by, cherry blossoms, neon signs, constant traffic: rumbling, humming, honking. His hotel room is compact, minimalist, clinically neat. A cubical oasis of quiet. There is a colour television glaring animations and blaring adverts: Rubik's Cubes, dishwashers, bikinis. Buy, buy, buy. In the market he smells seaweed, dried fish, sushi. No sizzling lamb fat or baking tandoors. There are also no armoured personnel carriers or circling gunships.

The conference hall is buzzing the next morning with delegates from Fiji to Nepal, from Malaysia to Mongolia, all in sleek suits. Nasruddin stands before them, with a sheaf of notes, a report. He clears his throat and begins to speak to this medley audience about the state of affairs in Afghanistan.

Halfway through there are perplexed frowns; whispering back and forth. A shocked Japanese technician interrupts him.

'Mister Saljuqi, you cannot be serious?'

'But I am.'

'You mean to tell me that in your country there are still hand-cranked telephones in use?'

'Yes, many. The network would collapse without them.'

'Equipment invented in the last century?'

'Yes, used every day.'

'So these phones have no number buttons, no touch tone?'

'None. Many are rotary dial. Even a few pre-rotary.'

A murmuring ripples through the hall. The Japanese delegate had, mere minutes earlier, delineated the rapid spread of analogue cellular systems, mobile phones, throughout Japan.

'So, what? An old-fashioned switchboard exchange?'

'Yes, we have exchange buildings in all the major cities.'

'You're serious?'

'Yes. In fact, my wife was an operator.'

The other men around the conference table take some more minutes of convincing before they can accept Saljuqi's report.

Nasruddin is Afghanistan's representative at the Asia-Pacific telecommunications conference. At the end of his second year of conscription, after the waiting, the counting, the yearning, nothing happened. He was kept on for duty for an additional year. When he was finally discharged, after a total of twenty-six months in uniform, he returned to the Ministry of Telecommunications, where he was promoted to director. He attended evening classes at Kabul University, studying Persian literature, which his mother had taught him to love. Due to his high level of English, he was then permitted to finish work early three days a week while he studied English at a UN development programme. His new qualifications led to him being selected to attend a course on international postal statistics in Bangkok in 1985.

There he'd gawked at golden spires, temples terracing steeply skyward, statues of Buddha everywhere. Was this, he wondered, what it was once like in Afghanistan? In the Gandhara period, the Bamiyan era? It was his first time outside of Afghanistan.

A year later, and he is again travelling. As with the first trip, he has used a special working visa, which limits him to precisely the itinerary of the official trip. Once again, he had a stopover at Delhi. There, he waited a week for the paperwork to be processed. He scrutinised Mughal architecture, ambled along the shopping arcades of Connaught Place, watched a Bollywood film. He marvelled at the bindis, the red dots, on the women's foreheads.

He was issued a passport by the airport authorities and on returning home he will relinquish it. The government takes no chances. Azizeh is stuck at home anyway, as are Elyas and their five-year-old girl, Shamiem, so flight is impossible.

Back home, though the war rages on, literacy has inched up, and women are a common sight now in schools, factories, government. There are even a few women's militias. Anahita Ratebzad, one-time nurse and feminist activist, is deputy to the head of state. Women all over government territory are spreading their wings. And not just the more affluent, as in the time of Daoud. But there is little else to be cheerful about. At work Soviet technicians constantly monitor Nasruddin, check his work, approve or reject.

Kabul is a stronghold, but large swathes of the countryside are under the sway of the Mujahideen. Hamlets are flattened, goats riddled, wells poisoned. Neither side has much need of prisoners.

The economy is struggling. Herat and its hinterland remains a war zone, with frequent skirmishes and bombardments. The cypress-lined boulevards have been shredded, the parks cratered.

Nasruddin sits among Japanese peers at lunch. He does not tell them about the war. He tells them about Rumi, asks them about Bashō. He thinks the haikus they write here will intrigue his mother.

On the final morning of his trip, Nasruddin gazes out his hotel room window. He looks at the teeming street below. One of the pedestrians might be a telecommunications director: perhaps he is strolling home to his family, in their safe little apartment, with lights that stay on all night, powered by unsabotaged pylons, near a park maybe, with cherry blossoms, a school nearby, maybe even a safe university for when they grow up, one without conscription and campus assassinations and bloody riots. He sighs.

On the white wall, perfectly centred, is a woodblock print. Hokusai. A great wave towers over a fishing boat, sublime, terrifying, inescapable. Once man is caught under its frothy maw, there is no hope.

Nasruddin snaps his suitcase shut.

'Mister Saljuqi?'

A clerk pops his narrow head in the doorway, glancing about at the beige waiting room. On the wall, between a photo print of Mecca and a portrait of Ayatollah Khomeini, is a calendar: 1989. An Iranian flag hangs limp in one corner. A yellowing palm sits in another, drooping. A fly buzzes. Scattered about are some fidgety men, smoking incessantly, of various ages and means, but all with rings under their eyes, glancing up at the clerk and then back down at the mustard tiles.

Nasruddin raises his hand. Beside him sits Azizeh with

the toddler, Arsalan, on her knee, eight-year-old Shamiem and eleven-year-old Elyas. They are, ostensibly, back in Herat for a few weeks' holiday, well earned considering Nasruddin's continuous hard work at the Ministry of Telecommunications.

'The consul is ready to see you now. Please come this way.'

Nasruddin follows the clerk down a corridor and in through a double door to an office of dark wood with an exquisite rug. Azizeh and the children trail along quietly. Behind a chunky desk sits the Iranian consul, leafing through papers, a pen hovering over them, falcon-like, diving suddenly to check a box or scribble a detail. He motions for the newcomer to sit. Azizeh and the children huddle behind, mouse-like.

'Mister Saljuqi, a pleasure to meet you.'

They shake hands, Nasruddin leaning across the vast desk.

'Our friend in the ministry has told me you are a learned man. Highly qualified?'

'Well, Sir, I studied a degree in literature in Kabul.'

'Persian literature?'

'Indeed, Sir. It was a wonderful course.'

'And here we are in *this* city. If you stretch out your feet –'

'You kick a poet.'

'Ah yes,' chuckles the consul. 'The Pearl of Khorasan. This was all Persia at one time, ey?' He smiles wryly. 'No borders to cross.'

Nasruddin nods.

'Have you got your papers, Mister Saljuqi?'

Nasruddin takes a stack from his pocket and fans them out on the desk. The consul picks one up and scans it. His eyebrow cocks.

'"Fruit vendor," it says.'

He looks at Nasruddin. Nasruddin shrugs and nods, looking down at his toes.

'Mmm hmm.'

The consul scribbles something out on the document and bangs a stamp on it. He bundles the papers, taps them off the desk into neat alignment. He stands up, comes around the desk.

'Approved. You are welcome in the Islamic Republic of Iran.'

Azizeh sighs, squeezing the children. Nasruddin thanks him, scans the bottom of the document.

'But Sir, this says for only two weeks … that's not enough for –'

'Never mind that, Mister Saljuqi, it will do for now. A toe in the door, ey? Once you are there, you can apply for an extension. The trick is getting in.'

'And the visa itself?'

'The visa will be ready in a couple of days. My secretary will let you know.'

He grins and shows the family out.

A week later, in the darkness of the townhouse courtyard, the suitcases pile up. Both parties hug, those parting, those staying, those being ripped from the bed of reeds, those too firmly rooted. Nasruddin's younger brother shakes his hand. Abdul Azim is now a doctor. Tears stream down Nasruddin's mother's face. First Aamena saw her son married, then move to Kabul. Then her husband passed away. Now her son is leaving again, but where he will settle and when he will return are a mystery. Her blessed grandchildren are leaving her after so brief an enjoyment. Little Arsalan giggles and pulls her hair as she hugs him, ignorant of her tears.

The minibus arrives as a red blaze peeks over the ancient citadel, flooding the alleyways of Nasruddin's youth with a saffron dawn.

The minarets wail goodbye as old Herat sinks behind them

in the rear window, swallowed up by branches of mulberries and grapevines, until all that is left is the aching sun, arising.

> *If any one ask thee which is the pleasantest of cities,*
> *Thou mayest answer him aright that it is Herat.*
> *For the world is like the sea,*
> *And the province of Khorasan like a pearl-oyster therein,*
> *The city of Herat being as the pearl in the middle of the oyster.*[6]

The bus veers around a crater, a black star orbited by burnt engine parts, a hubcap, some exhaust pipe. In a distant field, over the rolling wheat, the domes of three tanks rise: rust-red crustacean shells. When Nasruddin squints, they become curved underbellies of dambura lutes: necks slanting up, yearning for a breeze to strum them. He prefers that.

Up ahead, a village looms.

There is a barrier, a nest of sandbags to one side. Militia are lounging about, chewing and spitting pumpkin seeds. They wear bits and bobs of officialdom: a grey cap here, a tunic there, some belt buckles, but mostly traditional garb. The minibus rolls to a halt, the handbrake coughs, and the driver rolls down his window. One of the militia hops to his feet and scurries up to the vehicle.

'Salaam brother – sorry, comrade. Comrade. What is your business here today?'

'We are simply passing through.'

'Passing through …'

The militiaman stretches his neck, blinking in at the hapless

---

6   From the writings of Jalāl ad-Dīn Muhammad Balkhī (1207–73), popularly known as Rumi. Born in the Khorasan region, he became one of the foremost poets and philosophers of the Islamic world and has grown increasingly popular throughout the West in recent decades.

passengers, mostly women and children, eyes darting here and there, mouth twitching. His lumpy little teeth set in bloody gums have the look of a row of grey beef-bone shards jutting out of shorwa soup. His neck retracts again, turning back to the driver.

'All in order? You can vouch for that? Because I' – he coughs – '*we* can remember your face.'

The driver nods his head.

'Yes, Sir.'

The militiaman laughs nervously, looks back to his colleagues, then at the driver again.

'So,' he mutters, 'you tell me I won't need to check these people?'

The driver opens the glove compartment. Inside is a pistol and a wad of Afghanis. He plucks the wad out and stuffs it into the militiaman's hand. The militiaman nods rapidly, stuffs the money into his tunic pocket, jerks around and waves to another, who drags the barrier to one side. The minibus heaves a collective sigh as it pulls off.

Nasruddin gazes numbly out the window. Vultures swirl over some remote rot. He is terrified but keeps his terror pressed down deep within him, dammed, pent, hidden from his family. He gazes at distant villages, many reduced to rubble, and imagines the war councils, the secluded caves, the elders and the young, hunched around campfires, oiling rifles, loading magazines and swapping tales of battle. He imagines the puff of a rocket and the searing flash as it punches into the side of the minibus. He pictures the front desk of the secret police headquarters in Herat, a family friend or neighbour arriving, whispering travel plans. Or perhaps someone who has noticed that he sold all his furniture in Kabul. He sees militiamen storming into the minibus and grabbing him, dragging him away from his children, beating him; he sees himself waking in a damp cell, fingernail-less. At every looming checkpoint, he feels these images, feels the cold sweat prickle his forehead.

There are sixty checkpoints. The journey from Herat to the border should take two hours. Today, it takes twelve. Each stop requires a bribe. Each bribe chomps into their savings. The sun swoops around them as they voyage; it saw them off from the east and welcomes them now in the west.

They pass the last militia checkpoint and are out of the maw of corruption. At the border, however, are more reliable officials, men who will care more about paperwork than paper money. The minibus comes to its terminus and they, finally, can spill out and suck in the fresh air, the scent of surrounding apple blossoms. They are coated in a sticky film of fear mixed with sweat and dust.

But the biggest challenge still lies ahead. The border police.

Nasruddin has no official documentation, other than his papers, which claim he is a fruit vendor. All indication that he is highly educated and a high official is stuffed in an envelope in the townhouse in Herat. His brother is guarding it until it can be posted to Iran, only after they have safely arrived.

They are shown into a doorway, a two-storey building. Nasruddin goes first, the family file in behind him. The children are silent. Azizeh looks at him, nods. Inside, the guard greets them, motions for the papers through his partition. Nasruddin slips them across. The guard looks up through his eyebrows, past the shopkeeper to his wife and children. Nasruddin strains to look unstrained. 'Does he see the quiver in my hand?' he thinks. 'Does he see the softness of my fingers? How they have hauled, hoisted, hammered only files, books, keyboards? Will he hear the schooling in my voice?'

'Thank you, comrade,' says the guard.

The papers slide back across.

'Next.'

They emerge from under the low ceiling, through a narrow threshold, out into the vast starry night. They cross a broad yard and into the Iranian guardhouse. Then, suddenly, they are in a new country. It is Nasruddin's third time outside of Afghanistan. His family have never before left.

That night, in a guestroom in the border town, the children whisper excitedly all night. Nasruddin looks at Azizeh through the darkness. They are both smiling.

Next morning, they climb aboard another bus. This time, there are no militiamen or bribes. The three-hour journey takes three hours. The sun bathes them rather than glares, lights rather than exposes.

They descend from rusty hilltops, red ridges in the deep blue sky, into lush green fields and striped saffron beds, from which, in the distance, rises a metropolis.

In Mashhad they meet some of Nasruddin's relatives.[7] The plan is to go to the US. Nasruddin's sister moved there three years ago with her husband. They soon learn about a change in US policy, however, which makes them suddenly ineligible. Unless they try from Pakistan. Nasruddin makes his plans and applies for an exit visa from the Iranian government. Then they are packing up again, clambering again aboard a bus, a day's drive south, along blistering roads, among leaden crags, jagged along the heavy sky like a column of shattered tanks.

They skirt an oblivion of scorched salt flats until they reach the city of Zahedan in the southeast corner of Iran, near the border with Pakistan.

From the conifer-lined streets of Zahedan they hire a car. The

---

7   Mashhad is located in the northeast of Iran and is the second most populous city in the country. Many Afghan refugees gravitate there after crossing the border.

town has tripled in size, swollen with Afghan refugees. They drive down into the desert, forty minutes towards the border. In the distance, a volcano rubs the hazy heavens.

Up ahead, on the shimmering road, a checkpoint materialises. When the car pulls in an officer sticks his head in the window.

'Who do we have here?' he says to the hired driver.

'I am just the driver, Sir.'

The officer gazes over at Nasruddin.

'You heading for the border?'

'I am, Sir.'

The officer stares at him a moment, then stands up.

'Driver, follow me.'

He hops into a jeep and they follow, off road. The children are confused.

'It is okay,' Nasruddin tells them. 'Don't worry.'

The car pulls in and again the officer sticks his head in.

'Okay, you Sir, follow me. The rest, you can wait here.'

The officer leads Nasruddin into a barracks, down a corridor and into a room where a dozen or more fresh-faced recruits are seated in a circle under a ceiling fan. They all straighten on sight of the officer.

'Gentlemen, we have today a fine specimen, fresh from real life.'

The men murmur, shuffle in their seats. The officer turns to Saljuqi.

'Where, may I ask, are you going, Sir?'

'To Pakistan, Sir.'

'Pakistan? Why?'

'I have some business there.'

'Business? What kind of business?'

'I am a shopkeeper, Sir.'

'A shopkeeper, is it?'

'Yes Sir, I have a small place, nothing special, in —'

'What sort of shopkeeper brings his whole family with him on business?'

The officer turns around, eyeing the men.

'Well, what do you say, lads? What does he look like to you?'

One raises his hand slowly.

'Eh, a shopkeeper, Sir?'

The officer laughs. Some of the men chuckle. Then he bellows.

'Are you all half-witted? There are drug dealers and spies and pimps crossing the border every day, plying their dirty little trades at will. And you are all Iran has standing in their way.' He passes his hand over his face. 'Shopkeeper? This man is lying through his teeth! Is it really so difficult for you? Can't you see his hands? Can't you notice the awkward way he wears these peasant clothes? Can you not see it in his face, in his gait, in his very eyes, that he is a man of learning? Of position?'

The men look at their toes sheepishly.

The officer laughs.

'Okay, Sir, thank you for helping me train these buffoons. A sorry lot.'

'Train?'

'Of course! Did you think it was a real interrogation?'

'You mean, I can go?'

'Yes. Goodbye now.'

Nasruddin nods awkwardly, glances at the students, and leaves.

The silhouettes of the tents sink into the setting sun like saw-teeth. The hired car has dropped them at a border camp. They stay overnight. A howl wakes Nasruddin in the dark. He slips back into an uneasy sleep, bunched together with his family, between them and the tent flaps.

In the morning, a bus drives them to the border fence. An officer drags open a gate and points across the sands.

'That is Taftan,' he says. 'The first village in Pakistan.'

They trudge across that shimmering wasteland, the hunched figure of Nasruddin against the azure, then Azizeh, then the children, hauling their meagre luggage as best as they can.

In Taftan they hunch under an awning around their little pyramid of cases while Nasruddin asks around for a driver to hire. He hopes his man has good tyres.

Then they plunge into the desert, its endless sea of sand, hour after hour, until, towards evening, the mountains rise up from the sea, like serried waves, petrified, undulating into the distance. By nightfall they are in a valley of orchards and then, twinkling between branches, is Quetta. They check into a railway hotel overnight.

In the morning, they rise early and walk around to the station. There is a long queue for tickets. After finally purchasing them, they make their way to the platform, its shelter spreading rusty wings, like a protective egret. It is teeming with people, squatting, smoking, playing cards, hugging, arguing, snoozing on top of bags and sacks. Poultry flutter and squawk in wicker cages, vendors stroll up and down, selling snacks. Skinny dogs, ribbed, ribald, sniff about.

'Stay close,' Azizeh tells the children.

'Yes Mama,' they reply, staring wide-eyed, gathering even tighter.

Nasruddin keeps his eyes stitched to them. To lose one, even for a moment, in this swirling vortex of humanity, among countless strangers, is unthinkable. They seem so delicate, so innocent, like raw hatchlings.

With a surge of the crowd and screech of brakes the locomotive puffs in, carriages gasping to a stop. Somehow they make it through the scrum to the doors. Nasruddin launches the cases up to Azizeh and the children, who grab and scramble them aboard.

There are no connecting doors between carriages; they must make do with wherever they boarded. They find a corner and nestle in among the throng, amid the sweat and the smoke and the spices. As they lurch forward, a breeze billows through the glassless windows. Some passengers, the well-balanced and the firm-hearted, sit up on the sills and scramble out onto the roof to bask in the wind.

'Can we, Baba?'

'Absolutely not.'

Azizeh clucks her tongue at the children.

At every station, the tides of people collide at each carriage doorway. After some minutes, a whistle would shrill, the latecomers would scramble and the great beast would splutter huff, splutter huff, huff, huff and away.

Five hours pass in the humid carriage.

'Baba, I'm thirsty.'

'Me too.'

Nasruddin looks at Azizeh. She nods.

'Yes,' he says. 'Me too. Here is the next stop. Who is for tea?'

'Me, me!'

Nasruddin weaves and wends off the carriage, leaving his family behind, and moves across the platform to where an old man with a little cart sells bottles of tea. Nasruddin can smell the leaves brewing, feel the itch in his dry throat, as he drops the coins into the man's hand. There is a shriek and a splutter, huff. Nasruddin spins about, sees the blooms of steam with horror, barges through the crowd, drops the tea bottle with a smash. The train is crawling forward, as a forest of hands wave out the windows. He trips over a basket, barrels into an amputee, spilling his alms bowl, staggers out of the mass, running for the doorway.

'Baba! Baba!'

He sees their faces pass for a second, then the doorway is pulling ahead, he is running, running, the precipice of the platform charges at him and he leaps. Hands grab him and pull him aboard, away from the shuddering sleepers.

Nasruddin must wait for an hour, knowing they know nothing. At the next stop he dashes out, runs up the doors, one, two, three, and into his carriage. He hugs his family, wipes away their tears.

'I'm sorry,' he says. 'I'm sorry.'

'Cousin, Salaam!'

In the railway hotel a man in a slick tunic rounds the grubby old armchairs of the lobby and embraces Nasruddin.

'So glad to see you, Abdul. Hamdullah.'

'Welcome to Islamabad.'

'I thought we'd never get here.'

'You look tired. Come, let's eat.'

Abdul Malik is a grocer in a bustling street, dense and darkened by overhangs. They sleep at his place above the shop for a few nights until a nearby apartment can be found to rent. Meanwhile, Nasruddin's sister is applying to sponsor him for a visa, which, hopefully, will be acceptable now that he is in Pakistan.

'So,' says Nasruddin, down the faint line, 'it could take weeks.'

'Perhaps,' she crackles back, 'but you'll get a job easily. Just be patient. It'll be better than Mashhad, at least.'

'All the bosses want someone who speaks Punjabi.'

'Not all, I'm sure. Look, talk to Sediaq. Promise me you will.'

Sediaq Saljuqi is their father's cousin. An exile, former minister in the Daoud government, he has a well-established network in the city by now. He assures Nasruddin that he has excellent contacts, including some NGOs, and that a little bit of patience will win the day. But the savings, like a mud-pond in the desert, are shrinking day by day. Occasional dollars from his sister are a blessed rainfall, but the evaporation soon continues.

There is a short bridge he passes when he visits the grocery: slimy banks, sludge treacle down the middle, stench so thick you can chew it. He pictures the faces of his children, filthy and gaunt, peeking out from under it.

They say this valley was the cradle of civilisation.

In many ways, it still is. In the salubrious districts of government one can admire the forested hills, the leafy avenues; it is a planned city, and airy. Lush. But there are the other quarters, derelict tenements and makeshift slums, where the wretched of Afghanistan accumulate, spilling in from the adjacent city of Rawalpindi.

Nasruddin hears a story. Somewhere in India, a farmer and his wife lived a simple but happy life, on the edge of a hamlet, which was separated from the nearest town by a long mountain spur. When she became ill, the doctor, across in the town, rushed around to them on the looping road. After several hours he arrived, to find the wife dead. The next morning, the farmer began chiselling a nearby cliff-face, every day, much to the amusement of the local gossipers. Twenty years later, the spur was sliced in two. The laughter stopped. He had hewn a shortcut to town, so that the next sick person might live. From then on, they called him Mountain Man.

Nasruddin wonders, what path must I carve for my family? Can I carve it now, before it is too late? Not for the next man's wife, but for my own living Azizeh?

Three months pass. No job. Despite entreaties – from his relatives and his sister – it is time to return to a place where he can actually speak to most people: Mashhad.

Nasruddin writes to the Iranian consulate in Islamabad, applying for an exit visa. It is refused. Sediaq has a word with some contacts. The second application is successful.

Back at the border, after the train and the mountain corkscrews and the vast desert, they are allowed re-enter Iran, where they claim asylum. They are corralled in a camp on the outskirts of Zahedan.

It is a flapping city, a prison of tents, a canvas limbo. The wind whips sand across their cheeks. Nasruddin and his family settle in one of the filthy shelters, furnished with a few thin mats and blankets, stocked with a handful of tea leaves. There is no water; that can be found in an ever-crowded shack, five minutes' trek away. They huddle there, amid the greys and browns, the shadows and sheets, awaiting their fate.

2000. In a restaurant in Mashhad, Nasruddin sits pondering the news he has just received. He is in a shirt and tie, hair neatly brushed. A plate of shashlik kebabs arrives before him, but he barely nibbles them. He has come to accept Mashhad in these past seven years, but this news has set that bleak acceptance spinning.

The City of Martyrdom. Tourists and pilgrims flock here to see the Imam Reza shrine, which is mushroomed with domes of gold and blue, girdled with a spectrum of hotels and bazaars selling prayer rugs, prayer beads, prayer rings.

The vibrant streets had certainly been welcome after the month his family spent in that tent limbo. He reminds himself that they were some of the luckier residents; many of their neighbours received deportation notices, or languished interminably. He shudders and is thankful for the lamb sizzling below his nostrils. He is not rich, but, at least nowadays, he rarely starves. He worked at first as a teacher in two part-time jobs, rushing each lunchtime from a primary school across town to a secondary school, requiring three buses to get there, scoffing whatever morsel he could in transit. His pupils were mostly Afghan refugees. The resources were meagre, the classes jam-packed. After a year, however, he was appointed a clerk in the Afghan consulate, near the city centre, eventually becoming secretary to the consul himself; typing letters, organising files, carving out calm amid the chaos.

Rumours about home constantly swirl among the ever-swelling Afghan community. His chest aches by day, his sleep is ragged at night. Much has changed in the motherland.

In 1989 the Soviets dematerialised: a trail of burnt materiel, winding into the deep north, of steel carcasses and putrefying ideals. Their Afghan comrades struggled on for another three years, far longer than anyone would have expected, until they finally collapsed in the spring of 1992, ending with President Najibullah and his brother swinging, mutilated, from traffic lights. With the communists defeated, Afghanistan became once again irrelevant to the wider world. Warlords – many of them high on modern weaponry and medieval ideas – scrambled for the crumbs of the country, the remnants that had somehow survived over a decade of destruction. Afghanistan was a goat carcass battled over by Buzkashi horsemen. It was a mangled place, scarred by ruins and acned with landmines.

Kabul has been decimated under a rain of rockets. Ismail Khan, the Mujahideen warlord, has made a personal emirate of Herat.

In 1994 a new power emerged in the Pakistani borderlands. Young men, often refugees, schooled in fundamentalist madrasas, they swept the provinces like a wildfire, toppling warlord after warlord and engulfing the capital within two years, welcomed as liberators. They call themselves the Students – the Taliban. A new centralised state, a new ideology, though as with the communists they have not quite established total territorial control. Massoud, the Lion of Panjshir, still reigns in the north.

It is now mandatory to wear a beard, a turban, traditional clothes. Women have vanished, only ghosts remain: burkas billowing in the streets, whispers overheard in window grates. Prisons overflow, music stills, stadiums sport beheadings. Poppy fields finance the fighting.

And yet, even among such salted ruins and wounds, tiny sprouts dare to blossom. At home, Nasruddin hears, there is a Golden Needle Sewing Society. Once a week they congregate at the appointed home. When the coast is clear, they drop their spools and slip books from their burkas: Dostoevsky, Orwell, Joyce. And, of course, Rumi.

The Iranians have their own issues. They are still reconstructing after a brutal war with Iraq, slogging through a slew of sanctions. There can be a certain callousness towards the refugees. Nasruddin often wonders is it safe here. The children at school, Azizeh at the market or at home in their tiny bedsit, where she minds the fourth baby, Shamoon. He worries about the increasing xenophobia, like the bigotry he met at the UNHCR. He did two months of interpreting there, loving it, until some angry locals interceded and told him he better back off from their livelihoods, that he might find himself unwelcome soon. Iranian work for Iranians. So ended that job.

'We are watching,' they said. 'Waiting.'

Zaheda still sends what she can. She may live in America, but she is a childminder with a teacher husband and many needy relatives.

In Mashhad, in the shadow of the shrines and penthouse suites, there is teeming poverty, especially among the burgeoning, bursting Afghan communities, where refugees arrive daily in their rags to eke out some existence in the squalor, in mucky camps or lean-to slums. A sex industry is sizzling beneath the city's crust of piety; flash-pan marriages, night-long loopholes. An impious itinerary: shrine, shish, Sigheh. It may not be most pilgrims' experience, but even a tiny percentage of the travelling masses is more than enough.

Nasruddin heard a rumour that the UN was admitting those with higher qualifications, higher experience, ushering them up the queue. Whether that was true or not, he was seen to when he arrived, interviewed in their office. That was many months ago.

How will he break the news he has just received to Azizeh? Nasruddin chews the skewered meat, closing his eyes, savouring the sweet vinegar marinade, the succulent lamb, what might be his last kebab for a long time. He is out of work. But by his own choice, his own notice. What is it they eat *over there*, he muses, trying to recall the handful of those pale people he had met during his golden student days, those glorious spring afternoons in the porches of the Great Mosque. Yes, that is right, they too eat lamb. Lamb something. Stew?

The enormity is rushing in now, reality storming surreality. He pays and hurries home.

Azizeh, across the aisle, clicks in her safety belt and helps Shamoon fix his, pointing at the little lighted sign. Nasruddin strains to gaze out the portholes, down past the wing and the engine. Below, the sea heaves and tosses, green then blue then spuming. A beach appears, then dunes, fields, greener than they would have thought possible, as green as the gardens of paradise. The Emerald Isle.

So different. So soft. Not scorched, carved, rippled. Not salt flats, gullies or desert.

It took three months for the Iranian authorities to finally permit them an exit visa. Now, suddenly, they are landing.

They leave the airport and drive through the drizzle and the morning traffic to a leafy neighbourhood of old red-brick terraces, not far from the city centre. The owner of the bed and breakfast meets them in the short driveway, between a flowerbed and a carpet-like lawn. He has salt and pepper hair, rosy cheeks and a cardigan.

'How are yous doing, yous are very welcome. *Salama lickum*, Mister Saljuqi.' He shakes Nasruddin's hand vigorously. 'Jim is my name, folks, anything yous need at all at all, you're only to ask and I'll have it sorted in a jiffy.'

'Thank you, Sir,' said Nasruddin, not quite catching the outburst in its entirety. There is no mistaking the smile and the handshake, though. The guesthouse owner and the case worker help them unload their suitcases and then they are shown to their rooms.

In the sitting room Jim pours tea along with a torrent of pleasantries. Rain patters the windows but warmth swirls around them where they sit on the couch, which takes up a third of the room. There are no piled cushions to recline on, the dinner table is visible in the dining room and everyone wears their shoes indoors. The Pope is hanging over the mantelpiece alongside a football team in green jerseys.

'Rotten morning, hey?

Nasruddin nods uncertainly.

'How about some fizzy orange?'

Shamoon and Arsalan grin when Jim comes back with the bottle.

'So.' Jim claps his hands, rubs them together. 'Herself has the fry on inside, is there any way yous prefer it? Eggs? Beans? A few rashers I suppose?'

'Rashers?'

'Rashers – eh … bacon, you know, from a pig. Oink, oink.'

Shamoon giggles.

'Sir,' says Nasruddin. 'I'm afraid we cannot eat the … *rasher.*'

Jim's eyebrows shoot up.

'I'm after completely forgetting. Sorry, hang on.'

He rushes out. Nasruddin looks over at Azizeh, Elyas and Shamiem. They shrug. Jim rushes back in.

'We've a bit of stew in there, how does that sound?'

'Stew? With the lamb?'

'Lamb stew, the very one!'

Nasruddin smiles.

Nasruddin is plodding down the narrow staircase when Arsalan barges in the front door. His schoolbag, slung over one shoulder, is smeared with muck. This is their temporary place, a transition between the guesthouse and a new home.

'Son, what is it?'

'It is nothing, Baba.'

He tries to shrug past. Nasruddin grabs him, turns his face. It is bruised, swollen around the eyes. There is some crusted blood in the nostril.

'What have they done, my boy?'

Arsalan looks away.

'What happened?'

'They punched me.'

'They? Who?'

His son shakes his head, scowling.

'Who? In the school? Tell me!'

'Some of the lads from over around the corner.'

'Why? What did you do?'

'Nothing. Nothing. They hate me. They hate *us*.'

'They are ignorant, they –'

'Baba. They called me a dirty Paki.'

Nasruddin sighs deeply, painfully. Arsalan pounds up the staircase, shuts the bedroom door. We need to get into a new place, thinks Nasruddin. Surely some landlord will accept us soon. He wonders which he prefers: a punch or a polite excuse. Or, as happened a few weeks earlier, the crash of glass in the sitting room. Nasruddin had peered in to see, on the Persian rug, half a brick nestled among sparkling shards.

A hundred thousand welcomes there may be, but Ireland is a country of many more hundreds of thousands. Not all welcoming, all the time, to all comers.

Like reeds on the River Hari, they have been plucked and put far away, out of sight, out of mind, to wither. They lived in the bed and breakfast for many months, through the winter of 2000. They moved into their temporary house, in a neglected neighbourhood, bedecked with boarded windows and graffiti, in time to hear of the collapse of the Twin Towers. Now, local youths are pummelling his son and American bombs are pummelling Afghanistan.

Nasruddin strolls through the dusk-daubed streets, past Daniel O'Connell on his pedestal, under the outstretched arms of Jim Larkin and through the bustle among the bullet-chipped columns of the General Post Office. He continues up the street and then around the corner where bronze swans surge up out of the remembrance pool, a mirror, still but fiery. There is a slight stiffness in his gait now, an unhurried creakiness. He crosses the road and trudges up steps and in the doorway of a grand old Georgian townhouse. He is giving a talk at the Irish Writers Centre.

'Mister Saljuqi!'

'Ah, Professor Bailey, good evening. How are you? How was the flight?'

'Good, a bit bumpy, but, you know …'

'Thank you for coming, old friend.'

They shake hands, grinning. Both have aged since that night at the Grand Hotel in Herat. Out are the thick hairdos and the bell-bottoms. In are some wrinkles and some grey hairs. But, fleeting decades and changing fashions notwithstanding, they have always kept in touch. For the last fourteen years this has been easy – only the Irish Sea separates them now, not two continents.

'How could I not?' says the professor. 'Besides, I read the book and I loved it. Fascinating stuff.'

Behind the rostrum, Nasruddin taps the microphone, adjusts it. He takes in the chamber: its cardinal-red walls and oil paintings, the wainscoting and the rich stucco moulding, the tables at the back piled high with fresh copies of his book: *From Dunbura to Guitar: the Diaspora of Afghan Musicians*. He gazes down at the rows of chairs, filled with people, many Irish, many not, their murmuring petering out as a hundred eyes turn to him.

'I can always remember the music,' he begins. 'As a boy, growing up in Herat, it was a constant leitmotif in our lives: dunburas strumming in teahouses, harmoniums echoing up from hidden peristyles, the muezzin's cry at dawn …'

This is Nasruddin's ninth book. He has become a cultural ambassador for Afghanistan in Ireland, a role that he grew into almost from the very start, while living in the guesthouse. A journalist had been working there part-time, and she had urged him to represent his country at a multi-media conference she was organising. His calligraphy exhibit, along with his engaging explanations, attracted attention, and soon he was on the road with his artefacts, headed for Galway. There, he met more intelligentsia, eager to learn about this distant civilisation from an angle other than that shown nightly on news screens.

Since those early days, he has travelled all over Ireland, the UK and beyond, giving talks and exhibitions on calligraphy, painting, craftsmanship, photographic history and musicology. He has been widely interviewed on radio and in the papers. Many of his writings have been translated and can be found on bookshelves across central Asia from Kunduz to Shiraz.

Nasruddin serves as a consultant for a variety of projects, including work on migrant integration with the Ministry of Justice, and soon he will begin work as a cultural consultant on *The Breadwinner*, which will go on to be nominated for an Oscar.

Not content with his cultural offerings, he sought to create a safe harbour for the newcomers from his beleaguered homeland. Within a year of arrival he established the Afghan Community of Ireland, where he could meet newly arriving Afghans and share with them his experience, his contacts and his hope. They organised the first Nowruz celebrations in Ireland, starting in 2003 with a handful of Afghans and their Irish friends but growing in the following years into a community event celebrated annually in a string of famous hotels, an Afghan grill restaurant and even, one year, at the Chester Beatty Library.[8]

The Saljuqis were finally accepted into a new house, in a quiet, leafy avenue, well out in suburbia. The children excelled in their new school, mastered the slang and the idiosyncrasies

---

8   Nowruz is a new year festival with Zoroastrian origins celebrated in many
     Persianate cultures.

of their peers, developed long-lasting friendships, flourished in university and, in the end, embarked on their own journeys, happier reedsongs.

Elyas earned a degree in computer science and got hired as a consultant for an Irish firm over in the US. Shamiem and Arsalan are both in London, she as a teacher, he working with University College London. Shamoon has just finished a second master's in pharmacology at University College Dublin. A whole new generation of Saljuqis, carrying knowledge out into the world.

'… the development and evolution of music, therefore, cannot be claimed by any one region or race. Musicians learn from each other. They communicate through their universal language, those mystical, those primordial vibrations, from Tehran to Texas, from Kabul to Killarney. That, I hope, is an example we can all aspire to.' Nasruddin gazes out over the rapt faces. Breathes. 'Thank you.'

As the applause fades out, he can hear the chirping bulbuls beyond the farmhouse portico, their flitting in the mulberries, the chorus of crickets. Baba and Babayi are listening while Mama, with dusk on her brow, like a mythical peri, recites, once again, her favourite poet:

'Raise your words, not your voice. It is rain that grows flowers, not thunder.'

AFTERWORD

Zarhawar successfully made it back to America with his wife and their new baby. Hawraz and his family waited many more months in Kuala Lumpur, but they also travelled to the US eventually. They and the eight other voyagers in this book are the lucky few: a tiny, an infinitesimal minority of the global displaced population who manage to get resettled in an affluent society. As of now (2018), there are over sixty-five million displaced people in the world, sixty-five *million* people fleeing a litany of dangers, including drought, rising sea levels and bloodshed. That is equal to the entire population of the United Kingdom. They are joined by more outlanders every hour. Each has a story.

RECOMMENDED READING

Chomsky, Noam, *How the World Works* (Hamish Hamilton, London, 2011)

Finkelstein, Norman G., *Image and Reality of the Israel–Palestine Conflict* (Verso, London, 2003)

Hickel, Jason, *The Divide: A Brief Guide to Global Inequality and its Solutions* (William Heinemann, London, 2017)

Hosseini, Khaled, *A Thousand Splendid Suns* (Riverhead Books, New York, 2008)

Jabra, Jabra I., *The Ship* (Three Continents Press, Washington, 1985)

Martinez, Raoul, *Creating Freedom: Power, Control and the Fight for our Future* (Canongate Books, Edinburgh, 2017)

Okorie, Melatu Uche, *This Hostel Life* (Skein Press, Dublin, 2018)

Orwell, George, *Burmese Days* (Harper & Brothers, New York, 1934)

Pollak, Sorcha, *New to the Parish: Stories of Love, War and Adventure from Ireland's Immigrants* (New Island Books, Dublin, 2018)

Rahimi, Atiq, *Earth and Ashes* (Vintage, London, 2003)

Said, Edward W., *Orientalism* (Penguin, London, 2003)

Van Bruinessen, Martin, *Agha, Shaikh and State: The Social and Political Structures of Kurdistan* (Zed Books, London, 1992)

ABOUT SAMOS VOLUNTEERS

Thank you for reading. The proceeds of your purchase, this very moment, are zipping towards the sun-parched island of Samos, where Samos Volunteers will use them to aid in their tireless support of incoming refugees: outlanders all too similar to those you've just read about.

Samos Volunteers are a grassroots, independent movement. They provide help and support to refugees and asylum-seekers living in the camp and shelters on Samos, by instilling a sense of normality, combating boredom and empowering people while they wait for their asylum to be processed. They achieve this by identifying the needs of new arrivals, and sustaining educational activities and recreational projects for both children and adults.

To learn more, visit their website: samosvolunteers.org

Or find them on Facebook at: Samos Volunteers

And please don't forget to spread the word about this book and about Samos Volunteers among your family and friends. Once again: our sincere thanks.